Sarajevo

INTERPRETATIONS OF CULTURE IN THE NEW MILLENNIUM

Norman E. Whitten Jr.,
General Editor

A list of books in the series appears at the end of the book.

Sarajevo

A Bosnian Kaleidoscope

FRAN MARKOWITZ

UNIVERSITY OF ILLINOIS PRESS
Urbana, Chicago, and Springfield

Manufactured in the United States of America
1 2 3 4 5 C P 5 4 3 2 1
∞ This book is printed on acid-free paper.

Library of Congress Cataloging-in-Publication Data
Markowitz, Fran.
Sarajevo : a Bosnian kaleidoscope / Fran Markowitz.
p. cm. — (Interpretations of culture in the new millennium)
Includes bibliographical references and index.
ISBN 978-0-252-03526-5 (cloth : alk.)
ISBN 978-0-252-07713-5 (paper : alk.)
1. Sarajevo (Bosnia and Hercegovina)—Social life and customs.
2. Sarajevo (Bosnia and Hercegovina)—Social conditions.
3. Sarajevo (Bosnia and Hercegovina)—Ethnic relations.
4. Cultural pluralism—Bosnia and Hercegovina—Sarajevo.
5. City and town life—Bosnia and Hercegovina—Sarajevo.
6. Sarajevo (Bosnia and Hercegovina)—Politics and government.
7. Bosnia and Hercegovina—Politics and government.
8. Bosnia and Hercegovina—Ethnic relations.
I. Title.
DR1776.2.M37 2010
949.742—dc22 2009053626

Parts of chapters 3 and 4, table 4 in chapter 5, and table 5 in chapter 7 were published in a different form in "Census and Sensibilities in Sarajevo," by Fran Markowitz, *Comparative Studies in Society and History* 49, no.1 (January 2007): 40–73. Copyright © 2007 Society for Comparative Study of Society and History. Reprinted with the permission of Cambridge University Press.

Branimir Anzulovic's translation of Radovan Karadzic's poem "Sarajevo" is from Anzulovic's book *Heavenly Serbia: From Myth to Genocide* (New York: New York University Press, 1999), 129, and is reproduced with permission from New York University Press.

In memory of my father,
Alan Markowitz

אבא הוא אחד
עליו השלום

Contents

Conclusion

Illustrations

Map

Photos

Tables

Acknowledgments

Research for this book was supported in part by grants from the International Research & Exchanges Board (IREX) with funds provided by the National Endowment for the Humanities, the United States Department of State, which administers the Title VIII Program and the IREX Scholar Support Fund. None of these organizations is responsible for the views expressed. IREX provided me with a short-term travel grant that brought me to Sarajevo in August 1997 and then supported the longer-term research that I conducted from March until August 2004 with an Individual Advanced Research Opportunities (IARO) grant. I would like to acknowledge as well a special research grant from the discretionary funds of the Dean of the Faculty of Humanities and Social Sciences, Ben-Gurion University of the Negev, that supported two weeks of field research in August 2002. Thanks also go to the Institut za istoriju, my host institution in Sarajevo during 2004.

Several friends and colleagues have inspired or encouraged this project. Willingly or unwittingly they have each, in their own way, left an imprint on this work. I should like to mention by name Mladen Andrijasević, Mark Baskin, Tone Bringa, Robert Donia, Greta Weinfeld Ferušić, Gena Fine, John Fine, Melisa Forić, Tania Forte (of blessed memory), Ernest Grin, Mladen Grin, Michael Herzfeld, Éva Huseby-Darvas, Husnija Kamberović, Mak Kapetanović, Dragica Levi, William G. Lockwood, Gail Lyon, Carol Mann, Jay S. Markowitz, Klara Pelja, Amila Pustahija, Dafna Shir-Vertesh, Anders Stefansson, Michele Sumka, and Olga Supek.

Contending with the mirth and melancholy of Sarajevo and the challenge to represent the pulsating patterns of *Sarajevo: A Bosnian Kaleidoscope* as an engaging yet scholarly text combined to make this book's gestation period longer and more difficult than any of my previous writing projects. I appreciate the good will and patience of Norman Whitten and Joan Catapano at the University of Illinois Press. My thanks to the Press for assigning my manuscript to Barbara Wojhoski for gentle but firm copyediting.

The Department of Anthropology at the University of Michigan provided me with a spacious office and the wonderful resources of the Horace Rackham Graduate Library during my sabbatical year there in 2005–6. Before and after that year, I relied on the support of my "home team"—the sociologists and anthropologists of the Department of Behavioral Sciences, who now comprise the Department of Sociology and Anthropology at Ben-Gurion University of the Negev. Shmuel Ben-Dor (of blessed memory), Sara Helman, Daniel Maman, Uri Ram, and Alex Weingrod deserve special mention. Thanks go to department head Lev Grinberg for inviting me to inaugurate the biweekly seminar of our new Department of Sociology and Anthropology with a presentation of my work, and to Becky Kook for asking me to present at the monthly seminar of the Department of Politics and Government. It was a delight to work with Roni Blustein-Livnon of the Department of Geography, who drew the map on page xiv.

Mostly I wrote at home in my cozy house in Meitar, a small residential community in the foothills of Israel's northern Negev. My little brown dog, Lulu, and my pantherlike cat, Bertram, brought me out of my reveries at least once an hour with their demands that I open the door or go for a walk. But I didn't have to rely on my pets for distraction; I could always find reasons to trim the bougainvillea, wash the tile floors, or cook up a storm. My across-the-street neighbor, Vitti Rosenzweig Kones, kept me socially connected with kind conversation and culinary treats. Kathryn A. Kozaitis did the same from afar.

And, of course—*pa naravno!*—my deepest thanks go to the many Sarajevans who became part of my life: the lovely young women at my favorite bakery who dubbed me "super" just because I was able to make light conversation with them in their language; the taxi drivers and artisans, clerks and teachers who told me about the beauty of their city and the happiness of their Yugoslav lives, which really were characterized by *bratstvo i jedinstvo*; the politicians and academics who trusted me to get their stories right, and countless others. For comfort and a home-away-from-home, I am most grateful to the Sarajevo Jewish community, to Dragica Levi, Jakob and Nadja Finci, David and Blanka Kamhi, to Moric Albahari, and to Greta and Klara and Renata and Ernest and Grga and Nataša and all the ladies of La Bohoreta.

Hvala Vam puno! Hvala Vam ljepo! Živeli!

Pronunciation Guide

In the text I remain faithful to the spelling of personal and place names used in the local Bosnian-Croatian-Serbian language as rendered in Latin script. Following the convention set by Tone Bringa in her 1995 *Being Muslim the Bosnian Way,* this guide presents only those letters that are pronounced differently from English.

A a in father
C ts in tsar
Č ch in church
Ć soft ch in watch
Dž j in John
Đ dj
E e in let
H kh in khan
I ee in tee
J y in yes
Lj ll in million
Nj n in news
O o in oat
R rolled
Š sh in she
U oo in too
Ž zh, or s in pleasure

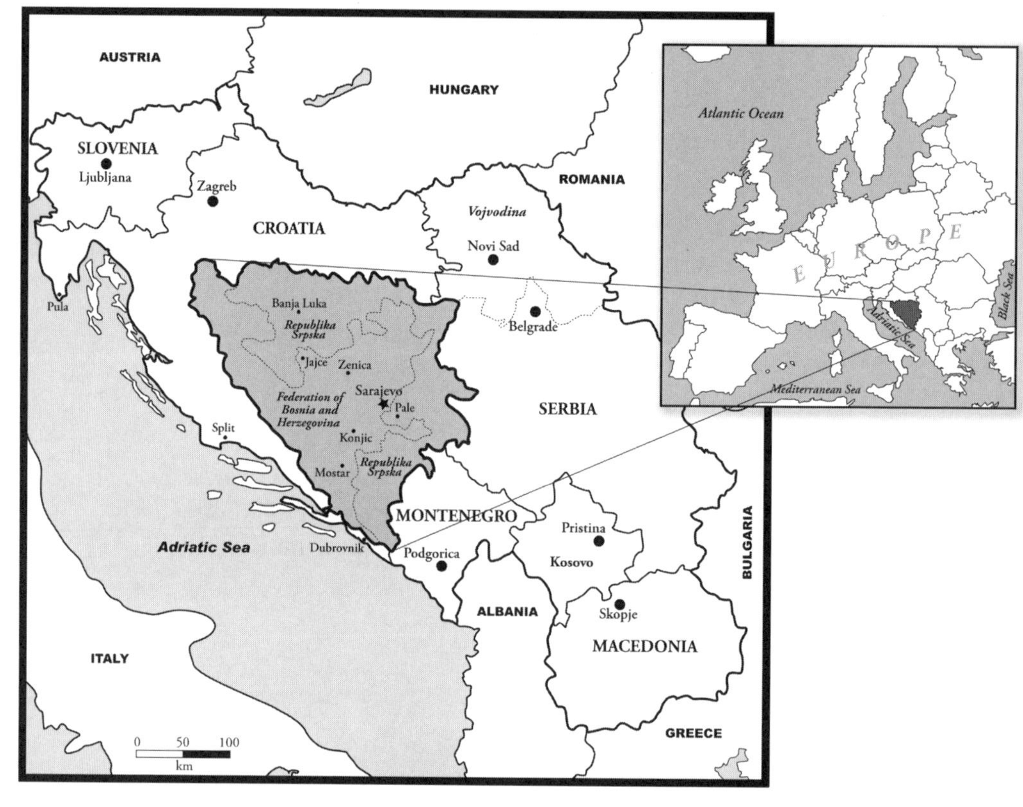

Bosnia-Herzegovina and Neighboring Countries. Drawn by Roni Blustein-Livnon.

Introductions

1

Meeting and Greeting the City

This book is about Sarajevo—its buildings, monuments, museums, and streets; its war scars, its histories, and its cultural legacies as narrated, categorized, and practiced by its people. This book is about the subjectivities of Sarajevans that have been formulated, adjusted, articulated, and squelched over centuries of political demands that transformed their country from an independent medieval kingdom to a westernmost province in the Ottoman Empire (1463–1878), to a territory of Habsburg Austria-Hungary (1878–1918), to part of two twentieth-century Yugoslavias, to the contemporary, ostensibly independent Republic of Bosnia-Herzegovina (BiH).[1] The book examines how Sarajevans navigate, negotiate, reproduce, and amend who it is that they think they are from within the authoritative discourses of history, in their interactions with the government, through their encounters with the built environment, and in comparison with other peoples and persons with whom they share neighborhood, city, country, and continent.

As the Berlin Wall and the Iron Curtain fell, Yugoslavia, which had vaingloriously straddled Europe's two sides, split apart. From 1992 through 1995, Sarajevo was held under the longest siege in twentieth-century history while all of Bosnia-Herzegovina suffered through a devastating war. That war destroyed the country's political and economic infrastructure and, having made a mockery of Yugoslavia's central slogan of *bratstvo i jedinstvo* (brotherhood and unity), shattered an implicit trust in the goodwill of all people(s). Prior to the war, many Bosnians had hoped to continue the grand European narrative of progress into the twenty-first century by taking all that was good in nonaligned, socialist Yugoslavia and making it better in a smaller, more manageable, inherently pluralistic Bosnian state. But that has not as yet come to pass. The Republic of Bosnia-Herzegovina, with its population divided into three constituent nations and its territory into two so-called entities, remains under the internationally mandated supervision of the Office of the High Representative (OHR) and is at best a shaky state. The OHR's self-proclaimed mission is to work with the country's people and the international community to ensure that Bosnia-Herzegovina is a peaceful, viable state on course to European integration. And that could happen; BiH could solidify into a territorially sovereign, united yet pluralistic, democratic European state. But it could also remain a protectorate of the European Union (EU) for the long term; it could be partitioned and parceled out to its closest neighbors; or it could erupt into another war. All these potential scenarios are intimately related; each is embedded in the constantly in-motion actions, debates, hopes, and fears that combine to forge Bosnia's future.

Rather than adhere to the convention of representing Bosnia through images of bridges that link separate sides or as a mosaic comprised of many disparate pieces (see, e.g., Hayden 2007; Bougarel, Helms, and Duijzings 2007b; Jansen 2005; cf. Andrić [1945] 1961), I have chosen for this book the metaphor of a kaleidoscope to convey the fluid and dynamic variety of Sarajevo, Bosnia's capital (see Richardson 2008).[2] With it I am suggesting that the city offers a multiplicity of ethnic, confessional, and philosophical trajectories that combine and separate, creating dozens of never-stable, always interrelated patterns. The hows and whys of Sarajevans' experiments with that diversity as they go about their daily lives is the focus of this book. It also analyzes the fact that while politicians, government bureaucrats, and social scientists use surveys, statistics, and history to determine who is who and what is what, these truth practices are open to contestation. It is in the kaleidoscopic alternation between constricted, monochromatic views and broader, multicolored configurations of power, culture, language, and polity that Sarajevo and its residents constitute, subjectify, and objectify themselves, their belongings, and (those of) others. It is also how they come to accept the certainty of some things while resisting and challenging other things.

Twisting a kaleidoscope reveals a plethora of patterns, but, like Sarajevo's offerings, they are not endless. They are constrained by the device and by the colors and quantity of the beads that it contains. Of course, all that can be altered by opening the tube to insert something new or to take something out. Nonetheless, the structure remains the same, and the old shapes and colors can linger palimpsest-like to inform and inspire the new components and their new configurations. In a sense, that is what happened in Bosnia during the last decades of the twentieth century and continues still, years after the millennium turned.

Although this book is not about the 1992–95 war, the negotiations that led to the Dayton Peace Accords, or the governmental structure of the Republic of Bosnia-Herzegovina, all these events and processes are present, if only in the scars that they have left on Sarajevo's sidewalks, on the bodies of its citizens, and in people's autobiographies. They are present, sometimes spectrally, sometimes in full body throughout the book; they intrude and cannot be ignored. Long gone are those rapturous days when anthropologists could put aside questions of politics, the brutalities of war, and the impact of government to concentrate on "culture." Today it is impossible to discuss culture—as categories, cognitive schemes, ways of going about in the world, belongings, rituals, languages, homes—except in connection with how it responds to, cracks, and reassembles in its confrontations with the political. How people see themselves, their children, their parents, the buildings that they pass every day, their across-the-hall neighbors, their country's leaders, the textbooks they once read and those that pupils are now reading are all part of the dynamic of culture that is articulated through the words, deeds, and works of people. And it changes, and it can change, sometimes through its own momentum, sometimes as the result of violence.

Sarajevo: A Bosnian Kaleidoscope is my take on how Sarajevans are negotiating their lives in conjunction with the larger dramas of nation and state building. It reacts against earlier portrayals of Bosnia's capital as an out-of-place Turkish or Muslim city in Europe, as a utopian site that defied the countryside around it, or as the sad result of a kind of historical determinism that produced representations of not yet modernized Serbs, Croats, and Bosniacs frozen in brutal Balkan acts. A critical, engaged urban anthropological analysis of contemporary Sarajevo, this ethnography refuses a singular trope. Envisioning Sarajevo as a Bosnian kaleidoscope situates the city in its cultural legacies and shows how its people resist and comply with an urbanism that provides the conditions for blurring boundaries and forging overlapping belongings, while also enabling the entrenchment of state practices that demand unequivocal national distinctions and unwavering loyalties.

Mirth and Melancholy in Sarajevo

Sarajevo makes me laugh. In its refusal to buckle down and knock out contradictory and competing ways to be, it elicits glee—from me.

I love walking across the bridges that link the banks of the Miljacka River: the ancient Goat Bridge, where caravans once trod en route to and from Istanbul; the Latin Bridge, where Gavrilo Princip took aim that fateful day in 1914 and shot dead Archduke Franz Ferdinand; and the Euro-modern metal structures that some say were inspired by the Eiffel Tower.

I love standing on the steps under the rosette window decorating the Catholic Cathedral of the Sacred Heart, watching the passersby as I wait for my friend Klara. Once seated in a café on the adjacent square, we are whisked out of noisy traffic into a bubble of Central European civility as white-shirted waiters with tea towels folded over their arms come to take our order. As we talk, the minarets of Ottoman-built stone mosques and the cupolas of the nineteenth-century Orthodox cathedral across the park flit into and out of our view. Just down the main thoroughfare named for Marshal Tito, an eternal flame burns brightly to commemorate all those Serb, Croat, Muslim, Roma, Jewish, Albanian, Montenegrin, Macedonian, Slovene, Yugoslav men, women, and children who fell as Partisans fighting against the Nazi occupation.

Not far from the double spires of the Catholic cathedral stands the pale yellow market hall, also built in the late nineteenth century. I love strolling its aisles as the vendors hawk their wares—yogurt, butter, eggs, cheese, meat, and the regional specialty *kajmak,* a pungent dairy product that is not quite sour cream and not quite cream cheese but a unique blend of its own—which I can sample and then purchase, or not. Or if I'm not in the mood for close contact, I can hop on a tram and rattle past the ultramodern glass and steel UNIS twin towers and the daffodil-colored Holiday Inn to shop in the antiseptically bright Merkator supermarket without having to talk to a soul.

I love that the arches and domes of Turkish stone buildings, the ornate facades commissioned by Austrian capitalists, and mega-sized concrete structures of socialist modernism stand side-by-side; that the sacred and profane transgress into each other's space; that government-produced apartment blocks, private places of purchase, houses of worship, and people's homes rub up against each other. I relish the variety of Sarajevo's built environment that provokes the imagination with a long list of possibilities for being in the world. The churches, mosques, and synagogues speak to the Abrahamic faiths, each to its own although they share a progenitor as well as urban space. Sarajevo's shops and markets represent diverse modes of production, interaction, and consumption; the government buildings, emerald green parks, museums, theaters, factories, garages, galleries, restaurants, and cafés all conjure a range of belongings and identities, and their alternatives.

1. Sarajevo's Roman Catholic Cathedral of the Sacred Heart

These styles of the city, carved in stone, and painted or printed on canvases and billboards, signs and menus, postcards and currency, speak to multiple histories and inspire imaginaries of possible futures in the present continuous of Sarajevo's motile public culture. Each structure instigates a slew of ideas about self and other and of faith and nation whether it was built on the socialist principles of worker self-management or in praise of a higher power; to accommodate bureaucrats or banknotes; or to display and deal in the whims of fashion or the pleasures of grilled meat and baked spinach pie.

There are enough goods and gods to go around and enough space for all to be displayed, adored, feared, or ignored. There is even a statue that declares, *Ecce Homo*—Here is Man—a lasting leftover from the 1984 Winter Olympic Games, which Sarajevo and the Socialist Federation of Yugoslavia so proudly hosted, a piece of urban sculpture that decorates a rose garden where men play chess, children chase pigeons, and Gypsies ply their wares.

In all these ways, Sarajevo is ludic, even extravagantly so, because it defies demands for consistency and any sense of Euro-modern national boundedness (Boon 1999). Catholic, Orthodox, Muslim, Jewish, Bosnian, Yugoslav, Austrian, Turkish, socialist, and humanistic sites—and those who pass through,

2. *Ecce Homo* sculpture in foreground; Sarajevo's Serbian Orthodox Cathedral in background

worship, socialize, purchase, consume, and just live there—touch one another, inducing intermingling and inviting improvisation (Amin and Thrift 2002, 10). By displaying their symbols and sending their messages, each structure contributes to the "multiplicity of histories that is spatial" (Massey 2000, 231): They are public reminders of Ottoman rule and of annexation into the Central European Habsburg Empire. They represent the spread of Islam, Serbian Orthodoxy, Roman Catholicism, and Sephardic Jewry. They are manifestations of two twentieth-century Yugoslav projects, as well as the idea that Yugoslavia was, and now Bosnia-Herzegovina is, comprised of rights-vested constituent nations. Certainly each structure can be plotted on a time line in terms of its completion date and classified as the product of a specific tradition (see, e.g., Neidhardt 2004; also Donia 2006), but in the city of today all buildings, and the faiths and nations that they represent, are contemporaries. Nestled together they embody the competing, coexisting, and intertwined results of convoluted pasts; they produce a copresence of difference that encourages Sarajevans to fashion and refashion their city as an exemplar of diversity and cosmopolitanism. That is why Sarajevo makes me laugh.

Nothing, however, is fixed, and everyone knows that things can change, that things have changed. The same stately nineteenth-century buildings that sheltered first the Austro-Hungarian imperial governors, followed by officials of the two Yugoslavias—with Nazi occupiers in between—now fly the flag of Bosnia-Herzegovina. No longer an Ottoman province, an Austrian crown territory, or a Yugoslav socialist republic, BiH has been recognized as independent since April 1992. But achieving state sovereignty and maintaining Bosnia's territorial integrity were won at great cost. The war of 1992–95, fought for and against the principle of ethnic cleansing, devastated the country and changed its landscape. More than one million people fled; thousands more were maimed and murdered. Cultural landmarks and the economic infrastructure were destroyed. Not until the highest elected representatives of Serbia, Croatia, and Bosnia-Herzegovina agreed in Dayton, Ohio, to distribute territory, resources, governing power, and rights among the country's three designated constituent nations—the nations of the Bosniacs, the Croats, and the Serbs—was a consensus reached on how to end the war (see Holbrooke 1999; Chandler 2000, 43).

While maintaining BiH's prewar boundaries, Presidents Milošević, Tudjman, and Izetbegović internally divided the country into two ethnically dominated entities—the Bosniac-Croat Federation of Bosnia-Herzegovina (the Federation, or FBiH, 51 percent of the territory, further divided into ten cantons), and the Republika Srpska (Serbian Republic, or RS, 49 percent of the territory)—and endowed these with more governing power than the unitary state. Further entrenching the idea that this state is a compromise wrested from the leaders of three incommensurable rights-vested groups, they established a trinational, three-person state presidency. Also, only Bosniacs, Croats, and Serbs are eligible to hold major government offices, leaving little if any room for mixed-ethnics, minorities, or those who consider themselves Bosnians with no ethnic affiliation. Although the Republic of Bosnia-Herzegovina exists formally as a unitary state, it operates more like a wary coalition of three statelets. In this confusing, overly bureaucratic, and often dysfunctional arrangement (see F. Friedman 2004; Moore with Buechenschuetz 2004; Gilbert 2006) Sarajevo serves as the capital of the Federation and of the entire country.

But that is not the end of it. The signing of the Dayton Accords both affirmed BiH's independence and made the country a protectorate of the international community by establishing a supragovernmental apparatus to ensure that the peace would hold. NATO-led international troops were deployed throughout the country first to assure implementation of the accords (Implementation Force, IFOR) and then to supervise stabilization (Stabilization Force, SFOR), while the Office of the High Representative was charged with overseeing the rule of law and guiding BiH on the path toward European integration.[3] SFOR was disbanded exactly ten years after the cessation of hostilities, but as of this writing in 2009, the sixth high representative, Valentin Inzko, continues to hold absolute power to overturn election results and parliamentary decisions should they fail to meet the demands of democracy as set forth in the Dayton Accords.[4] And so, as the wide array of humanitarian organizations that provided sorely needed resources to the city steadily decreases, the OHR remains ensconced in Sarajevo, where it supervises the reconstruction, if not the reconciliation, of a country ravaged by a hideous war.

From 1992 through 1995, when most of Central and Eastern Europe were peacefully working their way through difficult postsocialist transitions, Sarajevo was held in a thousand-day siege, causing the city to weep, burn, and bleed (see Andreas 2008). Civilians were wantonly shot; governmental, residential, and commercial sites were sprayed with sniper fire and blasted in grenade attacks. Millions of books, one-of-a-kind manuscripts, priceless artifacts, and major cultural landmarks were destroyed (see Bakaršić 1994). When I arrived in Sarajevo in August 1997, the airport was an unlit crater; the Old City was shattered; the National Museum was severely damaged; the UNIS twin towers were devoid of windows; the Holiday Inn's top floors were missing; and the Spanish Jewish Cemetery and the Olympic peaks surrounding the city were mined. SFOR troops and their vehicles were everywhere. Sarajevo's borders had been redrawn to place it entirely in the Bosniac-Croat Federation, and its centuries-old Serb population had dramatically decreased (see Donia 2006, 337–39; S. Ramet 1999, 282). So too had the Cyrillic script that once shared double billing with the Latin alphabet on marquees and billboards, newspapers and government documents, textbooks and shop signs.[5] These reminders of the near destruction of the city and its results are what made me, and so many others, sad in Sarajevo.

When I returned first in 2002 and then in 2004, the airport was brightly lit and computerized, and most of the city's damaged buildings were either repaired or in the throes of reconstruction. Cafés were full and shops were busy; most museums had reopened; children were going to school and their parents to work. SFOR's presence had greatly diminished, and daily life had resumed its normal rhythms and routines.

Telltale signs of the recent war, however, linger. Concrete hulks that were once department stores, hotels, and government complexes sit naked and foreboding in the city center. Once smooth sidewalks are pockmarked with craters left by sniper fire and grenade explosions, or they are filled with now faded crimson-colored cement to mark the spots where civilians had been shot dead. White marble obelisks dot municipal parks that do double duty as playgrounds and as cemeteries for Bosnian *šehids* (martyrs), those Muslim soldiers who died in the line of duty defending their homeland. Street signs and the doors of many elementary schools are colored green, and several sites and thoroughfares have been renamed to honor Bosniac leaders and wartime heroes (Robinson, Engelstoft, and Pobric 2001). Two new, gigantic mosques, gifts from foreign countries, dominate Sarajevo's outlying neighborhoods. Across the border in the RS, a big, elaborate Orthodox cathedral was erected to add symbolic strength and structural substance to Eastern—but what is popularly and contentiously known as Srpsko (Serbian)—Sarajevo. Reading these postwar scenes from afar, a renowned team of postmodern scholars, Sheldon Pollock, Homi Bhabha, Carol Breckenridge, and Dipesh Chakrabarty, declared of Sarajevo that "the cosmopolitan character of the city and all that it stood for were finally destroyed" (2002, 3).

Since 1990, nationalist politicians and their followers have been rallying Bosnians to identify politically with one or the other constituent nation, and the 1992–95 war forced everyone to take sides.[6] The Dayton Accords, which ended the war, affirmed the contention that Bosnia would be better off divided into mono-ethnic groups, and the constitution that derived from the

3. Grave of a Bosnian šehid in a Sarajevo municipal park

accords established borders, instituted a governing structure, and distributed resources based on that tripartite ethnic key. Although the overall urban scene and many of Sarajevans' everyday practices belie the belief that people and their products—food, clothing, home decor, language, neighborhood, loved ones, ancestors, and progeny—derive from and represent one and only one tradition, when those in power, backed by resources, arms, and the sanction of the international community, declare that everyone has a single ethnonational identity, well then, so be it. It takes a will of steel or sheer naïveté to reject the increasingly accepted knowledge that BiH is constituted of three separate nations representing three peoples, the Bosniacs, the Croats, and the Serbs (henceforth B-C-S), each holding constitutional rights to their own language, territory, governance, and culture. Yet it seems to me that pronouncements of the end of cosmopolitan Sarajevo, while they capture one sort of truth, also do violence to the people that they claim to represent. If we look beyond legal documents, population statistics, and voting results into the spontaneous words and everyday deeds of the people of Sarajevo, we might glean a different picture, one that derives from and reinforces a cherished common culture based on the familiar spectacle of multiplicity in the public domain (Karahasan 1993; Mahmutćehajić 2000; Pejanović 2004).

It is the constant shift between mirth and melancholy, heterogeneity and hybridity that keeps drawing me back to Sarajevo. It is what double dares me to write an ethnography that will do justice to the overlapping, necessarily interdependent processes and products of ethnic separatism and interethnic blends that constitute Sarajevo as "a cosmopolitan society and its enemies" (Beck 2002, 83). Yet even as I write of duality, I know that such binaries fail to capture what is and has always been happening in Bosnia, a special kind of Balkan and Central European borderland that encourages the blurring of boundaries even as it contributes to the maintenance of several separate groups who treasure and guard the distinctiveness of their traditions (see Ballinger 2003, 2004; Green 2005; Todorova 1997; cf. Berdahl 1999; Bhabha 1990; Rosaldo 1989). In commonsensical alternation between protecting the differences that represent ethnic divides and crossing, if not ignoring those barriers, Sarajevans' conventions and conversations attest to a dynamic of variegated, interdependent, and always changing cultural patterns.

With the key metaphor of kaleidoscope that informs this book, I am suggesting that along with the shattering experiences of war and a constitution that reinforces the entrenchment of either-or national(istic) belongings, the cityscape of Sarajevo and the long-term experiences of its residents serve as constant reminders of compatible ethnic, confessional, and philosophical trajectories, and the pleasures of cosmopolitanism. This is not to suggest that Sarajevans, Bosnians, and Yugoslavs have not long categorized themselves according to faith and ethnicity (see Lockwood 1975; Bringa 1995; Malcolm 1996; Donia 2006), but from 1945 until 1991 these categories were part of a wider Yugoslav discourse of socialist internationalism and an ethos of "brotherhood and unity" (Djilas 1991, 164–80; Ugrešić 1998; cf. Shoup 1968; Wachtel 1998; Zimmerman 1987). In Sarajevo high rates of intermarriage, the choice of generic first names for children, and a wide variety of cultural productions that transcended, mixed, or mocked the constraints of ethnic boundaries expressed interethnic tolerance and pan-ethnic solidarity (see, e.g., Donia and Fine 1994; Lampe 2000, 337; S. Ramet 1999). And then it all blew up in a gruesome war that ended only through official recognition of the mutual incompatibility of the claims, demands, and desires of Bosnia's Serbs, Croats, and Bosniacs, each bound to their own by blood and history. But that, too, is not the end of the story.

So, while it may certainly be the case that most people in Sarajevo and throughout Bosnia-Herzegovina view their capital, country, and society as a trinational hodgepodge of dissonant traditions that are better off "cleansed" into mono-ethnic groups and regions (Bozic 2006; Dahlman and Ó Tuathail

2005; Hayden 2007; cf. Sorabji 2006), as the book unfolds we will see that some of the same people who assert the rectitude of a trinational government and hardened ethnic divides sometimes abandon that stance to advocate for Bosnia's richly varied cultural heritage and Sarajevo's openness to diversity. Then they can shift again when faced with twenty-first-century facts that demonstrate that once-multiethnic Sarajevo is now dominated by Muslim Bosniacs, just as Banja Luka is predominately Orthodox Serb, and much of Herzegovina is overwhelmingly Catholic Croat. The continuously constricting and expanding patterns of a kaleidoscope capture the idea that even if the B-C-S scheme guides people's thoughts, acts, and feelings, it is intimately interlocked with a practical hybridity that also pervades everyday life.

Sarajevo: A Bosnian Kaleidoscope is a happy and sad tale about the contemporary nation- and state-building projects that connect heterogeneity to hybridity and impinge upon the people and places that are Sarajevo. Instead of accepting the conclusion that ethnic cleansing has become hegemonic—the seemingly natural, morally correct standard of political and cultural life—as well as a demographic fait accompli, the book tells a story, or a number of stories, about how the people of Sarajevo think about, represent, and interact with one another as ethnically marked and marking social actors. Taking the position that it is important to link "the little poetics of everyday interaction with the grand dramas of official pomp and historiography in order to break down illusions of scale" (Herzfeld 1997a, 25), this book refuses unilinear cause-and-effect models. Instead, it strives to illuminate the competing yet dialectically engaged stances of tolerance, cosmopolitanism, multiculturalism, and hostility, ethnic exclusivity, nationalism, and their ever-changing results specific to the reconfiguration of geographies, polities, and identities that, for lack of better names, we call postwar Sarajevo and post-Dayton Bosnia-Herzegovina.

Steeped in History: How Sarajevo Came to Be What It Is

I am not a historian, and in the overview that follows I rely primarily on the works of American historians (Donia 2006; Donia and Fine 1994; Fine 1975); British historians (Hastings 1997; Malcolm 1996); and Bosnian historians (Filipović 2007; Lovrenović 2001). As a cultural anthropologist, I do know that although Sarajevans frequently and fervently invoke the past to explain their country's present, very few people in Western Europe and the Anglo-American world are familiar with southeastern Europe, with the exception of ancient Greece's foundational contributions to Western civilization. This lack of knowledge may be due to the different vicissitudes that befell the Balkans and the countries bordering the Atlantic Ocean. By the end of the fifteenth century, Spain, Portugal, England, France, and the Netherlands had become centralized states and maritime powers. At the same time, the kingdoms and principalities of the Balkans had been conquered and colonized by the Ottoman Turks. While the countries of Western Europe established colonies in Africa, Asia, and the New World and became metropoles of global empires, Bosnia and many of its neighbors became colonies and disappeared from the map of Europe (Todorova 1997, 2004; Wolf 1982; Wolff 1994).

In the preface to his history of Bosnia, British historian Noel Malcolm declares, "The great religions and great powers of European history had overlapped and combined there: the empires of Rome, Charlemagne, the Ottomans and the Austro-Hungarians, and the faiths of Western Christianity, Eastern Christianity, Judaism and Islam" (1996, xix). This description evokes a fluid site of ethnic diversity and religious tolerance; Bosnia is portrayed more as a welcoming crossroads of faiths and nations than a battlefield made bloody by invading armies and sporadic uprisings (see also Donia and Fine 1994). Indeed, this description of *colonized* Bosnia is remarkably close to the hybrid "third space" that Homi Bhabha (1990, 1994) delineated as the optimistic result of *postcolonialism*. Be that as it may, the history of colonialism and foreign intervention in the Balkans resulted in different cultural constellations and political orientations from those of Europe's western and northern parts (Herzfeld 1997b). These differences contribute in no small part to the several overlapping causes of the violence that reduced the aspiring Republic of Bosnia-Herzegovina to a weak postwar state and rendered its diverse and fluid population into three separate Bosniac, Croat, and Serb nations. Perhaps too that history has paved the way for late-twentieth-century international intervention and Bosnia's ongoing supervision in the twenty-first (Bose 2002; Glenny 2001). How did this situation come about? What is this history in which Sarajevo is steeped?

Archeological and linguistic evidence indicates that late in the sixth century Slavic populations began to enter southeastern Europe, where they settled and intermingled with the indigenous peoples.[7] Some scholars claim that these Slaveni were "all one people" who divided over time into the Croats in the West and the Serbs in the East (e.g., Donia and Fine 1994, 14), while others suggest that "the Serbs and the Croats were, from the earliest times, distinct but closely connected, living and migrating in tandem" (Malcolm 1996, 8). Whether or not there were always Serbs and Croats in Bosnia—and this issue remains a bone of contention—it does seem clear that although sometimes under the domain of Hungary or Croatia to the west or of Serbia to the south and the east, Bosnia has long been recognized as a named, bounded territory, whose inhabitants were known as Bosnians (Donia and Fine 1994, 14; Magaš 2003, 19; Malcolm 1996, 11–12).[8] It is also undisputed that by the end of the twelfth century, Bosnia operated as an independent state.[9] That state expanded in size and power throughout the thirteenth and fourteenth centuries.

From the start, Bosnia differed from other European states in that three churches operated unimpeded on its soil. The loosely structured Bosnian Church, condemned as heretical after its thirteenth-century break with Rome, claimed adherents throughout the country, while the Orthodox Church concentrated its activities in Hum, or Herzegovina. The Franciscan order erected over a dozen Roman Catholic monasteries in the late fourteenth and early fifteenth centuries, which offered services in lieu of parish churches (Donia and Fine 1994, 17–23; Fine 1975). Religious pluralism persisted under Bosnia's Catholic kings until the medieval state's final years. In 1459, threatened by attacks from Turkish troops and fearful of being left alone to fight the impending battle, King Stephen Tomaš capitulated to pressure from Rome to persecute the Bosnian Church, and he broke it just four years before his kingdom fell (Malcolm 1996, 23). Over the centuries, however, the defunct Bosnian Church took on mythical proportions, and in contemporary BiH its teachings are invoked to explain why Islam made greater inroads in Bosnia than anywhere else in Europe (see chapter 3; cf. Donia and Fine 1994, 22–25).

After their victory in 1463, the Ottoman Turks began an intense period of construction in Bosnia. They built roads, bridges, and towns, which stimulated commerce and the growth of urban trades and crafts (Heywood 1996, 31; Lovrenović 2001, 92). Fifteen years after its founding, Sarajevo already boasted a mosque, a Sufi lodge, a bathhouse, a piped water system, a bridge over the Miljacka River, an inn for travelers, and the *serai*, or governor's court, which gave the city its name (Malcolm 1996, 67). A *bezistan* (covered cloth market), a library, a *medressa* (Islamic school), and another large mosque were added toward the end of the fifteenth century (Donia 2006, 17–20).

By the beginning of the sixteenth century, Sarajevo had grown from a new, exclusively Turkish garrison town to a multiconfessional city of 23,500. Small groups of Catholic merchants from Dubrovnik made temporary homes in Sarajevo, while an Orthodox church erected by the 1530s attests to a permanent Christian presence. A small number of Jews from among the thousands expelled from Spain in 1492 made their way to Bosnia. Most resettled in Sarajevo by the mid-sixteenth century, where they built a synagogue, established a community, and developed the city's cloth trade (Levy 1996, 11–15). In its treatment of the Jews, Bosnia again proved exceptional, for unlike in nearby Venice and Dubrovnik, Sarajevo's Jews were never confined to ghettoes.

Although certainly its church and synagogue were smaller in stature than its mosques with their towering minarets (Donia 2006, 15–16), Sarajevo developed architecturally, socially, and spiritually into a city of four faiths. Of life in sixteenth-century Sarajevo, Malcolm declares, "It was good, by Balkan standards or indeed by any standards of the time" (1996, 68). My friends Klara and Amar concur. In 2004 they fondly mentioned to me that centuries before the French *philosophes* articulated their ideas about the rights of man, these very rights were put into practice in Ottoman Sarajevo. Wealthy men who built new family homes were expected to contribute a public water fountain and place of worship for the enjoyment of all the people in the neighborhood (see Donia 2006, 17–19), and municipal statutes required that each home builder respect the rights of his neighbors to an unimpeded, outside view.

Along with leaving their legacy in religion, art, architecture, commerce, and trade, the Ottomans also bequeathed their *millet* system to Bosnia-Herzegovina. *Millet* means both "religion" and "religious community," and it was the major criterion by which the Ottomans classified, counted, and taxed the population. Several benefits accrued to adherents of Islam (Donia 2006, 15), but throughout Ottoman-ruled Europe most Christians kept true to their faith. The Bosnians, however, again proved exceptional as thousands embraced Islam.[10] As they reflect on the history of their people, their city, and their country, present-day Bosniacs, Croats, and Serbs offer differing interpretations of these conversions and the long-lasting effects of Ottoman rule (see chapters 3 and 7).

Over the course of the four-hundred-year Ottoman reign, several attempts were made by Christians from within and outside Bosnia-Herzegovina to overthrow the Turks. Prince Eugene of Savoy, bolstered by powerful Habsburg armies, made incursions into Bosnia in 1687 and on the night of October 23–24 burned most of Sarajevo to the ground after its leaders refused to capitulate. The Turks eventually regained their footing, repelled the Austrian troops, and rebuilt most of the city, but Sarajevo never recouped its former glory (Donia 2006, 24–25).

The final blow to Ottoman rule occurred in the middle of the nineteenth century following a spreading rebellion in Herzegovina, which drew armed support from Serbia, Macedonia, and Russia. Fearful of upheaval in the heart of Europe, the Great Powers convened to settle the conflicts, and with the signing of the August 1878 Treaty of Berlin they rearranged the map of the

Balkans. Romania, Serbia, Montenegro, and Bulgaria were recognized as autonomous, while the right to occupy and administer—but not to annex—Ottoman Bosnia-Herzegovina was granted to Austria-Hungary. The Habsburgs waited thirty years and in 1908 annexed BiH into their empire (see Donia 2006, 38, 106–7; McCarthy 1996, 78–82).

While leaving intact the self-supporting philanthropic, educational, and social organizations that each of Sarajevo's religious communities had established over the centuries, the Austrians added a "second face" to the city (Donia 2006, 27). Toward the intertwined goals of modernization and the development of a united Bosnian national identity, Prime Minister/Finance Minister Benjamin Kallay built railroads, encouraged the founding of new factories and commercial enterprises, and established secular educational institutions. Under his ambitious leadership, new governmental buildings were erected, including the elaborate Vijećnica (City Hall). A neo-Gothic Catholic cathedral was constructed near the recently completed Serbian Orthodox church, and new roads and walkways extended Sarajevo's reach. Perhaps Kallay's most significant project was the establishment of the stately Landsmuseum, or Zemaljski Muzej, known today as the National Museum of Bosnia-Herzegovina. Its concentration on the flora, fauna, archeology, and ethnology of the region was aimed at demonstrating *Bošnjastvo* (Bosnianness), the commonalities linking all the people and places of Bosnia-Herzegovina into one national entity. However, competing popular movements of "Croat and Serb nationalism spread among the Catholic and Orthodox Bosnians through the very networks of priests, schoolteachers and educated newspaper readers which Austro-Hungarian policy had helped to bring into being," dooming Kallay's "Bošnjak project" (Malcolm 1996, 147–48; see also Lovrenović 2001, 150–52). Nonetheless, its artifacts remain in place in the National Museum, and in the early 1990s Bosnian Muslim elites revitalized the term *Bošnjak,* which has since entered daily discourse as the official term for Bosnian Muslims (see chapters 3 and 4).

Prior to the 1992–95 wars, Sarajevo was best known as the city where, in protest to Austrian rule, Gavrilo Princip assassinated Archduke Franz Ferdinand and his wife, Princess Sophia, a deed that sparked World War I. Even though that war resulted in the collapse of both the Ottoman and the Austro-Hungarian Empires, Bosnia-Herzegovina did not gain independence. Instead, it was incorporated into the new South Slav, or Yugoslav, Kingdom of Serbs, Croats, and Slovenes. Two decades later, Europe was again a battlefield, and on April 10, 1941, BiH was absorbed into the fascist Independent State of Croatia. With this new conquest began mass persecutions against Bosnia's

Serbs, Gypsies, and Jews (see Djilas 1991, 121–25). By the end of World War II, the Jewish population was reduced from some twelve to fourteen thousand to a mere one thousand souls, and "one of the old and formative components of the Bosnian pattern was torn out, one that had shaped its urban culture and entire ambience" (Lovrenović 2001, 170; also Malcolm 1996, chapter 9; and chapter 6 of this volume).

During World War II, Bosnia became the principal battlefield of the Partisans, a multiethnic, socialist resistance army led by Josip Broz Tito, in two overlapping wars: One was against the Nazi occupiers. The other was a complicated civil war against both the Ustaše army of fascist Croatia, and the Četniks, the Serb and Montenegrin right-wing loyalist army, which were waging war against each other and ravaging the civilian population. In the midst of these wars, on November 29, 1943, Tito held a conference in Jajce, the medieval capital of the Kingdom of Bosnia, where he proclaimed the new Yugoslav Federation. By May 1945, the Partisans emerged victorious and implemented Tito's plan for a Communist Party–led Yugoslav Federation of six republics where each and every South Slav people was guaranteed equal rights.[11]

Tito's death in 1980 coincided with the onset of an enduring economic crisis and a decline in living standards after almost four decades of Yugoslavia's uninterrupted progress. Ongoing tensions among the republics were exacerbated by president of Serbia Slobodan Milošević's militant assertion of Serb nationalism, and in 1990 the Yugoslav League of Communists lost its unity and monopoly. By the end of that year, multiparty elections were held in all six republics, which resulted in absolute or relative majorities for nationalist parties.

What are now generally referred to as the Yugoslav wars, or the wars of Yugoslav secession, began in June 1991 after the republics of Slovenia and Croatia declared independence and the Yugoslav National Army (JNA), headquartered in Belgrade, took military action to keep them in the federation. Tucked into Yugoslavia's northwest corner, where it shared an internal border only with Croatia, Slovenia was the most ethnically homogeneous republic in the federation and had only a tiny Serb minority, and the JNA gave up the fight there in a matter of weeks (see Rothschild 1993, 259; Woodward 1995, 166–68). But hostilities were brutal in Croatia, especially in its eastern border region, where Serbs comprised a significant portion of the population (see Denich 2000; Grandits and Promitzer 2000), and the war raged there for several years.

In Bosnia-Herzegovina, citizens were called upon to vote on a referendum for independence during the two-day period of February 29–March 1, 1992.

Over 95 percent of those who cast their ballots did so in favor of independence, but many Bosnian Serbs who wished to remain within Serb-dominated rump Yugoslavia protested the legality of the referendum and stayed away from the polls. Nonetheless, approximately 65 percent of the citizenry voted for secession, and on April 6, 1992, the Republic of Bosnia-Herzegovina was recognized as a sovereign state by the United States and the European Community (now the European Union). Within days, Sarajevo fell victim to a strangling siege perpetrated by radical Serb militias that had established themselves in the surrounding mountains. Three armies—the Army of the Serbian Republic, the Croatian Defense Council of Herzeg-Bosna, and the Army of Bosnia-Herzegovina—and various militias waged war for almost three years. Thousands of troops and civilians were injured or murdered; nearly two million people, mainly women and children, became war refugees; and irreplaceable cultural landmarks were wantonly destroyed.

Western analysts disagree on the prime cause of the 1992–95 wars in Bosnia (see Stokes et al. 1996; S. Ramet 2005). Some point to long-suppressed ethnic hatreds boiling over with the final collapse of Tito's communism (e.g., Cohen 1995, 246–47; Kaplan 1994). Others cite the rise of political elites or megalomaniacal leaders in Serbia and Croatia, "who had nothing to gain from the transition" (Silber and Little 1997, 25) and remobilized the Yugoslav population into ethnic communities (Gagnon 2004) where nationalist myths were manipulated into violence (Donia and Fine 1994; Malcolm 1996; Perica 2002). Still others blame the actions and inaction of the European Community and the United States following the structural collapse of Yugoslavia's unique multicultural society and political-economic position at the end of the Cold War (Campbell 1999; Woodward 1995). But just about everyone agrees in his or her assessment of how that war was conducted: Military campaigns were fiercest and civilians faced the harshest brutality in areas where people had lived together as friends and neighbors who crossed, blurred, and sometimes dissolved ethnic divides (Bringa 1995; Denich 2000; Maas 1996; Sudetic 1998).

Counterpoised against those who attribute the recent wars in Bosnia to the inability of ethnically mixed populations to live together without a strong government ruling from above were the people of "the towns and cities of Bosnia-Herzegovina [who] presented a formidable obstacle to the nationalist propaganda aimed at making national states appear the natural condition" (Woodward 1995, 234). Sarajevans and foreign observers who chronicled events in the war-besieged city described a fierce determination to continue its centuries-long cosmopolitan spirit of multiculturalism and tolerance (e.g.,

Dizdarević 1994; Kurspahić 1997; Mahmutćehajić 2003; Mann 2001; Pejanović 2004; Tanović-Miller 2001; cf. Andreas 2008). They attribute the violence of the 1992–95 war to outsiders, those radical Serbs to the east and Croats to the west who, thwarted by BiH's crazy-quilt distribution of Muslims, Serbs, and Croats in its efforts to make territorially coterminous nation-states, waged a war to separate out the population and divide up the results.

The Dayton Peace Accords, which finally ended the war, maintained the territorial integrity of Bosnia-Herzegovina but endorsed its ethnically cleansed results by declaring the Bosniacs, the Croats, and the Serbs the country's incommensurable constituent groups, each vested with collective rights to its own language, history, and self-governance. Throughout the book, I ask: How have Bosnia's overlapping cultural legacies of colonialism, cosmopolitanism, and Yugoslav socialism, and the familiar, often fluid identities that developed over time solidified since Dayton through law and governmental practices? How are these legacies, identities, and practices being interpreted, accepted, challenged, or co-opted by Sarajevans as they go about their daily lives? But before delving into the ethnography that seeks to answer these questions, I must take a slight detour to contextualize my involvement in the processes and events that are at the heart of the book.

Methods

Although I did not know it at the time, field research for *Sarajevo: A Bosnian Kaleidoscope* began over twenty-five years ago when I first set foot in Yugoslavia. I arrived in Zagreb, then the capital of the Socialist Republic of Croatia, in October 1982 as the accompanying spouse of an American doctoral student who had won a coveted Fulbright Fellowship. While my husband traveled across town to spend his days with colleagues in an academic institute, I slung a canvas bag over my shoulder and trod uphill to the outdoor market to purchase the fruits and vegetables that were plentiful in summer but pitiful in winter, dairy products, bread, and an occasional chicken, with head and feet intact. My first lessons in Yugoslavia's languages and cultures occurred up there on the Dolac, where I asked for everything I needed in the amount of *po' kilo* (half a kilo, a little more than a pound) and paid for my purchases by allowing each vendor to pluck the appropriate bill from the fan of multicolored dinars that I clutched in my outstretched hand. My communications skills became more sophisticated with time, for in addition to homemaking duties, I enrolled in a course for international students at Zagreb University and studied what my textbook proclaimed to be the "Hrvatsko-Srpski jezik," or the Croat-Serbian language. I also audited a Russian language course and sat in on several sociology classes.

As an unexpected but welcome side effect, I began to meet many interesting and generous people from whom I learned about Yugoslavia's perplexing and paradoxical political structure. Some of them were, and remain to this day, committed Yugoslavs, but others expressed longings for an independent Croatia, comprised solely of "western people" more like Slovenians, Austrians, and Germans rather than the "primitive" Bosnians, Serbs, Macedonians, Montenegrins, and Albanians, their fellow Yugoslavs to the east (see Bakić-Hayden 1996).

Over the course of that 1982–83 year, I traveled twice to Sarajevo. I delighted in the multicultural aura of the city; its mosques, churches, and synagogues; its Yugo-rock groups and avant-garde theatrical troupes; and the brightly colored carpets, pounded copper coffee sets, and delicate filigree jewelry for sale in the Old City with its fountains, pigeons, and the smoky aroma of grilled meats. An extra air of excitement pervaded Sarajevo as it prepared to host the 1984 Winter Olympic Games.

Less than a decade later, Sarajevo was under siege. How could that have happened? Nothing in my Yugoslavia experience had prepared me for such violence. Along with so many others inside and beyond the borders of Bosnia-Herzegovina, I was certain that the hostilities were a freakish turn of events and would end in a matter of weeks. But they worsened as I prepared for my move from Chicago to another international hotspot, Israel.

At the same time that Yugoslavia became an inferno, the mood was optimistic in Israel with the August 1993 signing of the Oslo Accords. Following the precedent set in 1977–79, when it provided sanctuary to scores of Vietnamese boat people, the State of Israel extended an offer of refuge to one hundred Bosnian war refugees. Eighty-five men, women, and children who had been living in or near the Pula refugee camp on Croatia's Istrian coast took up this offer, and after the initial confusion of arrival, they settled into the semi-attached houses of Kibbutz Beit Oren.[12] The children enrolled in school and the adults went to work. I spent several long weekends commiserating with these families about the tragedy of the war and how and why they were waiting it out in Israel (Markowitz 1995, 1996).

Those visits, coupled with the brutal images televised via CNN and the BBC of a city deprived of electricity, water, foodstuffs, and communications, jarred my memories of a jubilantly multicultural, multiethnic city called Sarajevo. The recent triumph of the Olympic Games and the centuries-long crazy-quilt pattern of peoples and faiths that had characterized Bosnia were being bombed into oblivion in the name of a new hygienic program called ethnic cleansing. How to understand this tragedy? Was there anything that I could do?

As the war wound down, I turned to my fellow anthropologist Olga Supek, and together we wrote a proposal for research aimed at exploring how extended, often ethnically mixed kin networks were rallying to rebuild war-shattered homes and communities. In August 1997, we traveled to Sarajevo to confer with Bosnian colleagues and assess the feasibility of our project. Against the backdrop of a bombed city, its rather dazed inhabitants seemed to repeat mechanically, "Bio je rat—biče bolje" (There was a war; things will be better). The only two degreed ethnologists in Sarajevo at the time endorsed our project but with the caveat that we wait at least two years to conduct the study. They also informed us that we would have to change our methodology. Toward the goal of reinvigorating anthropology at Sarajevo University, we planned to collaborate with local doctoral students to conduct the bulk of the ethnography. But unbeknown to us, unlike the universities in Belgrade, Ljubljana, and Zagreb, Sarajevo University never did have a Department of Ethnology.[13] Our Sarajevo colleagues advised that one or both of us conduct a small ethnographic project in the capital and avoid fieldwork in the small towns or villages, which had been ethnically cleansed.

Five years passed before I returned to Sarajevo with a new research plan. "Ethnic Entanglements: Sarajevo's Cultural Legacies in Discourse and Practice" moved the emphasis away from postwar trauma and the reintegration of refugees to the impact of colonialism, socialism, hybridity, and heterogeneity—and "ethnic cleansing"—in the daily life practices and identity narratives of Sarajevans.[14]

Sarajevo had changed since my last visit. The SFOR troops that were ubiquitous in 1997 held a much lower profile, and Sarajevans were more eager to talk than they had been five years earlier. They told jokes about everything from the "Rolling Stones amplifiers" and "Pershing missile" minarets on the new mosques, to the "Ninjas," those few yet striking women who covered themselves from head to toe in flowing Muslim garb, to the reams of paper required for privatizing apartments, and to the seemingly endless disappearing acts of indicted war criminals. But the dazed optimism of 1997 had just about disappeared as well. Along with their jokes, Sarajevans of varied ethnic backgrounds voiced disappointment with their country's sluggish rate of economic recovery and its bizarre, ineffective political system. Some expressed alarm at a rising Islamic presence. Just about everyone, from young people to pensioners, mentioned fear of another war.

4. "Pershing Missile" minaret

When I came for full-time fieldwork in March 2004, I planned to investigate the effect of Sarajevo's multiple legacies on the current state-building project by participating in the daily life of the city and engaging in face-to-face conversations with a variety of ethnically marked and marking Sarajevans. My research strategies included participant observation within the networks of several key hosts and interviews with representatives of major cultural organizations (Bosniac, Croat, Jewish, Serb, Slovenian, and intercultural) and political parties. I also attended public forums of the Congress of Bosniac Intellectuals and of two independent, ecumenical discussion groups—Krug/Circle 99 and Među Nama (Among Us)—and joined in various festivals and commemorative services. Most important, I engaged in conversations with and among a wide range of individuals aged twenty-one to eighty. Many of my conversation partners were young people—students, teachers, sales clerks, museum workers, nongovernmental organization (NGO) staff—but my closest Sarajevo friends were considerably older. Most of the representatives of the cultural organizations and political parties with whom I met were middle-aged and university educated, and all but two were men.

In addition to these methods, I also consulted Yugoslav census data and the results of a population count conducted in the Federation during 2002 (see esp. chapter 4). A few months into fieldwork, I sought an additional way to capture how Sarajevans declare their ethnic identity when engaged in interactions with the state, and I learned that marriage registry forms request, among other things, that brides and grooms indicate their *nacionalna pripadnost* (national, or ethnic, belonging). Unlike the census, which requires citizens to reply orally to a field interviewer, applicants at the marriage registry write in the requested data—name, address, profession, national belonging, and so on—as they wish. Thanks to the kind administrators of Sarajevo's Centar Općina (Center District), I was able to record the *nacionalna pripadnost* entries of the almost five thousand brides and almost five thousand grooms who registered their marriages there from the beginning of 1996 through the end of 2003.

In April 2008, I paid my latest visit to Sarajevo. I took a walking tour of the city with a certified tour guide, visited key sites on my own, and spent time with several friends from my earlier fieldwork. Sitting in the living room of Lebiba's high-rise apartment with her eight-year old daughter and tiny infant son, I couldn't help but reminisce about our first meeting in August 1997. While we talked about her growing family and their much improved financial situation, Lebiba and I wondered out loud, How postwar is postwar Sarajevo?

Ultimately, the descriptions I offer of Sarajevans narrating who they and their neighbors are as they go about living their lives comprise a specific text, written with no small measure of trepidation from the hands and through the eyes of a particular observer. This book is not meant to be, nor can it be, *the* definitive ethnography of Sarajevo after the war. Others have written and will write their stories quite differently. Nonetheless, what I have to say is written in the spirit of "getting things right" (Farmer 2004; Scheper-Hughes 1995), by which I mean not only reporting facts on the ground but also listening to, taking seriously, and engaging with the many conflicting interpretations of what those facts mean for the variously self-defined Sarajevans who enliven their city as they live in it.

2

Practices of Place

Living in and Enlivening Sarajevo

Cities are complex, exciting, and challenging places, densely populated man-made environments characterized by the interdependence of occupational and spatial specializations (Durkheim 1964; Gottdiener 1985; Park 1926; Weber 1966; Wirth 1938) and permeated with difference (Simmel 1950a; I. M. Young 1990). Cities are cerebral and tangible, expressive and sensual; they are places of production and consumption, work and leisure, private homes and public institutions that "support unimaginably diverse social practices" (Amin and Thrift 2002, 3).

When portrayed as fat black dots in world atlases or viewed from airplanes, mountaintops, or the upper floors of a skyscraper, cities appear permanently fixed in the terrain, bounded and complete, spatially integrated according to a grand plan. From below, however, the city reveals a profusion of styles in its boulevards and alleys, parks and plazas, theaters and temples, markets, marquees, and monuments. This ongoing contrast between the wholeness of a city and its fragments, its permanence and its openness to change produces an everyday experience of multiplicity, paradox, and choice.

Cities, then, are dynamic contact zones whose populations are as diverse as their layouts. Urban life supports such diversity through the interdependence of specialized labor, and an array of markets; cultural, ethnic and religious institutions; and residential communities. In the workplace, in their apartment buildings, in school, on the streets, in shops, and on the bus, urbanites regularly rub shoulders with others who are in some way different from themselves. In that context of "diversity in proximity" (More 1975), they daily confront, reinforce, test, and cross group boundaries. Through intercultural contacts and multiethnic connections, city dwellers are constantly constructing new modes of belonging (Baumann 1996); their identities tend to be particularly fluid, hybrid, and cosmopolitan (Bauman 1996; Hall 1996; Hannerz 1996).

All that notwithstanding, cities can also be effective sites for the articulation of nationalistic projects that enforce religious and racial distinctions and solidify ethnic hierarchies (Holston and Appadurai 1999, 2). Cities, with their monumental architecture, ritual displays, and time and traffic regulations (Rotenberg 1992; Singer 1991; Wheatley 1969), are fertile ground for the dissemination of top-down hegemony, which seeps into and shapes the intricate intimacies of urbanites' domestic space and personal lives (Bourdieu 1984). And yet, even as swastika-draped Berlin, filled with Nazi troops and Hitler Youth appeared to manifest the goals of the Thousand Year Reich, and Soviet Moscow, enmeshed in a network of ruby red stars—from the tops of the Romanov-built Kremlin, Lenin's tomb, and Stalin's wedding-cake skyscrapers, to the caps of Red Army soldiers and the ties of Pioneer schoolchildren—displayed the right and might of Communism, the palimpsest-like copresence of contradictory forms in both cities never failed to stimulate competing, subversive visions (see Benjamin 1979; Bulgakov 1996; Huyssen 1997; Voinovich 1986).

Because cities are spatial compendiums of multiple histories that coexist with, flow into, and disrupt one another, the "authoritarian project is not always successful" there (Short 2000, 19; cf. Derrida 2001; Lefebvre 1996; Simmel 1950b). And as much as they seem to be certain and complete, cities are also ambiguous texts replete with contradictory meanings, waiting to be read, redacted, and rewritten. The continuously in-motion results of "flesh and stone in interaction" (Amin and Thrift 2002, 10) make cities complex places open to multiple interpretations.

The city of Sarajevo has never produced unanimity of categorization or experience. In scholarly tomes, Bosnia's capital has been dubbed a typical Balkan city (Todorov 1983) and included as an example of Mediterranean European urban life (Kenny and Kertzer 1983). Late-twentieth-century Sarajevo has been described as an Ottoman city with an enduringly Turkish appearance (Spangler 1983, 80); as a city in which Central Europe and Turkey meet and combine (Karahasan 1993, 90–92); and as the most Yugoslav of Yugoslav cities (Donia and Fine 1994, 192), a multiethnic and multicultural city where no one national group held the majority (Simmons 2002; Woodward 1995, 234; Žiga 2001, 58). With its churches, mosques, and synagogues in close proximity, Sarajevo was the "European Jerusalem" (Koštović 2001), a city of pluralism, religious tolerance, and mutual understanding (Mahmutćehajić 2000, 46; 2003).

Perhaps it was the 1961 Nobel Prize–winning author, Ivo Andrić, whose description of Sarajevo has proven the most prophetic. He said of Sarajevo that it is "a real city: [a] city aging and dying, and at the same time, a city being reborn and reshaped" (1970, 12).

When those words were published in 1970, Sarajevo was a bustling hub where "the peoples of Bosnia and Hercegovina for the first time [had] their destiny in their own hands and [were] leaving a new imprint on this ancient city" (Andrić 1970, 10). Renovation of the Ottoman-built Baščaršija and the residential, administrative, and cultural facilities of Austrian-built Marjindvor turned Sarajevo into a favored tourist spot for people throughout Yugoslavia and vacationers from abroad. At the same time, new high-rise apartment neighborhoods, equipped with sports arenas and cultural facilities, extended Sarajevo's city limits outward. All this construction provided an enviable array of jobs for the growing city's ethnically diverse, upwardly mobile population (see Donia 2006, 229–34).

5. Sarajevo's Baščaršija

By the early 1980s, multiethnic Sarajevo was Yugoslavia's center of multicultural creativity (Lampe 2000, 337; P. Ramet 1984; S. Ramet 1999; Tahmiščić 1970, 6).[1] Selected to host the XIV Winter Olympic Games, in 1984 Sarajevo received worldwide recognition as a beautiful, interesting, and well-organized city, characterized by warm hospitality, cultural vibrancy, and a surprisingly high standard of living.[2]

In addition to the ethnic diversity and religious pluralism of its structures and its people, Sarajevo was also characterized by a reassuring rhythm, by the peaceful predictability of its pace and tempo: In the mornings traffic grew heavy as tramlines, buses, and private automobiles moved people from one end of the city to another, from outlying residential neighborhoods into the center. In the renovated Baščaršija, silversmiths created delicate filigree jewelry, and coppersmiths pounded out plates and platters; popular music from Radio Sarajevo poured out into the street, while smoke from the grilled-meat restaurants wafted past colorful displays of brightly patterned carpets, up-to-date leather goods, and contemporary art and literature. In the outdoor city markets, seasonal fruits and vegetables, dairy products, breads, and meat were fresh and plentiful. In the new office buildings, managers, economists, engineers, clerks, and architects were at work implementing Yugoslav policies, planning new apartment communities, factories, hydroelectric facilities, bridges, schools, and sports complexes at home and in nonaligned countries abroad. People knew what to expect when they went to shop; when they stopped in at a café; when they entered a government office, a hospital, or a library. They knew what awaited them at work or at school, and they knew how to do their jobs.

Sarajevo's easy-going sociability came to an abrupt halt in the spring of 1992, when radical Serb forces in the surrounding hills launched a campaign of violence against the city. The goal of that campaign was to eliminate pluralism in the built environment and to destroy the everyday practices of Sarajevans' "common life" (Donia 2006; Filipović 2007; Karahasan 1993; Pejanović 2004).[3] It was to prove once and for all the fallacy of a hybrid Bosnia and the necessity for its ethnically based partition (see Donia 2006, 313–16; Simmons 2001; Woodward 1995, 192–93).

The first steps taken toward that end were the disruption of urban public space by sniper fire and mortar attacks. The first civilian casualties were gunned down at a peaceful demonstration in front of the BiH Assembly Building on April 5–6, 1992, putting an end to the hopes of thousands for a coalition "Government of National Salvation" (Donia 2006, 282–86).[4] Less than a month later, on the night of May 2, 1992, the Austrian-built Main

Post Office was firebombed, cutting thousands of telephone lines and sending the city's mail up in smoke. From their positions on the mountains, the aggressors quickly gained control of over 80 percent of Sarajevo's water and electricity supplies and shut these off. It is hard to imagine a European city in the late twentieth century deprived of electricity and the darkness that descends upon it at nightfall.

The shelling of both public buildings and private homes drastically altered the cityscape. Mosques and churches, once exclusively houses of worship, now served as makeshift distribution centers for the parcels of humanitarian aid that came from abroad. Sarajevo's Ashkenazi synagogue became the city's sole radio-communication base, as well as a soup kitchen, pharmacy, and medical clinic. Nothing was as it had been, and the aggression against the normal operations of an economically diversified, modern, multiethnic city shook the confidence of its inhabitants, undermining the trust that had undergirded their diversity (Simmons 2001, 625). Nonetheless, despite the dire conditions and the bullets that they faced, many Sarajevans remained resolute in asserting their desire for pluralism by performing daily acts of courage, ingenuity, and kindness (see, e.g., Dizdarević 1994; Donia 2006, 287, 317–21; Kurspahić 1997; Mann 2001; Pejanović 2004).

By the end of the siege in December 1995, Sarajevans were dazed and disoriented. Everyone could point to a bullet hole, grenade crater, or bodily scar to show the effects of the war. Sarajevo was no longer a bustling, economically and spatially specialized, interdependent city of cosmopolitans (Pollack et al. 2002, 3). It was a wounded city whose populace had changed. Everyone was much thinner. There were many newcomers to the city, marked in their clothes and accents as villagers, while many native sons and daughters had disappeared. So too had the roofs, windows, and walls of several buildings. Khaki-uniformed SFOR troops and their vehicles patrolled everywhere. The markets were slowly replenished, but instead of Yugoslav dinars, prices remained fixed in deutsche marks, and it was often easier to find a can of Coca-Cola or a bottle of German beer than fresh produce. People began once again to cluster in cafés, to stroll their city streets, to look things over, to remember what had once been and enjoy the present while trying to put aside recent horrors. In August 1997, Lebiba, a member of the ethnology staff in the BiH National Museum, where salaries had not been paid for months, pointed to Sarajevo's full cafés as she told me that everyone was using what little money they had to purchase the small luxuries that they had missed during the war. They were buying candy and toys for their children and paying a mark or two to sip soft drinks, coffee, or beer seated at tables under brightly colored umbrellas out in public.

At the same time, the crimson "roses of Sarajevo" embedded in the sidewalk, the commemorative plaques on the facades of many buildings, and scores of newly renamed streets (Robinson, Engelstoft, and Pobric 2001) reminded passersby of the war and continue to do so over a decade later. On April 6, 2003, "Opkoljeno [Besieged] Sarajevo" opened at the Historical Museum. Documenting the siege through photographs, government documents, newspaper articles, posters, and artifacts, the exhibit has become a permanent fixture. Offered as a "living museum," the display keeps alive Opkoljeno Sarajevo and tangibly connects it to the postwar city beyond its doors.

Early in the twenty-first century, that city has been described as a sad victim of urbicide (Simmons 2001); as a mockery of its former multiethnic self (Kampschror 2001; Simmons 2002); as an uncertain capital (Cataruzza 2001); and as a wounded, struggling, postwar city (Stefansson 2003, 4). Optimistic voices are sometimes heard from among the gloomy descriptions. On the basis of its history of tolerance, compassion, and pluralism (Weine 2000) and its placement at "the crossroads of civilization," Sarajevo has been called "the fastest changing city in Europe" (Somun 2003). Robert Donia closes his biography of Sarajevo by noting that despite the violence done to them, "Sarajevans have demonstrated the capacity and the will to revitalize the city's common life and preserve its legacy of diversity" (2006, 356).

In this chapter, I explore Donia's assertion by examining Sarajevans' place-making and self-making practices. Accompanying Sarajevans in their comings and goings, we will observe how they engage bodily with their surroundings and listen to the stories that they tell about sites on their routes. I will show how habitual strolls through Austrian-, Ottoman-, and Yugoslav-built ground are a means by which Sarajevans prioritize their identity as *Sarajlije*, "literally, the people of Sarajevo" (Stefansson 2004, 16) while they piece their city back together again, normalizing it as a pluralistic and peaceful place.

Two separate but interrelated forms of movement provide the ethnographic material for this chapter. The first to be considered is the *šetanje*, or evening promenade, when Sarajevans take to the streets and trace a well-worn path through the city center. The footprints that Sarajevans leave night after night display their belonging to the entire city and attest to Sarajevo's territorial integrity. In that way, the stylistically varied city becomes one with its residents—it is they who own the streets; it is they who demonstrate the openness of an urban sphere that has enough flexibility to offer novelty to its habitués and extend hospitality to strangers. Yet at the same time, the nightly promenade exacts a particular bodily performance, a rhythm and a directionality, that creates a center and a periphery, so that this seemingly inclusive practice might also exclude.

Sarajevans are also reconnecting (to) the city as they stop at particular places and tell stories about them. Friends and acquaintances often brought me to certain sites that they then described as unique and integral to Sarajevo's special spirit or character. Just as important, sometimes their narratives of place contextualized important events in their personal lives, linking these to the tales they told of what Sarajevo represents to them as an inclusive human habitat and a symbol of resilience.

Overall, this chapter demonstrates that through their movements across the multiply layered urban text, Sarajevans are rereading the war-scarred city and revivifying it as the historically rich, multiethnic site of European civility and sociability that it once was and may still be. Of course, as several cultural anthropologists have taken pains to demonstrate (see, e.g., Blu 1996; Feld and Basso 1996; Henkel 2007; E. Hirsch 1995; Richardson 2005), different people, through their place-making and self-making practices come to perceive and inhabit the city in different ways, and the people of Sarajevo are no exception. Let us now join them on the šetanje.

Place-Making and Self-Making in the Šetanje

Every evening when the weather is fine, and some nights when it is not, Sarajevans are out strolling their city's major thoroughfares. Many begin with a tram or bus ride that brings them from the outlying high-rise apartment complexes that were built as part of socialist Yugoslavia's urban development plan. Others tread downhill from older neighborhoods into the city center. Sarajevo is a walker's city. Its sidewalks are broad and clean, encouraging pedestrians to look up, to stare ahead, or to glance from side to side. As they walk, they can take in the sights of the city and seek out familiar faces.

As has been the case in towns and cities throughout Mediterranean Europe (Del Negro 2004; Vućinić 1999), the Austro-Hungarian Empire (Hanak 1998), and Russia (Bushnell 1988), Sarajevans have been taking to the streets as a leisurely pursuit since at least the beginning of the twentieth century. In Yugoslav Sarajevo, the tempo would slow in the evening as pedestrians converged on the city center. They promenaded in couples and small groups along Tito Street, where they met up, as if by chance, with coworkers, neighbors, and friends. The eclectic architecture, various kinds of street performances, the changing array of consumer goods and commodities, and the continual test of recognizing faces in the friendly crowd kept Sarajevans stimulated, challenged, and discriminating. Underlying the excitement was the reassuring certainty that urban life in socialist Sarajevo was peaceful, predictable, and permeated with good-will.

In early 1992, an ambience of fear began to seep into the safe and secure public domain of civilian urban space. When the shelling of Sarajevo began in April and May, gasoline stations, tramlines, and depots were destroyed, and walking, once a leisurely pursuit and highly social evening practice, became the sole means for getting from one place to another. Sarajevans quickened their pace; they darted and crouched, trotted and ran. Walking-scurrying-running was now the only way to move about. Those thousands of Sarajevans who braved the streets to get to their workplaces, who continued to walk to friends' homes and to the theater, to volunteer their services at the synagogue's communication station or at one of the local hospitals, turned walking from a slow-paced stroll into a political act of defiance (Certeau 1984, 98; cf. Jansen 2001). They did so to nourish the "spirit of Sarajevo" and assert their commitment to an urban way of life based on difference and creativity.

Sarajevans came back outdoors after the war and resumed doing what they had always done. But now those actions held different meanings. One evening in early April 2004, Seka, Vera, and I left a hearty dinner party. Not many people were on the streets. It was rather late, and the weather was brisk. Seka and Vera headed toward a tram stop. I told them that I would prefer to walk. They joined me. After a few blocks, Seka turned off toward her home, while Vera and I continued west. Vera told me that we were treading the route that she had walked early every morning and late each afternoon when Sarajevo was under siege. She and all those other Sarajevans walked in the dark through "Sniper's Alley" and along other dangerous paths just so that they could get to work even if their workplaces were cold and unlit. Walking and working were the ways they resisted the assault on their city and refused capitulation. "Now I am more likely to take the tram. When I walk here at night I remember all those days of walking, walking as quickly as I could, and remember the danger and the dark." In 2004 she compared those extraordinary war years with the peaceful present, and through that comparison Vera affirmed her continuing commitment to the multiethnic staff of the institute where she is employed and to the long history of tolerance in Sarajevo.

The šetanje takes place on Sarajevo's major east-west/west-east avenues that traverse the city center. Stalwart strollers cover the area that is bound on the west by Austrian-built Marjindvor and on the east by the Turkish-built Baščaršija, but many people join the promenade at points along the way. They cover some distance, stop in a café for a coffee or an ice cream, return to their starting point, and then head home. If you were to begin in Marjindvor, you might start your stroll at Saint Joseph's Catholic Church. That church, erected in 1940 according to the nineteenth-century design of architect Karlo Paržik, marks the transition between the central city and Novo [New] Sarajevo on one side and the National Museum complex on the other. You would step down the church's stone steps, turn left, and proceed to Ulica Maršala Tita.

Sarajevo is the only capital city of the new states of former Yugoslavia that has retained the name of Marshal Tito for its main street. But Tito Street does not extend all the way through the city; a compromise was struck that kept Tito's name only on one part of the broad thoroughfare. After it enters Sarajevo's commercial district, Tito Street meets a promontory that houses a stone niche and an eternal flame commemorating the Partisans who fell in the April 1945 battle that liberated Sarajevo. Then it forks into two. On the left side, it continues as the highly trafficked Ulica Mula Mustafe Bašeskije, while on the right it becomes the Ferhadija pedestrian mall, where the šetanje proceeds. Ferhadija empties into Saraći in the heart of the Baščaršija, which dead-ends into a perpendicular street near the eastern city limit. Strollers either turn around and retrace their steps to head home or disperse into one of the many cafés or *ćevabdžinice*, restaurants specializing in grilled kebabs called *ćevape* or *ćevabćići*. There are no McDonald's or Burger King chains in Sarajevo.

From a window overlooking the city, the šetanje appears not as groups of individual people walking at different rhythms and paces but as two parallel undulating ribbons of humanity traversing Sarajevo's city center; one moves east to west, while the other goes west to east. On fine spring days or summer evenings, it seems as much a fixed part of the city as the Miljacka River or the

6. Šetanje on Tito Street, April 2008

tramlines that run through it. But unlike the river, the promenade peaks and fades; it traverses the city from seven until ten o'clock on summer evenings, and from six until nine in spring and fall. It disappears in the winter. Yet with no reminder, no announcement or call it begins again as the weather changes.

The šetanje leads nowhere; it is simply movement, and it is never complete. There is always another day, still more people to meet and greet, still the curiosity of viewing the sights and sites—have they changed or remained the same? Although people move east to west and west to east, directionality is irrelevant to the šetanje, which seems to be the mechanical repetition of moving live bodies "always forthcoming and already past" (Deleuze 1990, 80). That movement is process, the process of becoming one with the city, becoming Sarajlije, the people of Sarajevo.

If destination and directionality are irrelevant to the evening stroll, then centrality is at its core. People who live in outlying neighborhoods could more easily stroll on those paths. But they come by bus, tram, or car to walk in the city center to assert their inclusion among the Sarajlije. By leaving their footprints there night after night, they trace a presence of self on the pavement and make the city theirs.

When people stroll through Sarajevo, they interpret their habitat through a certain kind of movement, and that repetitive movement is learned through the lived body (pace Merleau-Ponty 1962; cf. Del Negro 2004). When I began to join the evening promenade, I felt awkward, out of the flow. My rhythm was wrong; I was walking too fast. Like those self-occupied flaneurs and flaneuses seeking new discoveries in urban, capitalist Europe, my scrutiny of the crowd kept me separate from it (Valentine 2001, 225; Gilloch 1996, 26, 140–43). It took many an evening before I could weave myself into the ribbon of strollers, before I was able to *šetati* (walk) with no purpose except to become one with the movement through the city.

As you pass the buildings, or as the buildings float past you, you might notice that some people are outside the urban flow. There is the little boy who sits propped up against a gray nineteenth-century facade on the Ferhadija pedestrian mall. He opens and closes an accordion to produce the same five notes one after another. Every so often, someone drops a coin onto his cardboard platform and moves on. I have never heard the boy talk. I have never seen him pocket the change. He just goes on making his sounds as a living fixture of the city.

Across from the boy there might be a corn vendor or someone selling cotton candy. There are also a few tables stacked with CDs, offered for sale by grown men while recorded music blasts from a stereo player. There might also be black-eyed Gypsy women draped in flowered shawls, cradling infants

7. Šetanje on Ferhadija, April 2004

as older children sit at their feet extending a cupped palm upward toward the more prosperous people promenading past. But these displays of what Elzbieta Gozdziak (1995) calls the theater of poverty occur with less frequency over the years, while the number of vendors and their goods increases.

Romany men often huddle together by the stone niche behind the eternal flame. I wonder: Why have they staked out that place? Why are they not joining the šetanje? Is it to keep an eye on their charges? Or is it to preserve their distinction by refusing to melt into the crowd while also asserting the centrality of their connection to multiethnic Bosnia?

Nearby, spray-painted in capital letters on a brick building are the words *Ovo Je Naš Kvart*: This is our neighborhood; this is our turf. The Gypsy men standing together alongside the monument to all the peoples of Bosnia who fought against fascism in order to live together in brotherhood and unity might be declaring to their erstwhile neighbors that "our turf" is also theirs. They might also be sending the message: We have always been part of this city although rarely acknowledged. We are part and apart, and always will be, whether those in power are Bosniacs, Croats, or Serbs; Muslims, Catholics, or Orthodox; worker self-managing socialists or market-oriented capitalists (see chapter 5).

When everyone else is sedentary, to walk means to resist, to protest the status quo, to control space (Jansen 2001, 39). But when everyone else is walking, then standing still can be a political act. Perhaps the stationary stance taken by these Roma says, "Look, Tito is dead and the Partisans and their message are forgotten. But we do not forget."

These analyses of the šetanje might strike a chord with some strollers. But if you were to ask them why they were walking up and down Tito Street, in all likelihood they would reply that they were out for the evening air, enjoying some exercise, and looking around to see what there is to see. Dozens of people have told me, "We have a saying here, 'If out on the evening stroll between Marjindvor and the Baščaršija you don't greet at least one hundred people, then you are not truly a Sarajevan.'"

The šetanje is a *teatro mundi* (Sennett 2000, 384), a moving public arena of sociability (cf. Zukin 1995, 190, 259–60). Unlike those modern urban theorists who wrote of the anonymity of the city as they meandered its streets and byways, becoming blasé as they passed one sensually stimulating scene after another (see esp. Benjamin 1979; Simmel 1950a; also Hannerz 1980), Sarajevans do not get lost or lose themselves in the crowd. Individuals, couples, and groups of friends display their singularity even as they blend into the serpentine thread of humanity winding its way through the urban core. People come out of their homes to participate in the public culture of their city; they take up the gait of the crowd to see and be seen.

As they stroll, they reinforce what they already know through the bodily praxis of movement: that their city and they themselves are products of a rich and diverse history—or of a multiplicity of histories that converge in Sarajevo's people and their products. They might note the historical era of each building and the national affiliation of its patrons, but then again, they might not. These facts fade into the background because the foreground is occupied by fellow strollers. Familiar faces provide a reason to slow down, stop, exchange pleasantries, perhaps step out of the promenade to sit in a café, drink coffee, and then move on.

A group of teenaged girls, arms interlinked, heels clicking on the pavement, are chatting and laughing as they walk by. They come to a stop in front of the Imperijal Kafe's ice-cream stand. Does the sign announce *sladoled* or *gelato,* or both? The lines are long but fast-moving. In 2004, for half a euro, or 1 KM, the anachronistic-sounding Konvertibilni Mark that in Bosnia-Herzegovina replaced the Yugoslav dinar, you could have the tastiest frozen treat in Sarajevo.

The girls clutch their ice-cream cones and move back into the strolling crowd. Here and there are distinguished gentlemen in white shirts, ties, and suits, a bit frayed at the edge. They walk, sometimes arm in arm with their wives, who wear skirts and blazers, nylon stockings, and leather pumps. A gray-haired couple stops briefly in front of a bookstore window, looks to see what's new—there's nothing much—and starts to move on. But as they turn away from the shop, a younger man and his companions catch the gentleman's eye. "Good evening, Professor!" Introductions are made, pleasantries are exchanged; the group of five disengages and moves on.

One evening I was out walking with Melisa. Deep in the Baščaršija, she spied her cousin and a neighbor from suburban Vogošća, and we stopped to greet them. Then a couple I knew from the Jewish community hailed me as they approached. Another evening I was out with Amila. Every few steps, or so it seemed to me, we said hello to a schoolmate, a university colleague, friends of her parents, former teachers, neighbors. Late in July 2004, I ran into Nebojša when we were both strolling. He greeted me with a big smile and asked if I had already become a Sarajevan. I laughed while rolling my eyes. Then I came upon the secretary general of the Congress of Bosniac Intellectuals. He asked me the same question. Could it be that through my bodily practices, I was indeed becoming one with the Sarajlije?

Establishing a rhythm, leaving footprints, becoming part of the trail of humanity that makes the city a living organism with a pulse and a soul unite disparate individuals into an urban citizenry. As they walk through the city, Sarajevans embrace the porosity of their histories; they open themselves up to the sensual proximity of their neighbors, establishing trust as they seek sociability. The repetition of the nightly stroll signifies a citywide resistance to the divisiveness of nations and their demands. The šetanje is a collective insistence for the "right to habitat and to inhabit the city" (Lefebvre 1996, 173). It is open to everyone, for ice cream, for coffee, for the bodily practices of motion that allow all to perform as part of the theater of Sarajevo and to be(come) Sarajlije. As Karen Blu has noted, "Movement itself has a positive meaning for it suggests life, vitality, connection to others . . . [it] makes change on the social and political scene possible" (1996, 214–15). In that it animates Sarajevo and turns its animators into Sarajevans, the šetanje is the most social movement of them all.

Special Sites: Other Ways of Walking in the City

When I walk with Melisa or Amar, Klara or Greta, Amila or Mak, Ernest or Renata, these native sons and daughters always have something to point out to me: They tell me legends of Sulejman the Builder or the secrets of a mosque; they point out the details of a statue, link some buildings to dire historic events and others to happier times. But they don't do it consecutively, one building after another. They take me here or there; they point out this or that, for instance, the pet store where Klara bought her son the parrot that had to be let go when the siege, which everyone thought would last two, three, four months at most, turned into two years. These places are more than *lieux de mémoire* (Nora 1989), for they also give cause to mull over the present and inspire possible futures.

On a warm, humid day in August 2002, twenty-two-year-old Ernest brought me from the airport to his family's apartment up on a hill above central Sarajevo. As twilight cast its cooling veil over the city, we left the apartment and proceeded downhill over cracked sidewalks. I wondered: Were they simply old, untended, and needing repair, or was their damage caused by wartime grenade explosions and missile fire? Our path continued through a grassy park dotted with shiny white marble obelisks engraved with Latin and Arabic letters. Later I would learn that these headstones marked the graves of Bosnian šehids, Muslim soldiers who died defending their country during the 1992–95 war (see Bougarel 2007). But Ernest did not explain any of this to me at that time. He was walking with determination to a site that he defined as central to his city. We ignored the towers, steeples, and minarets that loomed before us to focus on the stone niche built into a promontory located smack in the center of the city where Marshal Tito Street ends.

As we approached the niche, Ernest stopped and audibly gasped. "This is the eternal flame to the Partisans—everyone in Yugoslavia from all groups and nations who fought against fascism in World War II, who fought with Tito against the Nazi occupation. Look, this is Bosnia to me: Every group, every nation is engraved in the stone, and together they were victorious. My grandfather was a Partisan; you'll meet others at the Jewish community. But what I don't understand is why the flame is out. No one would ever have let this happen." As he invoked a time past, Ernest bent down and flicked his lighter over the small opening of a slim gas pipe. That should have produced a controlled blaze, but it did not. Ernest flicked his lighter several more times. Each flick failed to restore the no longer eternal flame. After a few moments, some passersby out for their evening stroll told him to stop wasting his time. There was a general gas outage in the city center.

Visibly relieved, Ernest resumed his narrative. Pointing to the letters and words engraved in stone, he told me that this place was most important to him because it symbolizes the coming together of people from Bosnia's many subgroups to do something together, something that no one group could have done alone. This coming together for the common good to fight against the Nazis, to build a different kind of country, a country for everyone, was morally correct and historically important. Ernest showed me that the eternal flame and its niche in the city center stand metonymically for the unity amid diversity that makes Bosnia unique and valuable.

Ernest recited to me all the groups that the flame represents, inscribed as they are into the very essence of the encircling stone. The pride in his voice compounded as he spoke of his grandfather's participation and that of other Jewish acquaintances in Tito's Partisans. Yet along with that pride of the past, on that August evening in 2002 Ernest was mortified that independent Bosnia-Herzegovina, his native country, could not support its most important monument. We were standing in the middle of the city in an empty space, devoid of its brightly burning flame. This was not how things always were and certainly not as they should be. The next day, when we revisited the site the gas problem had been solved; the flame was ablaze, and Ernest's spirits were much improved. But the scene from the previous evening remained with us, and Ernest wondered aloud if the public disrespect he had perceived was really accidental. Could it be that the *bratstvo i jedinstvo* vision of Tito and the blood spilled by people of diverse ethnic groups were no longer valued in nationally divided Bosnia?

Two years later when twenty-one-year-old Amar, a journalism student at the university, took me to see his favorite Sarajevo sites, the eternal flame was not on the itinerary. We stopped at each of the stone bridges that cross the Miljacka River, looked at the mosques and the Clock Tower in the Baščaršija, and examined a variety of buildings erected in the late nineteenth and early twentieth centuries by the Austrians. Amar paid particular attention to the National Bank with its imposing statues flanking the doors. Sarajevans call this building the Čeka, from the verb *čekati,* which means "to wait," because its central location near many tram and bus stops makes it a prime meeting place. Amar also showed me that the Main Post Office, which had been firebombed in early May 1992, had been restored true to its original colors and details. He brought me inside and described how the building looked throughout the war without its roof. Now the postal clerks service their customers, and the building shows no signs of violence.

Of all the sites on his tour, Amar and I spent the most time looking at and discussing the still windowless Vijećnica. Completed in 1896 to serve as Sarajevo's city hall, the Vijećnica is an imposing structure built by the Austrians in a style that some call neo-Moorish, and others pseudo-Moorish. Its striped exterior, arches, and decorative trim evoke Andalusia and the Maghreb, although tourist guides note that a mosque in Cairo provided the architect with inspiration for the building. Suddenly it struck me as odd that Viennese Austrians had erected this building to be emblematic of their rule in Bosnia. I

8. The eternal flame to Tito's multiethnic Partisans, "the courageous and united fighters who spilled blood for Bosnia-Herzegovina"

turned to Amar and asked him what he thought of the Habsburgs' decision to commission a building that evokes the Alhambra of Moorish Spain and similar structures throughout Morocco and Tunisia. He replied that he is grateful to the Austrians, "who copied a building from Egypt, Cairo," he believes, "to recognize and credit the Orient, the Eastern Islamic influences in Sarajevo." I silently mulled over Edward Said's ideas about Orientalism (1978) and Milica Bakić-Hayden's (1996) insights about their relevance to the Balkans: The colonizing Austrians paid homage to Islam brought to Bosnia by the Ottoman Turks by erecting a building that evoked the East through an architectural style that synthesizes influences from Egypt, Spain, and the Maghreb.

During the socialist period, the Vijećnica ceased housing municipal officials and served instead as the National and University Library of Bosnia-Herzegovina. The building was firebombed during the night of August 25–26, 1992, by radical Bosnian Serbs who found its Muslim motifs antithetical to the country that they envisioned. The war raged on, and in June 1994, Maestro Zubin Mehta stood in the ruins of the Vijećnica, where he conducted the Sarajevo Symphony Orchestra and Chorus in a moving performance of Mozart's Requiem.

My conversation with Amar shifted to the wartime destruction of everything that even hinted at Sarajevo's Muslim heritage, including the thousands of volumes and one-of-a-kind handwritten manuscripts that were incinerated when Serbian ultranationalists tried to bomb the Vijećnica off the face of the earth (see Bakaršić 1994). When we stood there in the spring of 2004, the Vijećnica was still damaged. It was surrounded by scaffolding plastered with advertisements.

I visited the Vijećnica again on June 26 of that year along with a crowd of Sarajevans for the opening of a huge installation in the building's atrium by the renowned contemporary artist Jannis Kounellis. Consisting of books from the National Library's reserve, stones from Sarajevo's shattered buildings, and a variety of objects of everyday life, including clothing, shoes, and sewing machines, Kounellis's project filled in the blasted-out spaces of Sarajevo's most imposing building.

The newspaper *Oslobodjenje* reported that the twelve walled-in doors to the atrium constitute "one tale, uniquely emotive and political" (June 27, 2004, p. 20, my translation). I heard many people express their appreciation for the installation, and some of my acquaintances spoke of its emotional effect. Nataša told me when I met her there that she was very moved by the work: "It reminds me of everything that we lost, how the city was in siege. Look at all the books that were lost here. Kounellis insisted that the material he used rolled up in those cylinders came from our local markets and secondhand shops. And did you see the door stuffed with canvas bags? Those were the sacks used by humanitarian organizations for donated food." But others, particularly students in disciplines other than art history and architecture, voiced the opinion that although it is important that an internationally respected artist show his work in Sarajevo, perhaps the funds allocated to this project would have been better spent supporting local artists, replenishing the National Library, and renovating the Vijećnica. "Kounellis in Sarajevo" closed in September 2004, and the building was emptied of the exhibit.

Early one morning in April 2008, I walked over to the Vijećnica hoping to find it restored. But it was still enclosed in advertisement-plastered scaffolding. I mounted the front steps and saw something new. On either side of the padlocked doors were two commemorative plaques, both engraved in capital letters, one in Bosnian,[5] the other in English:

On this place Serbian criminals
in the night of 25–26 August 1992 set on fire
National and
University's Library
of Bosnia and Herzegovina
Over 2 millions of books, periodicals
and documents vanished in the flame.
Do not forget
Remember and warn!

9. The Vijećnica, June 2004

I was alone on the steps of the Vijećnica copying the inscriptions when two workmen emerged from around the side of the building. I began to tell them, "I was here in 2004 . . ." and before I could finish my sentence, one of them smiled, gestured toward the scaffolding, and interjected, "I isto!" Yes, I agreed, *i isto,* for with the exception of the plaques, everything is just the same as it had been four years ago.

Later that day, I took a walking tour of Sarajevo with licensed guide Zijad Jusufović.[6] As we passed by the Vijećnica, Zijad answered my question as to why Sarajevo's most famous building remains a ruin by recounting how various ministries and the two entities cannot agree on who will get what use of the building, including credit for its restoration. He insisted that there is enough money, that one million euros were pledged by the government of Spain, but that political infighting has impeded any progress toward bringing the Vijećnica back to its former glory.

Such has not been the case with the Museum of the City of Sarajevo, the former Museum of the Assassination, which was ransacked during the 1992–95 war. The new museum opened with a lovely ceremony in early April 2004. Celebrating the rare convergence of Catholic and Orthodox Easter, it featured an exhibit of Christian ritual items and colored eggs. Two baskets of fresh flora marked off a stage, where a small children's chorus sang a sweet song about the blossoms of spring. Professor Tomislav Išek noted in his introductory remarks that things associated with religion were simply not displayed in public before the war. But Melisa, who invited me to accompany her to the event, whispered to me that dyed eggs could be seen in many people's homes before and after the war as a normal part of the Easter holiday season. She always received some of those eggs from friends even though her family is Muslim. The newly appointed museum director told the gathering that this is only one of the many exhibits planned to show Sarajevo as a traditionally multicultural and multireligious city.

In April 2008, the museum did not highlight Sarajevo's ethnic pluralism or multiculturalism. It featured the period 1878–1914, when Sarajevo and all of Bosnia-Herzegovina were under Austrian rule. But unlike the earlier Museum of the Assassination (1953–92), which celebrated Gavrilo Princip and his colleagues in Mlada [Young] Bosna as freedom-fighters determined to liberate their country from foreign occupation, the exhibit and short film about the 1914 assassination portray it as a terrorist act.

"During Communism Gavrilo Princip was a hero," Zijad explained. "Today he is an enemy in half the country. In the Republika Srpska . . . he is still a hero. In the Banja Luka museum [of Republika Srpska], there is a Cyrillic sign glorifying the killer." He continued, "During the war this museum stood empty—all its contents were stolen, destroyed. The footprints were stolen. There is no consensus to put the footprints back, so a copy was made and it sits here."

Instead of Gavrilo Princip's footprints immortally imprinted in the sidewalk outside the museum, a new sign in capital letters marks the spot:

> From this place on 28 June 1914
> Gavrilo Princip assassinated the heir
> to the Austro-Hungarian throne
> Franz Ferdinand and his wife Sofia

"The result of that assassination," Zijad reminded us, "was that one month later the First World War began, which resulted in the death of 10 million people and four empires—the Turkish, the Russian, the Austro-Hungarian, and the German kaiser's. Then began the new history." Except for the opening ceremony in 2004 and Zijad's tour in 2008, none of my Sarajevo hosts ever suggested that we visit the former Museum of the Assassination.

Minutes before arriving at what everyone once called Princip Bridge but now call the Latin Bridge, Zijad had brought us to Despić House, the home of a wealthy Serb merchant whose family had bequeathed it to the City of Sarajevo. In 2004 Klara brought me to Svrzo's House, the home of a rich Muslim family that had become part of the Museum of the City of Sarajevo in the early 1950s (see chapter 7). She also wanted to show me Despić House, but it had not yet been restored. It only reopened to the public in late 2007. In April 2008, the young woman museum guide pointed out that the interior design of Despić House was the same as that of Muslim homes; "Although it is an Orthodox house, it is Oriental in style." Orthodox homes, she showed us, differed from Muslim ones only in their use of darker colors and in the icons on the wall of each room.

The most remarkable feature of Despić House is the last will and testament of the family patriarch, Makso Despić, which is posted prominently on the entryway wall. Printed in Latin and Cyrillic script in Bosnian and Serbian and translated into English, it describes Despić's refusal of long and expensive funeral ceremonies. Dated after his pilgrimage to Jerusalem in March 29, 1921, it states his postmortem wishes. Zijad read aloud its most striking provision,

> After my death, I leave to the poor without any difference in religion:
>
> To the Serbian poor—1,000 dinars
> To the Roman Catholic poor—500 dinars

To the Muslim poor—500 dinars
To the Jewish poor—500 dinars

After a brief silence, he asked rhetorically, "And where is the spirit of Makso Despić today?"

Seven years earlier, freelance journalist Beth Kampschror raised the same question. "In 2001," she wrote, "the only things remaining of Sarajevo's so-called multi-ethnic character are the religious buildings of four faiths pressed together in the city center." The diversity of Sarajevo's emblematic architecture, which for centuries attested to the coexistence of different religions, styles, and visions, seemed to her in Muslim-dominated Sarajevo incongruous and out of place.

Bosnia-Herzegovina's fragmented state government often fails to support the mixed heritage of Sarajevo's built environment. Representatives of the B-C-S constituent nations bicker with one another about ownership of preexisting structures like the National Museum of Bosnia-Herzegovina and the Vijećnica, while each group builds more and bigger shrines to itself. Scores of new mosques have sprung up throughout Sarajevo—in 2008 there was a total of 158, according to Zijad—many of which are architecturally incompatible with their surroundings. New Orthodox cathedrals in Eastern Sarajevo mark the entity divide between the Federation and the RS. On March 12, 2008, BalkanInsight.com reported that an association of Serbs in Sarajevo plans to erect a twenty-six-meter-high and eighteen-meter-wide cross on Mount Trebević, which would be visible from almost every corner of the city. When I met with Melisa a month later, she told me about that plan and, reminding me of the giant concrete cross erected by Croats in Mostar, she informed me that petitions were circulating to block it. When she was approached to add her name to one of those petitions, Melisa, who practices a liberal form of Islam, said that she would certainly sign but only if a clause is included to limit the building of mosques. No such clause has been added.

Many Sarajevans, like Melisa, Zijad, Klara, Amar, Nebojša, and Ernest, strive to reassert the openness of their city through their bodily practices, their memories, their narratives, and their desires. Yet for those who "long for the order of the singular story and the legibility of the smoothness of a surface," the spatial simultaneity of several philosophical, religious, and historical trajectories can be experienced as an inexorable problem (Massey 2000, 229). The challenges of everyday, borderland urbanism vex the neat, incommensurable categories of linear history and national exclusivity. At the same time, however, they provide rich materials for living lives of diverse experiences and imagining a wide range of possible futures.

As I listen to Sarajevans narrating stories of place, I am reminded that it is not only cutting-edge social theorists who view space as the manifestation of intersecting, synchronic legacies. The people of Sarajevo are continuously evaluating and putting to use those legacies as they confront a building, a person, a thing that seems to resonate with their notions of place or what is out of place. Susan Crane rightly notes that "collective memory ultimately is located not in sites but in individuals" (1997, 1381).

In this chapter, I have focused on the revivification of Sarajevo as a city of difference, a site of cosmopolitanism, and a familiar home filled with the delights of memory, familiar faces, and possible futures. I have presented ordinary Sarajevans' spatial practices as attempts to reassert an easygoing urban lifestyle in which encounters with diversity are part of the quotidian; in which variety is valued as an important aesthetic as well as social stimulus. When walking in the city, whether as part of the evening šetanje or accompanied by one or two close friends, Sarajevans reorient themselves to the altered cityscape, reconnect to particular places, and try to override the aberration of the recent war. In articulating the links between their lived bodies and the city that they inhabit, Sarajevans' words and footprints enact trajectories of trust in the present and hope for a peaceful, pluralistic future. Walking and talking through the heart of their city combine to push official identities as Bosniacs, Croats, Serbs, or Others into the background as they enact instead the self-making projects of Sarajlije, cosmopolitan citizens of a modern, open world.

But this trajectory is not embraced by everyone, nor is it advocated at all times by those who may be walking the walk. The guidelines of the 1995 Dayton Accords have solidified into law and have taken on a logic of their own. This logic of incommensurable ethnic groups vies with the once and future mixity of Sarajevo and vexes its present.

Bosniacs, Croats, and Serbs

The Constituent Nations of Bosnia-Herzegovina

3

National Legibility

Lines of History, Surges of Ethnicity

The Turkish conquests are regarded as the greatest tragedy in the history of the Croats and Serbs.

Aleksa Djilas, *The Contested Country*

The conversion to Islam of most of the Bosnian population . . . represents the most conspicuous and most significant event of her modern history.

Mustafa Imamović, *Bošnjaci / Bosniaks*

Sarajevo's diversity of structures elicits varied, often intertwined, and sometimes contradictory reactions from its residents. As we have seen, Sarajevans strolling their city's streets might view the buildings in front of them as part of a wider urban scene that cannot be reduced to its parts. Then again, they might focus on one structure after another, noting their size, shape, and color, and seeing in each of them something unique. They might point to the materials from which they are made or to their functions as a restaurant or market, school or court, museum or church, mosque, residence, factory, or registry.

Sometimes Sarajevans will link a place to a historical event or to a personal moment in their own lives, but more often than not, the very first thing that they do when they view a building is classify it according to age and style. They will attribute rounded and arched stone structures to the Ottomans or just call them Muslim or Turkish; they will connect onion domes and smoky colors to the Serbs, and assign rectangular, steepled, and colonnaded edifices to the Austrians or simply label them Central European. Some structures, like the Vijećnica with its Moorish motifs erected by the Habsburgs late in the nineteenth century, defy this neat scheme. In so doing, they speak metonymically to the variety of substances and styles attesting to Sarajevo's centuries-long mixed heritage.

The same commonsensical categories used to identify features in the built environment come to bear when Sarajevans attempt to distinguish personal identity from within the varied population. Like its buildings and bridges, the residents of Sarajevo come in many shapes and sizes, ages and styles. They are men and women, parents and children, and members of various professions. They were all once Yugoslavs. Now they are citizens of Bosnia-Herzegovina and residents of the Canton of Sarajevo in the Bosniac-Croat Federation. Some are Sarajlije with deep urban roots; others are newcomers (see Gagnon 2004, 4; Stefansson 2007). Those who lived through the siege of Sarajevo might differentiate themselves from those who fled (Stefansson 2004), while the UN, the OHR, and the Federation document and distinguish between returning refugees and returning internally displaced persons (see Stefansson 2003; Federacija Bosne i Hercegovine 2008). Yet all at some time cross these divides by categorizing themselves and their fellow citizens according to religious background, neighborhood, and economic, educational, artistic, and athletic accomplishments.

The diversity of Sarajevans' identities and belongings is often overshadowed by a ubiquitous emphasis on nationality, or what English speakers would call ethnicity.[1] "Ethnicity and nationalism," Rogers Brubaker (2004, 152) warns, "need to be understood as particular ways of talking about and experiencing the social world and a particular way of framing political claims, not as real boundaries inscribed in the nature of things." That warning has long been taken to heart by academic analysts, but since the beginning of the twentieth century it has rarely been heeded in decisions regarding European politics.

When in 1882 Ernest Renan asked the crucial question, "Qu'est-ce qu'une nation?" (What is a nation?) ([1882] 1996), the answer was far from clear. Europeans used physical appearance, language, and religion to distinguish one group from another, accompanying the prevailing romantic notions of nation as "a soul," "spiritual principle," or "character." To counter these metaphysical ideas with a materially based concept, Russian revolutionary leader Vladimir Lenin directed his protégé Joseph Stalin to write the definitive *Marxism and the National Colonial Question.* Published in 1913, it offered a concise definition: "A nation is a historically constituted, stable community of people, formed on the basis of a common language, territory, economic life, and psychological make-up manifested in a common culture" ([1913] 1975, 22). This definition not only underwrote Soviet nationalities policy (see F. Hirsch 2005) but also guided international decision makers at the end of World War I in selecting which peoples from among the fallen Ottoman and Austro-Hungarian Empires were to be awarded autonomous states. Although they were certainly treated as different from the majority populations among whom they lived, Europe's Gypsies and Jews were not deemed nations because they were unstable communities, speakers of many languages, and territorially dispersed. The Slavic-speaking peoples of southeastern Europe posed a similar dilemma: their overlapping, incongruous linguistic, territorial, and economic boundaries posed questions of legibility. Were they ethnicities or nations?

In 1918 the question was resolved in Versailles by the creation of a new state that combined the Serbian kingdom and Montenegro, both independent since the 1878 Treaty of Berlin, with Croatia, Slovenia, and Bosnia-Herzegovina, which were now decoupled from the defunct Austro-Hungarian Empire. The resulting Kingdom of Serbs, Croats, and Slovenes was based on the idea that "Croat, Serb and Slovene were to be regarded as no more than ethnicities within a Southern Slav nation" (Hastings 1997, 125). But the monarch reigning over the kingdom was unquestionably Serb, and its name rendered invisible many peoples that had struggled to gain national recognition (e.g., Montenegrins and Macedonians). In 1929, in an effort to represent the collective aspirations of all South Slavs, the state's name changed to Yugoslavia. Yet that linguistic switch did little to abate demands for greater Croatian autonomy or to remedy the indignation of smaller groups whose desires for recognition went unheeded (see Banac 1984).

In 1941 that first Yugoslavia succumbed to Nazi occupation, and the vicious civil war that ensued between the fascist Croatian Ustaše and the right-wing loyalist Serbian Četniks seemed to attest to the failure of the Yugoslav project (Shoup 1968, 10–11). At the same time, however, Josip Broz Tito rallied a multiethnic force of Partisans that ultimately emerged victorious, and Yugoslavia was reborn as a socialist federation in 1945. To resolve its problematic national question, during the formative postwar years Yugoslavia's Communist Party pursued a solution that "was calculated to limit controversy to an absolutely irreducible minimum. In place of the former three 'tribes,' or nationalities, five Slav nationalities (not counting Slav minorities) were recognized after World War II: Serbs, Croats, Slovenes, Macedonians, and Montenegrins" (Shoup 1968, 3; see also Wachtel 1998, 130–31). Also, the rights of minorities to "their cultural development and the free use of their language" were provided for in Article 13 of the 1946 Yugoslav Constitution.

Bosnia-Herzegovina posed a special challenge to the new federation because its Croats, Serbs, and Muslims all claimed it as (part of) their national homeland. During the first twenty years of Tito's regime, Bosnian Muslims were treated as a religious group, which rendered them politically invisible and impotent. Until constitutional changes were made, first at the republic level in

1963 and then statewide six years later (F. Friedman 1996, 159; Woodward 1995, 36), the people who today call themselves Bosniacs were counted in Yugoslavia's first three censuses as Serbs, Croats, Yugoslavs, or Undeclared. Only in the 1971 census were they nominated into existence as the *Muslimanska nacija.* But the Muslims remained different from and less than Yugoslavia's other five nations because unlike the Croats, Macedonians, Montenegrins, Serbs, and Slovenes, they had no eponymous socialist republic to call their own.

Bosnia's crazy-quilt pattern of ethnic distribution was a key reason why Tito kept BiH together as the only nonnational republic in the federation (Pavlowitch 2002, 152). This same anomalous mixture, however, was also a key reason why in 1991, as Yugoslavia was disintegrating, Croatian President Tudjman and Serbian President Milošević conducted secret negotiations to partition Bosnia between their two republics (Burns 1992; Gagnon 2004, 12–13; Woodward 1995, 192–93). The reasoning behind their belief that BiH rightly belonged to Serbia and Croatia was that because "Bosnia had no 'nation' of its own, its existence . . . [was viewed] as artificial; a consequence of Ottoman rule and religious conversion." Contrarily, Croatia, with its Croat nation, and Serbia, with its nation of Serbs, were claimed as "natural" (Hastings 1997, 141–42; see also Mulaj 2005, 7).

These "natural" nations notwithstanding, on-the-ground patterns of Serbs, Muslims, and Croats living intermingled throughout Bosnia-Herzegovina thwarted plans for an immediate partition. To remedy that problem, radical Bosnian Serbs established a breakaway Serbian Republic, and radical Croats soon followed suit (F. Friedman 2004, 43; Gagnon 2004, 5). The Muslims, those who called themselves Yugoslavs, many minorities, and thousands of nonradical Croats and Serbs refused to comply and voted instead to live in their united, multiethnic Bosnian republic (see, e.g., Dizdarević 1994; Kurspahić 1997; Pejanović 2004). Immediately after that republic gained international recognition, ultranationalists instigated a war aimed at "ethnically cleansing" the population, which, when complete, would lead "naturally" to the country's division between Serbia and Croatia (Gagnon 2004; Velikonja 2003, 235–52).

As Bosnia-Herzegovina's vulnerability to Serb and Croat nationalist violence increased, the Muslims solidified their loose historical narratives into one tale that attested to their long-term existence as the Bosniac nation. The Bosniacs were thereby able to present equal, and perhaps even stronger, discursive claims to the territory and legacy of BiH than the Serbs and Croats. As the violence mounted and the country's population was forcibly unmixed, Bosnia-Herzegovina's multiethnic army was steadily Islamicized (see Bougarel 2007, 170–72).

In the summer of 1995, Sarajevo's major outdoor market was shelled for the second time, and thousands of unarmed Muslim boys and men were massacred in Srebrenica.[2] American President Bill Clinton responded by authorizing the United States to lead a massive NATO bombing of Serbian artillery throughout Bosnia, which forced a ceasefire from all parties.

The agreement to end the war was a difficult compromise wrested over a three-week period in November 1995 (see Holbrooke 1999). In short, the Dayton Peace Accords and the constitution that derived from them officially recognized that BiH's population is constituted of three incommensurable nations, each holding inalienable rights to their own language, history, culture, territory, and self-governance.

By the first years of the twenty-first century, the Bosniac-Croat-Serb national triad has become the "natural order of things" (Brubaker 2004, 152; cf. Foucault 1991, 95). Since in Bosnia-Herzegovina citizens' rights derive more from the collective rights of nations than from the idea of individual liberties (see McMahon 2004, 202; Mulaj 2005, 8), and because the ethnic key is an important consideration for filling jobs, university places, and political appointments, B-C-S affiliation assumes great importance in individuals' lives. Willingly or not, Sarajevans often find that they are first and foremost ethnically marked and marking actors, who are classified, and classify themselves, their neighbors, coworkers, and friends according to essentialistic national identities and loyalties (see Gagnon 2004, xviii).

I demonstrate in this chapter how the long and complicated history of the national question in Yugoslavia and the demand for legible, incommensurable constituent peoples in contemporary Bosnia-Herzegovina are intimately connected to a wider European discourse that places the nation at the center of politics. First, I focus on the historical narratives that circulate in support of rival B-C-S national claims and how they extend their reach into the present. I continue that discussion by exploring how the 1992–95 violence, coupled with demands for national rights, gave rise to exclusionary ethnic practices. We will meet Serbs, Croats, and Bosniacs in contemporary Sarajevo conforming to and resisting these demands as they try to live together—or resolve to live apart—in what they believe used to be and might again reemerge as their cosmopolitan, heterogeneous, "multi-multi" city called Sarajevo.

Seemingly Seamless Narratives of the Longue Durée

Who are the Serbs, the Croats, and the Bosniacs? Historians from without and within the former Yugoslavia tend to agree that prior to the nineteenth century the inhabitants of Bosnia considered themselves neither Serbs nor

Bosniacs nor Croats but people "from here," inhabitants of particular villages or regions (Bringa 1995, 33–35; pace Gellner 1983, 62). More broadly, they referred to themselves and were referred to as Bosnians (Filipović 2007; Magaš 2003, 19; Riedlmayer 1993), Bošnjani (Lovrenović 2001, 93), or as "the Slavs who lived in Bosnia" (Malcolm 1996, 12; cf. Djilas 1991, 7). Under Ottoman rule (1463–1878), the population was classified according to religion, and centuries of records document that Bosnia was home to Christians of the Roman Catholic and Orthodox churches, Muslims, and Jews. But in the latter part of the nineteenth century, when the Ottomans left Bosnia and it became part of the Austro-Hungarian Empire, "imported Croat and Serb national ideas won over its Catholic and Orthodox parts" (Magaš 2003, 19; see also Lovrenović 2001, 106; Malcolm 1996, 12). In socialist Yugoslavia, nationality merged with and superceded religion as the essential category of belonging (Shoup 1968; Wachtel 1998).

Sometimes citing, sometimes inspiring, sometimes contradicting, and at other times simply disregarding academic research, Bosniacs, Croats, and Serbs in Sarajevo, Mostar, and Pale find reasons to tell the story of their people. Most of the narratives of the longue durée that follow were told to me spontaneously by people attempting to understand how a war could have recently ravaged their country; to explain the need for ethnic vigilance; to rationalize their individual and family decisions to remain in, flee from, and/or return to Sarajevo; and to justify or oppose the trinational division of their country. It would be easy to present these historical narratives in three parts: Serb, Croat, and Bosniac; but that strategy would be inaccurate, for alongside, and sometimes contesting, the nationalist party line of each group are several variations, which become murkier the closer the accounts get to the present.

The following pages offer a glimpse into the ways that Sarajevans understand themselves as part of the broader legacy of their city and of their nation. Rival versions of the past do not necessarily lead to violent conflicts (Gagnon 2004); but keeping these historical contests alive through narratives of theft, martyrdom, denial, or vindication stirs the flames of discord, whether the events in question occurred in the Middle Ages, during the seventeenth or nineteenth centuries, during World War II, or in the 1990s. Narratives of the longue durée invariably insist on the autochthony of the teller's group; proof of nationhood (which sometimes includes the denial of others' national claims); and assertions of self-defense that often function to absolve the protagonist and his group from any wrongdoing or responsibility vis-à-vis others.

RESONANCES OF THE PAST IN THE PRESENT

One day in the spring of 2004, I came to visit Ajša Softić, the acting director of the Zemaljski Muzej, now known as the National Museum of BiH, which had suffered heavy artillery shelling during the war. On earlier visits in 1997 and 2002, its diligent multiethnic staff told me how, despite terrifying conditions, they saved the museum's collections from destruction. In 2004, thanks to funding from Sweden, other foreign governments, and a handful of NGOs, the exterior of the building had been repaired, and most of the museum's main archeology displays were once again open to the public. But the museum still lacked central heating; its employees waited months for their tiny salaries; and despite its 126 years of representing the land, flora, fauna, and people(s) of Bosnia-Herzegovina, in 2004 no governmental entity would embrace and financially support the museum.[3]

What's the problem? I naively asked. The acting director responded by informing me that neither the Bosniac-Croat Federation nor the unitary Republic of Bosnia-Herzegovina holds fiscal or administrative responsibility for the museum. The museum receives a paltry monthly budget from the Canton of Sarajevo. "But," she explained to me, "it has always been the sole museum of Bosnia and Herzegovina. Since it represents the entire country, it should be administered at the state level." The problem is that the state-level government is virtually nonfunctional. "We are administered on the state level, but there is nothing at the state level. We are the National Museum of Bosnia and Herzegovina, 126 years old, 126 years old. We survived the war, but we may not survive the peace."

Beyond fiscal difficulties, there are even bigger problems. "Look," Softić continued, "I am happy to have school groups come here; I wish there were more of them. Just a few weeks ago, I saw this school group from [predominately Croat] Kiseljak, which is right outside Sarajevo. It used to be just one of many small villages on the outskirts of our city. How they profited from the war! Now they are a big village with brand-new buildings and banks and cafés and factories. They were looking at this display on the prehistory of Bosnia, and suddenly I hear not the students but the *teacher* exclaim, 'Where are the Croats?' Have you ever heard anything so stupid?! And this is a teacher of history. That's what we've come to, a teacher of history demanding something about the Croats of the region before there were even Croats."

Historical and archeological evidence indicates that Slavic peoples, be they Slaveni, Serbs, or Croats, only entered southeastern Europe late in the sixth century (Donia and Fine 1994, 14; Malcolm 1996, 8). Nonetheless, this teacher of history was seeking to show her students the long-term connection of their Croatian people to the land of Bosnia-Herzegovina and expressed indignation when that connection could not be found in the museum's display. That may be a reason why Bosnian Croats are demanding the national right to establish their own museum.

A few weeks before my meeting with Ajša Softić at the Museum, I met a young woman while traveling by bus from Split in Croatia to Sarajevo. Vesna is a student at the University of Mostar, where she studies German and Croatian language and literature in preparation for a career as a high school teacher. In the course of our conversation, she told me about her university and the wartime division of Mostar into the Catholic west and the Muslim east. In response to my incredulous questions about the violent division of the city, she explained, "Our history shows that once, all the people of Bosnia and Herzegovina were Catholics. And some, but only in the east, were Orthodox, Christians with the patriarchate but not the pope. Then the Turks came with Islam, and some took this religion so they didn't have to be slaves or servants. That's the history. That's the way it was." Vesna went on to describe the onerous conditions of the Croat *kmets* (serfs) under Ottoman rule, how they held no rights to the land they tilled and no voice in the government. Skipping several centuries ahead, now, as she sees it, history has been vindicated as the Catholic Croats of Mostar reestablished themselves as the city's rightful ruler-residents by waving Croatia's checkerboard flag, founding their own university, insisting on their own language, and building monumental crosses and memorials to their recent martyrs.

Vesna, of course, is not alone in narrating a history of the region in which there was always a Croatian people that suffered under the Muslim yoke. Under the heading of "Bosnia and Herzegovina Myths for Dummies" on the official Web site of the predominantly Croat Canton of Herceg-Bosna is a retort to all those who might think otherwise: "[The idea of a] Bosnian 'nation' is part of recent (post 1991) Bosnian Muslim historiography—it is their central historical narrative. . . . Addiction to the fictions about Croatian and Serbian 'false ethnic identities' is ineluctably locked with another piece of wishful thinking—projections about the dreamt-on disappearance of both Croats and Serbs from the soil of Bosnia and Herzegovina."[4]

Bosnian Serbs in the Republika Srpska impart similar historical narratives. When I met with them in Pale in 2004, Saša, a law student at the University of East Sarajevo, and his girlfriend, Jelena, who studies English there, insisted that Serbs as a nation possess the right to secede from Bosnia-Herzegovina to form a state of their own, if not to join with Serbia.

> Jelena: We are Serbs and we should be part of Serbia. Throughout history it's been this way. Look, before the fifteenth century, when the Ottoman rulers came from Turkey, everyone in this region was Orthodox. They were Serbs. Then the Croats with their *banovi* [governors] under the Hungarians spread out from the West, and the Turks came and established their rule over Bosnia. Serbia too was under the Ottoman rule. And here, in Bosnia, some people in order to get rid of the high taxation and to get the privileges, converted to Islam. This was always part of Serbia. That's the history. Saša, you know the history better than I.

Saša took over to embellish the story with facts from modern history that emphasized Serbs' grievances. He reminded me that Serbia had sided with the Allies in both world wars, while Austria, Croatia, and Slovenia fought on the other side. His historical overview reached its finale with the formation of socialist Yugoslavia. Saša then returned to Jelena's main point: "There were no Bosniacs then. There was no Muslim nation until 1971. All of Bosnia's Muslims were Serbs or Croats."

Ideas of a Greater Serbia circulated for centuries through epic poetry and in the consolidated Serbian Orthodox church (Anzulovic 1999; Judah 2000, 1–32).[5] By 1844, Ilija Garašanin had formulated the *Načertanije,* or outline of a program for establishing an expanded Serbia, which was to have included Bosnia-Herzegovina, Croatia, Montenegro, and Vojvodina (Pavlowitch 2002, 39). A century and a half later, Bosnian mathematician Naza Tanović-Miller asserted that Garašanin's plan opened the floodgates for ideologues like the linguist Vuk Stefanović Karadžić (1787–1864), whose collection of ancient epics and the essay "Serbs All and Everywhere" promoted the idea that "Bosnians of all faiths were formerly Serbs" (2001, 174). That view is clearly displayed on the Serb *mreza* (network) Web site in a section titled "Bosnia Is Serbian Land," which ends with an important postscript: "Note: Muslims are mostly Serbs (and some Croats) who betrayed their Christian heritage for the benefits given to them by the Turkish (Islamic) Empire. In other words—they collaborated with the occupying enemy. They were, in modern terms—quislings."[6]

Despite the fierce rivalries between Serbs and Croats, whether in BiH or in Serbia or Croatia, by 1991 their major spokesmen and thousands of followers came to agree on one central point: The Turkish conquest was a great tragedy that disrupted the "natural" historical progress of their nations. No matter their differing interpretations of maps, linguistics, and demographics, Serbs and Croats agreed that the Bosnians who converted to Islam and the land upon which they lived were originally—and eternally—theirs. In the early 1990s, when radicalized Serbs and Croats fought over territorial boundaries, they concurred that despite the 1969 Yugoslav constitutional declaration to the contrary, Bosnia's Muslims were not a nation. Consequently, they do not merit self-governance, and Bosnia-Herzegovina should be split between the Croat and Serb nation-states.

FROM MUSLIMS TO BOSNIACS: REMEDYING MISNAMING

"[T]he Muslims," Tone Bringa stated over a decade ago, "seem finally to have become a neat ethno-national category its neighbors and the international community can deal with and understand. They have been forced by the war and the logic of the creation of nation-states to search for their origins and establish a 'legitimate' and continuous national history" (1995, 36). Ignored in the first half of the twentieth century in the Yugoslav kingdom and then overlooked in the first three censuses of socialist Yugoslavia, in the 1990s, when that country fragmented along its ethnic fault-lines, Bosnia's Muslims reacted to the more aggressive national histories of Serbs and Croats by claiming national rights of residence and self-rule via their own narratives of the longue durée and asserted a group label that connected them to European Bosnia.

The first time I encountered the word *Bošnjak* was in 1994 when visiting Bosnian refugees waiting out the war in Israel. Then and on subsequent visits, I often heard them refer to themselves and to BiH's president, Alija Izetbegović, as Bosniacs (Markowitz 1996). I was familiar with the word *Bosanci,* which means Bosnians, and *Muslimani,* which means Muslims, but since *Bošnjaci* was a new word for me I asked my hosts what it meant. "Oh, you know, Muslimani," Omer replied. "This is a new, more nationalistic word for the same group. That is, Bosnians with a Muslim family background as a national group, without all the stress on religion. Like Catholics are Croats and the Serbs are Orthodox, we Muslims—and most of us are secular like the Jews in this kibbutz—are calling ourselves Bosniacs."

Although I did not know it at the time, Omer's words echoed a decision taken at the end of 1992. A few months into the siege of Sarajevo, a group formed calling itself the Congress of Bosniac Intellectuals (Vijeće Kongresa Bošnjačkih Intelektualca, VKBI). During my first visit to the VKBI in 2002, its secretary general offered an explanation for the group's choice of eponym: "Until 1992, the term *Bošnjak* did not officially exist. It was used during the time of the Austro-Hungarian Empire but was eliminated in the two Yugoslavias. We chose *Bošnjaci* over *Muslimani* because the term *Muslims* holds the connotation [in Europe and the United States] of terror and fundamentalism. Or, if not that, it is just a religious term. We wanted not a purely religious label, but a national one." The VKBI's decision was later adopted by the Izetbegović-headed government, and its ruling Party for Democratic Action (the SDA, or Stranka za demokratsku akciju) "took over the label 'Bosniak' (in place of Muslim) from [its] rival party" (Woodward 1995, 315). From 1993 onward, the term *Bošnjak* began circulating with regularity, and by the time I began fieldwork in Sarajevo in 1997 it was used interchangeably with Muslim.

Following its founding, the VKBI, among other institutions, began publishing a wealth of books aimed at convincing readers that the Bosniacs are indeed an indigenous, European Slavic people with their own history, language, and culture. Some of these publications explicitly state that the designation *Muslimani* had been a deliberate misnaming of Bosnia's most original people (see esp. Imamović 2000), and that within the group the term *Bošnjak* has always been used despite suppression from without (Zulfikarpašić 1998, 48; see also Mašović 1998, 145).

In postwar Sarajevo, the eponym *Bošnjaci* has officially replaced *Muslimani* in the government and in the media, yet the VKBI continues to stress through its publications and in public forums the necessity of declaring the Bosniacs a nation and differentiating that nation, along with its language and traditions, from those of the Croats and the Serbs. Representatives of Bosniac political and cultural organizations, linguists and historians, artisans and taxi drivers all narrated to me incidents from the recent war to demonstrate just how fragile and misrecognized the Bosnian Muslims had been. These horror stories were usually supplemented with the reminder that until the Yugoslav census of 1971 they were denied the status of a national group. Plying me with statistics from Yugoslavia's first population counts, in 1997 an eminent emeritus professor of political science at Sarajevo University declared that until the census of 1971: "One year I'd choose Serb, the next year Croat, and then Yugoslav" (see also Bringa 1993, 86; Woodward 1995, 36).

Official Yugoslav government misrecognition notwithstanding, several analysts of Bosnia's Muslim population noted that ethnic distinctiveness had always been evident as it manifested itself in Bosnia's uniquely multicultural settings (e.g., Lockwood 1975; Bringa 1995; F. Friedman 1996). Haris Silajdžić, a retired university professor who served as BiH's prime minister and foreign minister during Alija Izetbegović's wartime government, took the opportunity of our conversation in June 2004 to review Bosnia's history.[7] Like many Bosniac intellectuals, he placed special emphasis on the continuity between present-day Bosniacs and the inhabitants of the medieval Bosnian state:

> Bosnia is one of the earliest European states. Centuries before the Ottomans, Bosnia was independent. And centuries before the Ottomans, Bosnia sat on the fault line.
>
> In Bosnia there was a religious movement. You could call it a sect or a movement, like the Cathars. People call them the Bogomils, but I prefer to call them, as did Martin Luther, the first pro-reformist church in the world. And there were Eastern influences, as in the earliest forms of Christianity, which as you know came from the Middle East. They did not like the cross and refused to display it, for the Messiah was killed on the cross. They did not like the pope and refused to give him their allegiance. . . . And there was the influence of Zoroastrianism. These were Christian forms of probably old Iranian religions. They called themselves *krstjiane,* Christians.
>
> There is an arc of heresies throughout the Mediterranean region, and Bosnia was at the heart of these. The Catholics wiped them out in Italy, southern France, and west through the Iberian Peninsula. But Bosnia is rugged territory. . . . But the pope would not recognize the crown on Bosnia's kings until they accepted Catholicism. . . . So there were conversions, but those people remained in Bosnia and Dalmatia, and Catholicism there was nominal. The last two Bosnian kings were Catholics, and they fought against their own population to Catholicize them. Those were rough and violent times, and the people were exhausted.
>
> The Ottomans came with Islam in 1463 with one simple story: There is only one God. The population was exhausted having been through difficult times. And there were voluntary mass conversions. There are different versions of this history, and we can never know for a fact what actually went on. Some say only the elite converted. I think the population wanted some relief. We don't know the entire truth except that now we have this population here: Islamic, indigenous, and Slavic. The Bosniacs did not have much of an idea of separate nations. . . . They were always known as Good Bosnians, good people, maybe like the Cathars who always took everyone in.

In a similar vein, Ajša Softić told me in 2004, "Bosnia has a five-hundred-year tradition of its own Islam. It has its own traditions as a democratic religion . . . traditions, symbols, more than religion or nation." That liberal and flexible interpretation of Islam, influenced by the destroyed Bosnian Church, and an accompanying lack of nationalist aggressiveness, she insisted, are the Bosniacs' key cultural characteristics (see also Mahmutćehajić 2003; Simmons 2002; Weine 2000).

After listening to Silajdžić and Softić and having read contradictory claims about the Muslim nation (e.g., F. Friedman 1996, 2004), I would suggest that by the 1990s Serbs, Croats, and Bosniacs had come to agree that the Muslim label failed to denote a historically deep and distinct people. Prime among the reasons for the failure is that "Bosnian Muslims" is a multivalent term that conjures up a prior existence as Christians at the very moment that it indexes present-day adherents, or lapsed adherents, of Islam. Unlike Bosnian Croat Catholics and Bosnian Orthodox Serbs, who can assert the longue durée of their nations via a seemingly seamless history of Christianity, during the fifteenth through eighteenth centuries thousands of Bosnians abandoned Christianity to become Muslims (see Donia and Fine 1994; Pinson 1996; Malcolm 1996; cf. Zulfikarpašić 1998). The historical shallowness of Islam vis-à-vis Christianity in Bosnia places contemporary Muslims at risk. Bosnia's Catholic and Orthodox tend to view them as the descendents of opportunistic and treacherous individuals who changed religions to gain social and economic advantages, rather than as a primordial ethnic group. That risk is further compounded because in their association with Islam, a foreign and threatening "Turkish" or "Asiatic" faith, Muslims—even if of Slavic "blood"—are construed as out of place in Europe (see esp. Ballard 1996; Mašović 1998, 148). Indeed, several Bosniacs took the opportunity of our conversations to insist that during the 1992–95 war, "Europe" (i.e., the European Community, now the European Union) refused to assist the Bosnian army because they viewed it as a band of armed Islamic fundamentalists.

As opposed to the term *Muslim,* which indexes Islam, the Bosniac eponym makes a direct link to Bosnia, which, although situated in the peripheral Balkans, is certainly part of Europe. It is the hope of many that in the years ahead, Bosnia's liberal and tolerant version of Islam will gain positive recognition *as European* and that BiH will ultimately move from Europe's margins into the center through integration into the European Union. After all, by the early twentieth century after annexation into the Austro-Hungarian Empire, Bosnia-Herzegovina and its inhabitants became part of Central Europe.

As to the word *Bošnjak,* it seems to be a relatively recent European reinvention. In the nineteenth century, it was the Austro-Hungarian-German-Slavic word for all residents of Bosnia-Herzegovina.[8] Despite the opening of the magnificent Zemaljski Muzej in Sarajevo, whose artifacts demonstrate the unity of all of Bosnia's people, Bošnjastvo, or Bosnianness, did not in its time catch on as a pan-ethnic, territorially rooted identity. Despite its failure to attract adherents during the latter part of the nineteenth century, at the end of the twentieth Bosnian Muslim elites picked up on this by now historically salient term while transforming its meaning from "all Bosnians" to index only one segment of them, the Muslim national group (cf. Filipović 2007).

Revitalization of the Bosniac eponym has put the Muslims on par with the Serbs and the Croats by filling a troublesome gap in the terminological table. Now that Bosniacs are to Muslims as Croats are to Catholics and Serbs are to Orthodox, Bosnia's Muslims-as-Bosniacs have gained recognition as a nation, as a rights-vested political force as well as a loosely organized "culture." During the negotiations that led to the signing of the Dayton Peace Accords, it was the Bošnjaci—and not the Muslimani—who along with the Serbs and the Croats were inscribed as Bosnia-Herzegovina's constituent nations.

Often couched in terms of national liberation, first from the oppression of the Ottoman Turks and then from Yugoslav Communism, in the 1990s nationalist Croats and Serbs asserted their claims to Bosnia-Herzegovina through narratives of the longue durée. Equating their late-twentieth-century ethnicity with the religious affiliations of yesteryear, popular Serb and Croat historiographies contend that because this or that medieval Bosnian king was Orthodox or Catholic, the inhabitants of contemporary Bosnia should "really" be seen as Croats or Serbs.[9] These narratives claim that since there has never been a Bosnian nation, there is no legitimate reason now for Bosnia-Herzegovina to be recognized as a state.

During the war, Bosnia's Muslims were told to accept who they "really" are—Croats or Serbs—or be expelled or exterminated. The Muslims complied in declaring who they really were, but in rallying under the Bosniac banner and asserting their nationhood, they rejected the demands of nationalist Serbs and Croats. They then joined the world of nations by working their way backward from the present to "establish a 'legitimate' and continuous national history" (Bringa 1995, 36) as they linked their version of Islam with the heretical Christianity practiced in medieval Bosnia. Using the same narrative structure as the Serbs and the Croats, the Bosniacs have articulated a longue durée that substantiates primordial claims to the land of Bosnia, which they declare has never been nor should ever be part of Serbia or Croatia.

Despite the incompatibility of their contents, Bosniacs, Croats, and Serbs use identical structures to tell their national histories. Conforming to Stalin's definition of the nation, their discursive results have all but drowned out other more fluid and ambiguous perspectives about the people(s) of Bosnia. With the support they receive from the international community, BiH constitutional decrees, educational institutions, census categories, and the ethnic key that drives political coalitions and government appointments, B-C-S narratives of the longue durée have been congealing into a "static truth" (pace Herzfeld 1997a, 10). Bosnia has always been and will forever be comprised of three incommensurable groups, each entitled to its own land, language, and culture.

Preaching and Practicing Ethnic Exclusivity

Sarajevo tour guides, museum exhibits, scholarly essays, and popular parlance stress Bosnia's multiculturalism, that is, the particular social milieu wherein Bosniacs, Croats, Serbs, Jews, Roma, and people from various other ethnic groups lived together for centuries. For some who discuss the "multi-multi" nature of Sarajevo, boundaries between groups are porous, and it is difficult to distinguish where one ethnicity begins and another ends. Others stress the "common life" that formed as the result of several different cultural groups living in close contact with one another. No matter which interpretation of multiculturalism was emphasized, Sarajevans took great pride in their cosmopolitan city that extended hospitality to one and all and gave everyone a place.

But at the beginning of 1996 after the war ended, a mass exodus of Serbs left Sarajevo to settle in semirural conditions east of the city (Donia 2006, 338–39). A few years earlier, thousands of Muslims who had been driven from their towns and villages found refuge in Sarajevo. According to the 2002 FBiH count, the once extravagantly multiethnic city now has a 79 percent Bosniac majority, with small Serb and Croat minorities (Federacija Bosne i Herzegovine 2003a; see chapter 4). Across the entity divide, the area known popularly but contentiously as Srpsko Sarajevo is populated exclusively by Serbs (Armakolas 2007). Eighty-one miles southwest of Sarajevo, the city of Mostar spans the strikingly green Neretva River. In 1993, after combined Muslim and Croat troops repelled repeated attacks by the Serb-dominated Yugoslav National Army, Serbs were forced out of the city, and most of their homes and churches were destroyed. That Muslim-Croat coalition was short lived, and by November of that year, Mostar was forcibly split into two: Muslims were expelled from Catholic-Croat Mostar on the west bank of the river to live exclusively in Muslim Mostar on the east. Literally and symbolically splitting the city, the radical Croat army blasted the city's emblematic four-hundred-year-old Stari Most [Old Bridge] out of existence.

Despite the wantonly aggressive acts on the part of ultranationalist Serbs who placed Sarajevo under a strangling siege, and ultranationalist Croats who "ethnically cleansed" Mostar, individuals from both groups describe their situation as precarious in twenty-first-century Bosnia-Herzegovina. Serbs and Croats fear each other, but that fear only mounts when they discuss what they view as the country's worst possible scenario: life as an unprotected Christian minority in a predominately Muslim state. Foiled in their attempts to join Serbia, politicians and regular folk in the RS now laud the Dayton Accords for assurances that they will remain a self-governing entity able to protect their language, literature, and people. Representatives

10. "Don't Forget Srebrenica"

of Croat cultural organizations in Sarajevo and spokespeople for the Croat University of Mostar voiced similar concerns: It is only with vigilance and under the protection of the law that they can preserve their Croatian heritage under the onslaught of a quickly growing and power-hungry Muslim Bosniac nation. For their part, although Bosniacs tend to support a stronger central government and BiH without entities, they too have been developing exclusionary ethnic practices that complement their newly established national consciousness. Wartime experiences, culminating with the slaughter at Srebrenica, give them cause to fear their Serb and Croat compatriots.

WHO CAUSED THE WAR?

Throughout my stay in 2004, people often asked me why in the world I was in Sarajevo. By 2002 journalists, along with most military, administrative, and humanitarian-aid workers from what is referred to as the "international community" had long ago packed their bags and moved on to another war zone or trouble spot. What *was* I doing there? I was pushed to come up with an answer that convinced my interlocutors and was true to myself. I usually began by stating that when I lived in Zagreb during 1982–83, I paid a few visits to Bosnia and became fascinated by Sarajevo. And when the war broke out, I just couldn't believe it.

It was there, with the words, "war broke out," that I was interrupted. "What do you mean, 'the war broke out'? The war didn't break out. It had nothing to do with us here in Sarajevo. It is clear to everyone how that war started. Those"—and sometimes the next word uttered was, "Serbs," sometimes "Četniks," sometimes "aggressors"—"set themselves up in the hills and started firing down on us. It is no mystery; everyone knows how the war started. It did not break out. It was not a civil war." Haris Silajdžić, whom we met earlier in the chapter, explained, "What has happened here is part of a larger political design. Isn't it obvious? It should be obvious. These ethnic manifestations emerged out of a larger state-building design between the Serbs and the Croats to break up Bosnia. . . . In 1990 the picture was quite clear to everyone. . . . And because we had a very bad experience in World War II . . . being a minority, Bosniacs were alerted, but I could never have predicted that it would be so brutal and so bloody."

Listen, too, to Ibrahim Spahić, who coordinates cultural festivals and is a politician in his own right: "Everyone understands very clearly what happened in BiH and in ex-Yugoslavia. Milošević and Tudjman had those plans. I'm not giving you any Bosniac propaganda. It is simply the truth. Everyone knows what happened at Srebrenica. They organized concentration camps, raped girls and women, and slaughtered thousands of men. It is not the Serbian people who are responsible, but specific indicted war criminals who organized mass rapes and murders." And to Sanjin, who in 2004 was a twenty-five-year-old graduate student in literature: "The war didn't explode here. No, of course not. It came; it did not explode. In 1992 there were demonstrations here, right here. My father was there in those demonstrations against any war. . . . Many like him, who wanted a normal life, came to protest against war. Bosniacs, Croats, and Serbs were there—normal people who wanted a normal life. But the war came into Sarajevo. And when it came it changed everything."

These narratives confirmed much of what I had been hearing over the years. I had taken it to be a fact that after the referendum of March 1, 1992, armed aggressors positioned themselves on the mountains surrounding the valley in which Sarajevo sits. From there those radicalized Bosnian Serbs began attacks on civilians and laid siege to the city (see Pejanović 2004, 63–64). But when I went to those suburbs, villages, and recreation spots that are collectively but unofficially known as Srpsko Sarajevo, I was treated to quite a different perspective.

My first encounter took place there in August 2002 with Gordana, an attorney turned café owner. She responded furiously when I asked why she had moved away from the city in which she had spent her whole life, received an education, raised a family, and built a career: "I moved to the RS simply because of my name. We all feared what would happen to us. Don't you know how the war started in Sarajevo?" I told her that during the first weeks of April 1992 radical Serb forces surrounded the city and started shooting down from the hills. She corrected me:

> The war started with a wedding. A Serb family proceeded from its home in downtown Sarajevo to the Orthodox Church, as is the custom, carrying a Serbian flag in the procession. And with no provocation whatsoever, the father of the bride was shot dead.[10]
>
> Look, anyone who wants can move to the Republika Srpska; only we Serbs can't stay in Sarajevo. I can give you hundreds of examples of people here who were held with a gun to their head, intimidated, tortured by Muslim bandits. . . . More than ten thousand Serb civilians were killed in the war. . . . I didn't want to leave. I had to. That's why we ran in 1992; we were in danger because of our names. We were not religious; we were not SDS patriots. It was just our name.

Our conversation continued, and Ernest and Davor, who had accompanied me, joined in. Davor, the son of a Croat and a Serb, fled to Sweden during the war and has since resettled in London. He returns to Sarajevo whenever he can, this time for a few weeks to help his parents settle affairs with their apartment: "It takes at least twice as long to get your apartment privatized in Sarajevo if your name is Serb or Croat. And look what happened at the football game just two nights ago. Yugoslavia played Bosnia, and the Yugoslav team won 2–0. Loud shouts of *Allah Akbar* were heard all over the stadium and throughout the city; there were beatings, riots, at least one car was completely destroyed, hundreds were injured, sixteen hospitalized." He ended his comments by announcing, "Look, Osama bin Laden has a Bosnian passport," and rhetorically asked, "Do I have to say anything more?"

Jelena, who was born in Sarajevo but cannot remember living there, has been in Pale in the RS since her father was killed "by the Muslims" during the war. In 2004 Jelena attributed that war to the unconstitutional secession of Bosnia from Yugoslavia. Now that the war is over, she would like the RS to secede from Bosnia-Herzegovina and become part of Serbia (see also Armakolas 2007, 82–83): "So now you see what a confused place this is. Have you ever heard of any country that has three presidents? I think it is ridiculous, and if I could, I would want the Srpska Republika to be a part of Serbia." To my question, "Do you not feel any connection with Bosnia, with Sarajevo?" she replied: "Absolutely not. I go there as little as I can. And when I do, I feel that I am in a foreign country. There are Turkish words everywhere and those [gesturing] women all covered up from head to toe. The government of Bosnia is always talking about being part of Europe and entering the EU—that's a laugh! They are closer to the Middle East. All of that makes me feel very far away and distant. Pale is home."

Perhaps it is Danijela, an English teacher in Pale, whose family has since the 1960s lived in the nearby village of Lukavica, who expresses the sentiments of so many Bosnians, be they Bosniacs, Croats, Serbs, or Others. Blaming one group over another furthers no one:

> What makes me angry even today is making one people guilty. All sides should take blame for their actions. Children were dying on all sides, no exceptions. . . . With the war, we all lost. The people didn't get anything. . . . The only people who are well off are those who are in politics. . . . We don't have to like each other, but we still have to live together. The Muslims wanted their own state, the Croats wanted their own state, the Serbs wanted their own state, and in the end we got each other in one big apparatus that doesn't work.

11. Dobrinja, August 2002

Asja D., who in the summer of 2002 identified as a secular Muslim, grew up in Dobrinja, the neighborhood near the Sarajevo airport that during the war was one of the hardest hit (see Mann 2001). "After the war started I left for a two-week ski trip in Slovenia and only returned in January '96." Apprehensive that her peers in Sarajevo might scorn her, Asja was thrilled with the joyous homecoming she received from everyone, especially her two best friends, Bosnian Croats. She was about to end our conversation on that note. But something stopped her, and after a pause she shifted her tone:

> I was really optimistic, until yesterday. I'm working on a UNICEF project for children without parents. We're a team of six girls, three of us from Sarajevo, and three from Banja Luka in the RS. We went into the municipal offices of Banja Luka and right there on the walls were portraits of Karadžić and Arkan, indicted international war criminals. It really bothered me to go into the Banja Luka City Hall and see *war criminals'* portraits on the wall, along with icons and emblems of Yugoslavia. Ivica, one of the Banja Luka girls, said that they are heroes of her country and that Alija Izetbegović is a war criminal for her, and who am I to call them war criminals. I said, "It's not just me; it's the whole world." And then I realized for the first time that she was telling me that I am not part of her country and that she is not part of mine. The Republika Srpska, she is saying, has to be part of Serbia. This is the first time that it's occurred to me that part of this country doesn't want to be part of this country but sees itself as something else. Now I don't know anymore if it can work. It's like it's going to happen all over again, what happened with our parents ten years ago. Meantime, we have the international community here, but when they leave, what I'm thinking is: A war can happen all over again.

LANGUAGE AND LEARNING

During the 1990s, as the peoples of Yugoslavia demanded territorial and cultural autonomy, they insisted as well on the recognition of their languages. In the 1991 census, just over a quarter of Bosnia-Herzegovina's population named as their native language Serbo-Croatian (26.62%) or Croato-Serbian (1.41%), while the rest claimed Bosnian (37.12%), Serbian (18.85%), Croatian (13.56%), or no mother tongue (2.46%).

Prior to our flight from Zagreb to Sarajevo in 1997, Olga Supek and I wanted to confirm entry regulations with the embassy of Bosnia-Herzegovina. Olga opened the new Zagreb telephone book and turned to *A* for *ambasada* but found nothing there. "Surely there are still embassies in Zagreb," we joked. Suddenly Olga remembered an old-fashioned word, *veleposlanstvo,* and turned to the *V* section in the directory, where all the embassies were listed. On its Web site, the embassy [*veleposlanstvo*] of the Republic of Croatia to the United States lists its official language as "Croatian language and Latin alphabet." In 2006, the embassy of Serbia and Montenegro declared itself as such in English and in Serbian in Cyrillic script (амбасада). The embassy of Bosnia-Herzegovina to the United States only presents that title in English, but the Web site's homepage gives readers the option of clicking an alternate language button, *B/S/H jezik,* where the *B* stands for Bosnian, the *S* for Serbian, and the *H* for Hrvatski, or Croatian.

While many ex-Yugoslavs joke about the splitting of one language into three tongues (see chapter 7), the forging of new dictionaries and grammar books is a serious business. So too is the insistence that each B-C-S people holds the inalienable right to its own language. As a result, government documents and those of officially recognized NGOs are thrice printed, although there may be very little variation from one version to the others.

The biggest difference between the B-C-S languages is in the alphabet. Until the middle of 1992, Bosnia-Herzegovina's major daily newspaper, *Oslobodjenije,* was published in both the Latin and the Cyrillic scripts. School children throughout the republic learned their lessons one day or one week in *latinica,* the next day or week in *kirilica.* I remember feeling that something was missing when I entered postwar Sarajevo in August 1997, for along with the shock of seeing bombed-out, windowless buildings and bright crimson "roses" in the sidewalk memorializing recently spilled blood, there were hardly any signs, newspapers, books, or magazines in Cyrillic.

The biggest alphabet shock of all occurred to me at the tenth-anniversary celebration of the SGV, or Serbian Civil Council, in March 2004: All the signs and the organization's literature were published in the Latin alphabet. Were they saying with this orthographic decision that along with being Serbs, they are Sarajevans, part of a bigger, more cosmopolitan, multicultural world?[11] When, later in my stay, I asked some officers of Prosvjeta, Sarajevo's Serbian cultural organization, about their choice to publish in the Latin script, their response was that the Serbian language has a long history, and that it has always been written in both alphabets. I left it at that.

A few months later, my hosts in Pale, officials of the SDS in the Republika Srpska, took the opportunity of my visit to stress their satisfaction with the Dayton Accords, which granted to them 49 percent of the territory of Bosnia-Herzegovina and near autonomy as an entity. Calling the accords "our Bible," they told me, "The Muslims [in the FBiH] can build as many mosques as they wish, as long as we can have our churches and cathedrals." And then one asked rhetorically, "Tell me, where is Cyrillic in the Federation? We have *latinica* here, but there is not one letter in Cyrillic there."

A national language, as Ignatieff (1993, 10) suggests, assures each individual that she or he will be completely understood by co-nationals, "not merely what you say but what you mean." Because the Bosnian language includes several Turkish words and some Arabic expressions, many of BiH's Serbs and Croats reject inclusion in that language community and state unequivocally that they are speakers of Serbian or Croatian. Adding that the Bosniacs speak their own Muslim-inflected language, they contend that despite its recognition as such in the Dayton Accords, the term *Bosnian* is a misnomer, and they are demanding instead that it be called the Bosniac language (Grubišić 2003; Okey 2004). But it is not only Serbs and Croats who demand linguistic autonomy and their own national languages. "Unfortunately," Daria Sucic (1996) has noted, "Bosnian could have easily become the common name for the language shared by all Bosnian peoples, particularly as that name for the language had a long history of use in preceding centuries, [but] Muslim

12. Welcome to Republika Srpska, August 2002

linguists began at the beginning of the war to pursue the thesis that Bosnian was the language of Bosnian Muslims exclusively" (see chapter 7).

Today, the Web site of the Tourism Association of Sarajevo Canton displays its information in English, and in *lokalni jezik*, or the local language, without specifying the ethnicity or ethnicities of the local.[12] But at the University of Mostar, which was established during the war as a Croat institution, Croatian is used exclusively as the language of instruction and administration. Eighty-five miles to its northeast, the University of Eastern Sarajevo in the Republika Srpska was likewise founded as a Serbian institution, and the only language recognized there is Serbian. Over at the University of Sarajevo, Sanjin proudly told me that the linguistics and literature departments there emphasize plurality by teaching the languages and the literatures of Bosnia-Herzegovina. He declared of Sarajevo's intellectuals, "We don't have this shelving or boxing of people or things." This view, however, expresses nostalgia for how things once were and might yet be because across Bosnia-Herzegovina and in its capital city, one language with many regional dialects has in fact been divided up and boxed into three.

CULTURAL INSTITUTIONS

During 2004, I paid several visits to the cultural organizations that further the literary, artistic, and musical heritage of their respective groups. Like the national historical narratives that are identical in structure but different in their contents, the spokesmen for Croat Napredak, Bosniac Preporod, and Serb Prosvjeta each provided the same plotline when they told me about their organizations. These cultural societies, or their predecessors, they said, were founded as the nineteenth century turned to the twentieth to spread literacy among the people and to finance the secondary and higher education of young men.[13] In 1941, Nazi occupiers deemed Preporod and Prosvjeta illegal and shut them down. They reopened in the late 1940s, only to be banned again, along with Napredak early in Tito's regime.

In socialist Yugoslavia, "culture" was supposed to come as one workers' culture, and not in national packages. Of course, this policy was ironic since, with the exception of Bosnia-Herzegovina, the constituent republics of Yugoslavia came in national units, and so too did their citizens (Wachtel 1998). In 2004, spokespeople of the B-C-S cultural groups revealed that the demand for one Yugoslav workers' culture was an ideology that never quite took hold, and they described the reopening of their organizations in 1990 as the spontaneous expression of repressed national cultures. Yet at the same time that they discussed the right of their nation to preserve its uniqueness, they also mentioned the importance of its contribution to Sarajevo's common life and its attached tolerance for difference.

The spokesmen of Napredak, Preporod, and Prosvjeta each insisted to me that his organization is purely cultural and philanthropic, and that the organizations have no ties to political parties or politicians. Their aims are first and foremost the preservation and protection of their group's national heritage, and, second, the granting of scholarships to assist university students in their studies of language, literature, art, and history, and the creation of community through the organization's newsletter and its cultural events.

Professor B., who hosted me at Napredak, maintained that the organization's major goal is to assure that "this [Croatian] culture will not be forgotten." As he described Sarajevo's B-C-S cultural institutions, he used the word *povratak* (return) over and over, stressing that their revitalization was the "natural" outgrowth of democracy that occurred with the downfall of Yugoslavia's one-party and one-culture system. Skipping over the war years, Professor B. explained: "According to the constitution, we have that right, the right to a Croatian television and radio station in Bosnia-Herzegovina; the right to our language, people, culture, and history; the right to protect our nation from assimilation. These are our constitutional rights in today's political system. These are dangerous politics, and unfortunately, people are getting less tolerant and not more so now that there is one nation in the majority. . . . I can tell you more about this, our multicultural, multiconfessional way of life that used to be here in Sarajevo."

Over at Prosvjeta, which means "education" and "enlightenment," Dragan, the organization's president, stressed its autonomy from any and all political parties as well as from the Serbian Orthodox Church: "It would be better to be absolutely without funds than to be associated with the parties or with the church."

Prosvjeta, like Napredak and Preporod (the Bosniac cultural organization whose name means "renaissance" and is discussed in chapter 7), receives a small budget from the Ministry of Culture of the Canton of Sarajevo, "and an even smaller one from the Federation Ministry of Culture and Sport." Also, the organization relies on donations, for most of its members are pensioners who have a hard time affording the tiny monthly dues of 1 KM. Because of the members' advanced age, the future of Prosvjeta in Sarajevo is far from certain. Another member of Prosvjeta's advisory board, who had worked for years as a journalist, joined our conversation: "Because we are apolitical, we are not such a visible force in the city. Most of us have no nationalistic interests. I myself am a Serb married to a Muslim. My *ujak* [maternal uncle]

13. Mostar's newly rebuilt Stari Most, June 2004

is married to a Jew. The problem now is that most of our politicians are professional nationalists. It was never before like this."

Just as Professor B. at Napredak used the opportunity of our conversation to contrast contemporary Sarajevo with the not long ago time of his youth, Serbs at Prosvjeta also rued the lack of tolerance and multiculturalism in postwar Sarajevo. Perhaps the SGV celebration in March 2004, when just about every cultural organization, but no political party, was given an award for cooperation, should be viewed as an important moment in the reestablishment of "multi-multi" Sarajevo and Good Bosnia. Even more striking was the ribbon-cutting ceremony at Mostar's rebuilt Stari Most. Broadcast on television across the country, the opening of the new Old Bridge was accompanied by speeches, fireworks, and joyful music, all asserting a renewed commitment to Bosnia's long tradition of tolerance (see Hayden 2007, 108–10; Bougarel, Helms, and Duijzings 2007a, 2).

All these events would seem to bode favorably for an integrated, functioning, pluralistic Bosnian state working toward postwar reconciliation. Be that as it may, although its aim was to disband in June 2008, the Office of the High

Representative remains the final word in Bosnia-Herzegovina. The Federation and the RS remain intact as almost autonomous entities, and, as I show in the next chapter, B-C-S national divisions and personal identities may, over a decade after Dayton, be more entrenched and "natural" than ever.

4

Census and Sensibility

Confirming the Constitution

Convinced that a central task for anthropologists studying the contemporary world is to link the "little poetics of everyday interaction with the grand dramas of official pomp and historiography" (Herzfeld 1997a, 25), I make the case in this chapter for connections between the group belongings that we have heard Sarajevans narrate and seen practice and broader state projects of governance and control.

The "grand drama" to be considered here is the 2002 census of the FBiH, the first official population count in post-Dayton Bosnia-Herzegovina. Had Yugoslavia remained intact, or had the Bosnian Republic effected a peaceful secession, the regularly scheduled decennial census would have occurred in 2001. However, since in 2001 BiH had no unitary statewide statistics bureau, decisions regarding enumeration were made at the entity level. Insisting on continued use of the 1991 Yugoslav census data, the Republika Srpska declined to count its population. The Federation, however, conducted a "social mapping exercise" a year behind schedule. In that attempt to remain committed to bureaucratic regularity, FBiH's census can be considered a normal simplification strategy that characterizes all state projects of governmentality (Ferguson and Gupta 2002; Scott 1998; pace Foucault 1991). Yet inasmuch as the count used a categorical scheme that differed from previous procedures, the Federation's census should also be viewed as an extraordinary measure aimed at normalizing Bosnia-Herzegovina from an illegible, chaotic population to a peaceful, European tri-nation-state.

Following recent work in several disciplines that demonstrates how state bureaucracies hold the means to name, unname, count, and categorize their populations, and the power to discipline them into thinking of themselves along the very lines of such categorical counting (Anderson 1991; Appadurai 1996; Cohn 1990; Goldberg 1997; F. Hirsch 2005; Kertzer and Arel 2002; Urla 1993), my analysis of the FBiH census reveals that only a matter of years after the signing of the Dayton Peace Agreement (DPA), the B-C-S triad of incommensurable nations is congealing into Sarajevans' common sense. Put somewhat differently, I explore the idea that citizens' subjectivities and the demands of state are coalescing into what is increasingly experienced as the "natural" way of defining self and other.

Yet we should not forget that it took about a century for Sarajevans to switch their commonsensical thinking about identities from religious affiliation to nationality and that these categories continue to overlap and are often used interchangeably (Perica 2002; Velikonja 2003). In this chapter, Sarajevans are shown in their ongoing encounters with new demands from the Bosnian state to think and act in terms of a tripartite citizenry comprised of members of one and only one of the Bosniac, Croat, or Serb constituent nations.

I unravel these complicated and contentious issues, first by comparing the results of Yugoslavia's last 1991 census with the Federation's 2002 count. In the sections that follow, I present and analyze the most salient differences between the population categories used to frame these statistics: the transformation of Muslims into Bosniacs, and the reduction of a long catalog of ethnic options to a forced choice that mirrors the constitutional declaration that the Bosniacs, Croats, and Serbs are BiH's "constituent nations (along with Others)." The chapter ends by suggesting that although the postwar state in the figure of the census interviewer reminded 99 percent of the Federation's population that to count and be counted in Bosnia-Herzegovina means declaring a B-C-S national identity, that very state is fragile, divided, and uncertain. Off-census ways of belonging thus may rival what seems to be an increasingly accepted and acceptable tripartite ethnic scheme.

Counting to Be Counted

Yugoslavia's first census was taken two years after the formation of the post–World War II state and published a year later in 1948. The country's next census appeared in 1953. Thereafter, from 1961 until its demise, the Yugoslav Socialist Federation, along with the rest of Europe, counted and categorized its population every ten years. Statewide population reports and those of each of Yugoslavia's constituent socialist republics displayed, among other things, positive health indicators, economic growth, and increasing amounts of education with each subsequent cohort. And like other European states, the decennial census became a defining feature of Yugoslavia's sovereignty and modernity (Kertzer and Arel 2002, 7).

Yugoslavia's official list of nations and nationalities (minority groups) changed with almost every population count from the founding of the Yugoslav kingdom in 1918 to the end of the Socialist Federation in 1991. Immediately after the establishment of socialist Yugoslavia, the list of constituent nations expanded from three to five as Macedonians and Montenegrins joined the Serbs, the Croats, and the Slovenes. It took some time, however, for other groups to be added. In 2004 Greta remembered:

> In Belgrade after the Second World War, before we met each other, my husband had to register for his student identity card. In those days, there were no Bosniacs or Muslims. . . . My husband, who is not any more Muslim than you or I—he is atheist absolutely and only knows when it is Ramadan when someone invites him or tells him—registered as a Serb. As for me, I went and said, "I am a Jew." The clerk said, "That is not a category, for you [Jews] do not have a country." This was 1946 or 1947, before Israel was established. I showed him the number on my arm and said, "Because of being a Jew I was sent to a camp. Put me down as a Jew."

By 1961 the list of nationalities had grown to include groups whose constituents numbered less than 1 percent of the population along with the five nations, and a pan-ethnic, citizenship-based category of Yugoslavs. During the 1971 census, the addition of the *Muslimanska nacija* raised the number of Yugoslavia's constituent nations to six. In the 1981 population count, citizens had a choice of eighteen nationality categories in addition to the six nations. In scrupulously documenting *nacionalna pripadnost,* or ethnic belonging, the decennial censuses conferred official state recognition to minority groups with small numbers while simultaneously confirming the dominance of Yugoslavia's major nations, thereby giving substance to Tito's unifying slogan of *bratstvo i jedinstvo.*

In Bosnia-Herzegovina, one thing remained constant. Every ten years, the census confirmed it as Yugoslavia's only socialist republic with no majority group. It was consistently the most ethnically mixed region of the country and had the highest percentage of citizens who identified as *Jugoslaveni,* or Yugoslavs. Indexing a flexible hybrid identity, the Yugoslav category of belonging provided an alternative to forcing a single choice among individuals with mixed ethnic backgrounds and/or who preferred to identify with the socialist state's pan-ethnic or nonethnic universalistic goals. Tendencies toward heterogeneity and hybridity in the Bosnian population intensified when people moved from villages to towns and from towns to cities. In the 1991 census, whereas 5.6 percent of all Bosnians declared themselves Yugoslavs (table 1), that proportion rose to 10.7 percent in Sarajevo (table 2).

No decennial census was produced ten years later in independent Bosnia-Herzegovina. "B&H is the only European country which has not and will not organize a population census this year," notes Drazen Simic (2001) of AIM Sarajevo, and as a consequence, "no one will be able to know precisely the basic figure—the exact population of B&H, let alone a more detailed demographic picture of Bosnians and Herzegovinians." More telling than the lack of demographic statistics, Simic reiterates, is the fact itself that no census was taken. Bosnia's lack of population statistics stands out against

Table 1. Bosnia-Herzegovina's Population according to Ethnicity in the 1991 Yugoslav Census

Category	Total	Percentage
Crnogorci (Montenegrins)	10,071	0.2
Hrvati (Croats)	760,852	17.4
Makedonci (Macedonians)	1,596	0.1
Muslimani (Muslims)	1,902,956	43.5
Slovenci (Slovenes)	2,190	0.1
Srbi (Serbs)	1,366,104	31.2
Jugoslaveni (Yugoslavs)	242,682	5.6
Albanci (Albanians)	4,925	0.1
Česi (Czechs)	590	0.0
Italijani (Italians)	732	0.0
Jevreji (Jews)	426	0.0
Mađari (Hungarians)	893	0.0
Nijemci (Germans)	470	0.0
Poljaci (Poles)	526	0.0
Romi (Gypsies)	8,864	0.2
Rumuni (Romanians)	162	0.0
Rusi (Russians)	297	0.0
Rusini (Ruthenians)	133	0.0
Slovaci (Slovaks)	297	0.0
Turci (Turks)	267	0.0
Ukrajinci (Ukrainians)	3,929	0.1
Ostali (Others)	17,592	0.4
Undeclared	14,585	0.3
Regional affiliation	224	0.0
Unknown	35,670	0.8
Total	4,377,033	100%

Source: Federacija Bosne i Hercegovine 2003b, 61.

Yugoslavia's once impressive record of progress. As the only country on the continent without a census, Bosnia-Herzegovina seems to be drifting off on its own, away from modern Europe.

In 2001, remembering the bombed-out city I had seen in 1997, I could easily imagine Sarajevo stuck in a postwar morass, but that image changed immediately when I arrived at Sarajevo International Airport in August 2002. The brightly lit and computerized Euro-modern airport was nothing like the dark, dreary crater where I had landed five years earlier. In the city center, great changes were under way as well. In the reopened cafes, German beer, American soft drinks, and Italian espresso vied with thick Bosnian coffee, and unlike the dazed people I encountered shortly after the war, Sarajevans were now quite talkative. Many grumbled about the sluggish pace of economic recovery, the persistence of ethnic strife, and the tripartite division of the country. Some yearned for the glory days of Yugoslavia and complained that "Europe" was in no small measure responsible for the violence of the last decade. Several of the same people expressed fear that should the international community leave, Bosnia might erupt in another war.

Jokes, especially about all those experts from abroad (present company included?), were more conspicuous than complaints. Here's one that struck my fancy:

> Today, two journalists meet up in Sarajevo. One asks the other,
> "When did you arrive?"
> "Yesterday."
> "When will you leave?"
> "Tomorrow."
> "Why have you come?"
> "To write *Sarajevo: Yesterday, Today, and Tomorrow.*"

Along with these Sarajevo scenes something else caught my eye. Plastered on buildings recently renovated, on those that were still bullet-scarred and windowless, and over the skeletal hulks of what had once been apartment buildings, department stores, and government complexes, I saw posters announcing a "Federation-wide social mapping exercise." Featuring a family seated around the dining table, the posters iconically declared: The war is over. We are at home with our loved ones. Normalcy has resumed, and the time has come to do what we as a modern, European country have always done every ten years. The poster's text appealed to the citizenry to open their doors to "our interviewers" and participate in the project: to be counted—and count—in the population of Bosnia-Herzegovina.

When I returned to Sarajevo in March 2004, I was eager to see the results of that census. Remembering the posters but confused by the governmental structure of entities, cantons, and municipalities, I searched the capital for the BiH Statistics Bureau—to no avail. It took a few days of inquiries for me to understand that the posters I had seen announced not a statewide census but a count of the Federation only. The Republika Srpska had made no plans to count its inhabitants, and as of this writing there has yet to be an enumeration of the entire population of Bosnia-Herzegovina.[1]

Once I stopped searching for the nonexistent BiH Statistical Agency, it was easy to find the Federal (FBiH) Office of Statistics. It is located in the center of town across the way from the spruced-up bezistan, once the covered cloth market that now houses boutiques. Upon arrival I was directed to the statistical library, where I asked the librarian for the latest population census. He went to a nearby shelf and pulled out a hard-bound volume of the Federation's 2003 Statistical Yearbook and placed it on the desk in front of me. I opened it, scanned the table of contents, and turned to page 61, titled, "Population Grouped according to Ethnicity." What I found there were the Yugoslav census results from 1961, 1971, 1981, and 1991. I sighed audibly. The librarian asked, "What's the problem?" I told him that I remember seeing posters two years ago that announced a population survey. "Where are the results?" I asked. He looked me over, asked if I could wait a bit, and then left the room. He was gone for several minutes. When he returned, the librarian placed before me ten modest black and white booklets, one for each canton of the Federation (Federacija Bosne i Hercegovine 2003a). Those brochures contained the results of half of independent Bosnia-Herzegovina's first population count.[2]

I opened the first booklet at random to compare it with the last Yugoslav census. Remarkably, instead of the twenty-five categories used in 1991 to count and categorize the population on the basis of nationality (see table 1), in 2002 FBiH placed its citizens into only three named categories: Bosniacs, Croats, and Serbs. All the other nationalities that were part of Bosnia's ethnoscape had simply vanished. So too had the Yugoslavs, who, since the war, were no longer a categorical possibility. The Muslimani of 1991 had also disappeared, but unlike Bosnia's ethnic minorities and the Yugoslavs, reconstituted under the categorical label of Bošnjaci, they emerged from the count stronger than ever. The aggregated census results from the Federation's ten cantons demonstrate that the Bosniacs (1,690,280, now comprising 73% of the population) together with the Croats (504,717, 22%) and the Serbs (101,518, 4%) combined to form 99 percent of the population. The fourth listed option, *Ostali,* those Others who would not or could not be counted as Bosniacs, Croats, or Serbs, accounted for a mere 1 percent (22,457 persons).

Table 2. Comparative Enumerations of Sarajevo, 1991 and 2002

Ethnic Composition in Yugoslav Enumeration of Sarajevo, 1991

Total	Muslimani	Srbi	Hrvati	Jugoslaveni	Ostali
527,049	259,470	157,143	34,873	56,470	19,093
100%	49.2%	29.8%	6.6%	10.7%	3.6%

Source: Republika Bosne i Hercegovine 1993, 7.

Ethnic Composition in FBiH Enumeration of Sarajevo, 2002

Sarajevo	Total	Bošnjaci	Hrvati	Srbi	Ostali
Total	401,118	319,245	26,890	44,865	10,118
	100%	79.6%	6.7%	11.2%	2.5%
Centar	68,151	52,151	4,737	8,945	2,318
	100%	76.5%	7.0%	13.1%	3.4%

Source: Federacija Bosne i Hercegovine 2003a, Kanton Sarajevo u brojkama, 10.

In Sarajevo, where heterogeneity and hybridity always outstripped the countryside, the percentages differ somewhat from the total FBiH count. Sarajevo's residents include a greater proportion of Serbs and Ostali than in the general population. But the overall results here too confirmed the trinational structure of the new state. As table 2 shows, in the city as a whole and in the Centar Općina, where I lived, in 2002 the Ostali category had shrunk to parenthetical status.

Several social scientists have read preliminary census estimates for Bosnia as confirmation that after the 1992–95 war, ethnic segregation now characterizes regions that were once multiethnic and multiconfessional (see Cattaruzza 2001; Chaveneau-Lebrun 2001; Robin-Hunter 2001, after Hayden 1996). Although such a reading is certainly plausible, I suggest that the 2002 population survey pushed familiar but slippery notions into fixed categories. Administered under government auspices only six years after the end of a war waged on the principle of ethnic cleansing, the survey encouraged citizens to identify with the B-C-S scheme. The remainder of this chapter ethnographically explores that hunch.

Changing Names, Asserting Nation

As we have already seen in chapter 3, over the decade of the 1990s Sarajevo's Muslims transformed themselves discursively, historically, and constitutionally into the Bosniac nation. The word *Bošnjaci* has a long history that conjures associations with the medieval Bosnian state and with BiH's late-nineteenth-century inclusion in the Austro-Hungarian Empire. In the early

1990s during the siege of Sarajevo, it was chosen by Bosnian Muslim elites to replace the term *Muslimani,* which they agreed had become inappropriate, and by the time I began visiting postwar Sarajevo, the Bosniac eponym had officially superceded *Muslims* in the government and in the media. The 2002 FBiH census therefore eliminated the Muslim category as an affiliative option and installed *Bošnjaci* in its place. But what is not clear from the census is whether the state acted by fiat to turn FBiH Muslims, and perhaps some Yugoslavs and members of ethnic minorities, into Bosniacs, or if citizens, through their own declarations, made that switch in identity.

During interviews and in the course of casual conversations, I heard all kinds of people refer to themselves or to their neighbors as Bosniacs. Sometimes they used that term interchangeably with Muslims, and sometimes not. In addition to those spontaneous identity stories and the official FBiH census, I searched for a way to capture how Sarajevans define their ethnic belongings, especially to organs of the state. When couples register their marriages at the Matični Ured, or Registration Bureau, they are required to complete a form that asks for personal data, including ethnic belonging. During the summer months of 2004, I recorded the *nacionalna pripadnost* entries of the brides and grooms (for a total of 9,652 individuals) who registered their marriages at the Centar Općina from the beginning of 1996 through the end of 2003.[3]

Those data demonstrate a clear trend to abandon the Muslim label for Bosniac. Table 3 shows that in 1996 nearly 44 percent of all brides and grooms registered as Muslimani while almost a quarter declared themselves Bošnjaci. By 2003 only 12 percent defined themselves as Muslims, and over half the people who registered their marriage that year designated their national belonging as Bosniac.

The decision made by an elite group at the height of the siege of Sarajevo to call the Muslims of Bosnia Bosniacs was adopted in the state constitution

Table 3. Solidifying Bosniac Identity

	1996	1998	2000	2003
Bošnjaci	24.7%	36.3%	41.7%	52.8%
BM/MB[a]	5.2	5.2	3.8	1.6
BOS/BiH B,M[b]	0.4	0.3	0.3	0.2
Muslimani	43.6	25.2	20.2	12.4
Total of all registrants	73.9	67.0	66.0	67.0

Source: Matični Ured, Centar Općina, Sarajevo

[a] Bosniac-Muslim or Muslim-Bosniac.

[b] Bosnian Bosniac or Bosnian Muslim, or BiH Bosniac or BiH Muslim.

via the Dayton Peace Agreement to reify a people whose diffuseness had put them at risk. Solidifying the ambiguously labeled Muslims into the Bosniac nation responded to people's fears and desires by filling what had been a troublesome gap in the terminological table. Now that Bosnia's Muslims-as-Bosniacs have gained recognition as a nation as well as a cultural or religious group, Bosniac ethnopolitical identity has become fixed as fact. The state category and citizens' sensibilities have worked together to shape selves that correspond to the constitutional mandate of a Bosniac people.

What remains hidden in this analysis, however, is that even after adding up all the variously self-designated Bosniac and/or Muslim brides and grooms of Sarajevo's Centar district in 2003, these comprised only 67 percent of all the registrants. That proportion is almost 10 percent less than the 76.5 percent Bosniac figure reported in the census of the *općina* and offers a provocative hint that, the lessons of the recent war notwithstanding, not all Bosnians of Muslim background always choose to identify as members of the Bosniac national group. I discuss the issue of Bosnian hybridity in chapter 7, but now let us consider the pressures on everyone in Sarajevo to declare their affiliations via the B-C-S triad through the probe, "But what are you really?"

But What Are You Really?

The facts of the 2002 FBiH census overwhelmingly confirm FBiH as the Bosniac-Croat Federation and the B-C-S triad as Bosnia's constituent nations. Yet, as several analyses of nation building and state formation have revealed, no "facts," not even the hard data of maps and population statistics, speak for themselves (Anderson 1991; Appadurai 1996; Cohn 1990; F. Hirsch 2005). They show instead that the divisions and groupings chosen by bureaucrats and social scientists to count and classify populations are neither neutral nor natural. Although the census is presented as a transparent measure, its categories, objectified in government documents and disseminated via the media, become the means by which the population learns to think about and understand itself (Goldberg 1997; Kertzer and Arel 2002; Scott 1998; Urla 1993). Ordinary citizens often end up abandoning the labels that are not part of the census repertoire and instead adopt, use, and ultimately accept the state-mandated categories to talk about themselves and others. With discipline and practice, these categorical ways of counting become the seemingly natural units of culture and society, and the 2002 FBiH census is a case in point (see Markowitz 2007, 46, 68–69).

What is at stake here is a sense of belonging, a desire, if not the need, to count as an approved constituent nation member-citizen of the nation-state.

In 2004, twenty-one-year-old journalism student Amar, who holds politically liberal views, reflected,

> I am a Bosniac. That's what I call myself these days. My family is from a village outside Sarajevo, and my great-grandfather was a *hodža* [imam]. My mother is pretty conservative, but my brother and I don't observe [Islamic law] at all, like most Bosniacs. Look, until a few years ago I went around telling everyone I was a Bosanac until I realized that this category is illegal. It doesn't exist in our constitution. So I thought about it and decided that I wanted to count as one of the constituent groups of my country. And now, I feel like, yeah, I'm a Bosniac.

In 2002 the FBiH census takers rejected mixed or amorphous answers to questions about nationality. They did not leave it to individuals to think over their ethnic belonging and make their own decisions, as did Amar. Instead, they adjusted the respondents' replies or probed for the answers that they sought by asking the follow-up question, "But what are you really?" Here are a few examples:

Asja M., who spent most of the war as a university student in the United States, returned to Sarajevo in 2000. Two years later, she was visiting a friend when "the census-taker came and started asking a series of questions." She recalled, "My friend's mother answered the question about national belonging by saying, 'I am a Czech.' The interviewer told her, 'I have no Czechs on my list. Czechs are Catholic. I'll put you down as a Croat.' And my friend's mother did not object."

I have heard similar stories about the making of Serbs from Montenegrins or Macedonians and of Bosniacs from Albanians or Gypsies. The November 1999 report of the Bosnian Section of the Society for Threatened Peoples states, "Since the Constitution of B&H does not recognized the constitutionality [of the Romani people], these Roma do not have their representative in the government" and declare themselves as Bosniacs, who do.[4] Although the Roma, Albanians, Macedonians, Montenegrins, and other Others may keep alive an alternate off-census identity through social interaction among friends and family, by allowing themselves to be counted as B-C-S they end up conspiring with a state that renders their ethnicity too troublesome or too insignificant to count in the new scheme of things. These issues are considered in greater detail in chapters 5 and 6.

Most of the people who told me about being pushed to declare "who you really are" as Bosniac, Croat, or Serb are those who had always thought of themselves and went about their lives as Yugoslavs. Now, still resisting the tripartite division of their country, they refuse to articulate an ethnicity, or they assert that they are Bosnians, individual citizens of BiH. Amila was at home when the census taker called: "When that interviewer came to my house, she talked to my mom. Mom answered the question about national belonging by saying what she always says, Bosnian. 'Yes,' replied the census-taker, 'we are all Bosnians in Bosnia. But what are you really?' My mom insisted that she really *is* Bosnian. The census taker then asked another question: 'What is your family's religion?' My mom said that she and my dad are not observant, but that both her parents and his parents are Muslims. 'Aha,' said the interviewer, 'then you are Bosniacs,' and that is how she completed the form."

Susan Woodward notes that during the war "Serbs and Croats in Bosnia-Herzegovina who identified themselves as Bosnians rather than side with Bosnian Serb or Bosnian Croat nationalists were all classified with the enemy and vulnerable to treatment as traitors" (1995, 271). In August 2002, Nebojša, whose first name marks him as a Serb but whose hyphenated surname along with wartime service in the Bosnian army keeps everyone guessing, implicitly concurred with Woodward when he pointed out that the DPA and the FBiH census reflect earlier wartime practices. He explained that during the war demonstrating a specific ethno-religious identity was often the only route for gaining the humanitarian aid—foodstuffs, medicine, blankets, clothing—that was distributed through religious organizations. Nebojša explained, "If, during the war, I had declared myself as a Serb, life would have been at least 20 percent easier because I could have gotten humanitarian aid from Dobrotvor. Only ADRA of the Adventists and La Benevolencija of the Jewish Community were open to and helped everyone. Otherwise, Caritas only gave to Croats and other Catholics, Dobrotvor to the Orthodox, and don't get me started on Preporod and Merhamet, which only serviced the Muslims."

Since the end of the war, citizens who identify with groups that place them outside the B-C-S triad often have the hardest time landing jobs in government institutions and finding state-guaranteed mortgages, student loans, and scholarships. They are ineligible to hold office in the BiH presidency and are disqualified for many other state and entity offices. Bosnia's constitution in its insistence on tripartite power sharing "emphasizes national identities and downplays individual rights" (McMahon 2004, 202). There are no advantages to claiming an Other identity.

Important as they may be, these kinds of instrumental reasons for conforming to state-imposed demands for self-definition via the B-C-S scheme tell only one part of a wider, more complicated story. Several people from ethnically mixed families told me that along with understanding that unequivocal belongings are necessary in contemporary BiH, they have chosen to identify with only one side for emotional or ideological reasons. Sonja, the daughter of a Jewish father and a Croatian mother, had always thought of herself as Yugoslav, which gave her the flexibility of identifying with her country and being simultaneously a Jew and a Croat. But after returning from four years abroad and finding that she can no longer be a multiply constituted Yugoslav, Sonja joined the moderate Croatian New Initiative Party (HNI) because it best expresses her own vision for Bosnia-Herzegovina. And although she continues to attend functions in the Jewish community, Sonja has been identifying unequivocally as a Croat.

Politics of a different sort drive the ethnic identity decisions of Damir, Mak, and Azra. Thirty-year-old Damir, whose father is Bosniac and whose mother he described as Serbian Orthodox, told me that he is first and foremost a Bosnian. But when pushed to declare who he "really is," he will comply and say Bosniac, "because I fought in the BiH army during that war." Admitting to a patrilineal bias, he added, "I feel closer to that side of my family." Likewise Mak, who at age twelve barely escaped imprisonment and worse at the hands of irregular Serb forces when he and his Croat mother were part of a convoy fleeing besieged Sarajevo, identifies with his father as a Bosniac. Azra, however, wears a medallion of the Virgin Mary and calls herself a Croat although her deceased father was a Muslim and her surname, like those of Damir and Mak, indexes her as Bosniac. But Azra, who under the pretext of an employment opportunity in Italy was sold into prostitution by a Bosniac family friend, now disavows that identity.

Dubravko Horvat, president of the Sarajevo branch of the nationalist Croatian Democratic Union (HDZ), generously spent several hours with me one fine summer morning in 2004. After informing me how his views differ from those of fellow party members in Herzegovina—they want to secede from BiH and join the Republic of Croatia, whereas Horvat advocates "100 percent rights for [the Croat] 10 percent of the BiH population"—he told me that, unlike most Bosnian Croats, he remained throughout the war in Sarajevo, where he continued to work as head of a clinic in which just about all his colleagues were, and remain, Bosniacs. In fact, as he told me with a smile, he was then married to a Muslim woman. That marriage ended, and he married again; this time his wife is a Serb: "Tako je kod nas" (That's how it is with us). I asked about his children. He told me that he is raising his sister's daughter: "My sister was married to a Muslim man. At age five or so, their daughter came to me and asked, 'What am I?' I asked her what she wants to be. She said, 'I want to be like Grandma,' that is, like my mother, a Croat. And that's just fine. According to our constitution, she can be like her mother, or like her father, but she cannot be both. Funny, isn't it? We are allowed two passports [i.e., dual citizenship] but not dual nationality. That's not possible. Tako je kod nas."

Despite long-established social practices of intermarriage and cultural hybridity, the 2002 FBiH census has confirmed what many have been groping to say: To count and be counted in contemporary Bosnia-Herzegovina means being either a Bosniac, a Croat, or a Serb. Declaring a minority identity or refusing to conform to pressures for exclusive B-C-S affiliations invites assignment to a tiny residual category of Others, who, although BiH citizens, lack membership in the constituent nations of the Bosno-Herzegovinian tri-nation-state. The fact that almost 100 percent of FBiH's population was counted as Bosniac, Croat, or Serb suggests that citizens—and census takers in particular—have accepted the state's affiliative demands and avoid the Ostali label whenever possible.

I have argued here that the dramatic population shifts that changed Sarajevo from a city of multiplicity and blendings to one with a majority Bosniac population with clear Croat and Serb minorities, but hardly any others, may be as much a response to the tripartite structure of the new BiH state as an actual change in the ethnic composition of the city's inhabitants. In Sarajevo familiar but loose national categories have been congealing along hard and fast lines. Census and sensibilities are converging to affirm the desires of Bosnia's ruling nationalist parties and an increasingly impatient European Union that urges clarification and pacification of a troublesome intermixed population.

It is impossible to know the future ramifications of current demands for B-C-S legibility. Toward the end of the eighteenth century as the concept of nation was beginning to take shape, Johann Herder advised that "[t]he most natural state . . . is *one* nation with one national character. . . . Nothing therefore appears so directly opposite to the end of government as the unnatural enlargement of states, the wild mixture of various races and nations under one scepter" (from Herder's *Outline of a Philosophy of the History of Man,* quoted in R. J. C. Young 1995, 39). Nations, by definition, are bounded, pure, and unitary. Categorical imperatives that today push Bosnia's Czechs to become Croats, Macedonians to count as Serbs, and Albanians to merge with Bosniacs may result in the discovery that BiH's constituent nations have become diluted, if not polluted, and the 1990s projects of ethnic cleansing and national legibility will have failed after all.

Even centuries after the assimilation of Vlachs into the Serb nation, upon the publication of *Bosnia: A Short History* (1996), in which British historian

Noel Malcolm presents evidence to show that the ancestors of most of today's Bosnian Serbs were Romanized descendants of southeastern Europe's pre-Slav indigenous peoples, an outcry was raised by Serbs in Bosnia and in Belgrade. It was important, indeed mandatory, for contemporary Serbs to know that they and their nation were the direct descendants of those Orthodox Christian followers of Serbian King Lazar, who suffered a treacherous defeat in 1389 at Kosovo Field (Anzulic 1999). Although Malcolm concluded his chapter titled "Serbs and Vlachs" by emphasizing that "it is necessary to point out that there is little sense today in saying that the Bosnian Serbs are 'really' Vlachs [because] to call someone a Serb today is to use a concept constructed . . . of a combination of religion, language and the person's own sense of identification" (1996, 80–81), nationally sensitive Serbs vehemently reject this assertion about their ancestry by calling his work "classic war propaganda literature" (Ekmecic 2000)

Another possible future deriving from present demands for B-C-S identification could follow the lines of what first Ruby Jo Reeves Kennedy (1944) and then Will Herberg (1955) identified as the triple melting pot of the United States. Their still-cited and controversial work claims that national origins have receded in importance as compared to religion. Lines of unity and divide in U.S. society, they argue, are best understood as the coming together of people from varied ethnic backgrounds into the still-divided religious communities of Protestants, Catholics, and Jews. Perhaps in the years ahead, the people of Bosnia-Herzegovina might likewise redefine themselves in terms of the same categories in which they were counted and classified centuries ago under Ottoman rule. This time, however, no special privileges would be meted out to adherents of one religion over another.

To return to the present, although I have presented strong evidence to show the increasing exclusivity of the B-C-S triad, national lines that reject and divide are still not absolute. Even though they have been removed as named nationalities from the constitution and from the census, in contemporary Sarajevo Jews, Gypsies, Hungarians, Albanians, Slovenians, and Macedonians live on, sometimes as Ostali, and sometimes in their own right.

Ostali

The Other People(s)
of Bosnia-Herzegovina

5

Where Have All the Yugoslavs, Slovenes, and Gypsies Gone?

As we have already seen, the last Yugoslav census, which remains the only official census for the entire Republic of Bosnia-Herzegovina, listed twenty-five categories in its enumeration of national belongings and thereby conferred official state recognition on groups whose numbers are tiny as well as to the majority peoples of Yugoslavia (see table 1). Yet even in the heyday of brotherhood and unity, accompanying their seemingly egalitarian inclusiveness was a clustering among the categories that revealed an implicit hierarchy. In 1991, indexing their prime status as the indigenous nations of Yugoslavia, the list began with Montenegrins, Croats, Macedonians, (Bosnian) Muslims, Slovenes, and Serbs.[1] Following that list were fourteen additional eponyms: Albanians, Czechs, Italians, Jews, Hungarians, Germans, Poles, Roma (Gypsies), Romanians, Russians, Ruthenians, Slovaks, Turks, and Ukrainians, which formed among them a group of peoples whose ancestral homelands lie beyond the borders of Yugoslavia.[2] Mediating between the two clusters were the Jugoslaveni, a flexible hybrid identity that represented neither an autochthonous category of belonging nor an ethnic group but a citizenship-based alternative to forcing a single choice among the nationalities (Woodward 1995, 36; cf. Sekulic, Massey, and Hodson 1994; Wachtel 1998). The final four slots on the census accounted for persons declaring an affiliation beyond those listed ("Others" and "Regional affiliation"); those who did not declare an ethnicity; and those whom the census takers did not know how to categorize ("Undeclared" and "Unknown"). These slots provided the state with ways to document those persons who chose not to fit with its representation of collective identities while also giving citizens legitimate options for rejecting the state's categorical grid. In the 1991 census, 92.1 percent of Bosnia's population was counted as Muslims, Croats, and Serbs; Yugoslavs accounted for 5.6 percent; and the remaining 2.3 percent represented the smaller nationality groups and other or undeclared designations.

We then saw that what the state gives, the state can take away. With the FBiH 2002 population count came a drastic reduction in the number of national categories, from twenty-five to four. The three constituent nations—Bosniacs (73%), Croats (22%), and Serbs (4%)—combined to account for an astounding 99 percent of FBiH's inhabitants. In Sarajevo, always the most diverse place in multiethnic Bosnia, almost 15 percent were counted in 1991 as Yugoslavs, members of minority nationalities, and other designations. But in the 2002 postwar city, a mere 2.5 percent emerged as Ostali.

Where have all of Bosnia's Yugoslavs, Gypsies, and Slovenes gone? What happened to the 10,071 Montenegrins, the 4,925 Albanians, the 3,929 Ukrainians, the 893 Italians, and the 590 Czechs? Certainly some have emigrated, but so too have thousands of Bosniacs, Croats, and Serbs. Just as certainly, diligent field interviewers conformed to state demands for unnaming non–B-C-S groups and counted many of them among the three constituent nations. Yet even if the numbers tell a convincing story of state-driven ethnic consolidation, the actions and pronouncements of real people are not so simple or unequivocal. Although the B-C-S scheme often emerges in Sarajevans' narratives of belonging, alongside and sometimes replacing that scheme they also express an *off-census* sensibility as Albanians, Hungarians, Macedonians, Jews, Roma, Slovenes, and Bosnians.

Informed by Aihwa Ong's designation of cultural citizenship as "a dual process of self-making and being made by the state" (1996, 738), I explore in the next three chapters how the simplified population category of Ostali and the experientially based views of real people are dialectically locked together, sometimes hiding the existence of the groups that comprise BiH's others, and sometimes revealing it. Toward those ends, I begin chapter 5 by pondering the meanings and manifestations of the Ostali category. Next, the focus moves to those people who resist classification in the Other category, paying particular attention to Sarajevo's Slovenes and to the Roma.

Building on the argument made in chapter 4 that the FBiH census responds to state demands for consolidating and making legible a chaotic population by reifying its three major groups, throughout chapter 5 I consider the new entanglements that derive from the Ostali category. That discussion continues in chapter 6 as we take an intimate look at one community of Others, Sarajevo's Jews. I place Bosnian hybridity and an inclusive Bosnian identity on center stage in chapter 7 to demonstrate that although officially overlooked and unrecognized, these cultural legacies provide potential solutions to BiH's divisiveness, even as they pique lingering insecurities about B-C-S collective rights and national purity.

The Logic of Ostali

Breaking with Yugoslav precedents and confirming BiH's constitution, in 2002 the FBiH counted its citizens according to three named categories only, the constituent nations of the state. People who declared to the census takers that they were Yugoslavs, Albanians, Ruthenians, or Slovenes may well have been placed into one of the B-C-S categories anyway. Or if they insisted they that they were *really* neither Bosniac nor Croat nor Serb, they ended up within the tiny group of Ostali.

Who are the Ostali, and what is the logic behind the composition of that category? As absurdly confounding as the Chinese encyclopedia entry for animals made famous by Foucault (1973, xv) that combines "embalmed" with "tame" and "frenzied"; "sucking pigs" and "stray dogs" with "sirens," and all of these with "that from a long way off look like flies," the merging of long-standing minorities into parenthetically rights-vested Others imposes a new legibility on Bosnia's population. By ignoring specific ethnic, regional, and religious identities and placing individuals who claim membership in a wide range of cultural groups into one residual category, the state apparatus is erasing what had been seen and enacted in Yugoslavia as significant differences. At the same time, in a manner akin to that used by the Chinese encyclopedists to strengthen the boundary delineating humans from all other creatures, the marginal Ostali category reinforces the centrality of the B-C-S triad and marks only its internal divisions as significant.

The designation of Ostali, which amalgamates any and all ethnic minorities into one indistinguishable category of leftovers, has nothing to do with shared culture, language, or history. It has everything to do with the politics of Bosnia-Herzegovina. "Establishing discontinuities is not an easy task for history," Foucault has warned (1973, 50). But in less than a decade, independent Bosnia-Herzegovina, under the strong arm of the OHR, has established an order that separates all other peoples from the B-C-S constituent nations. The FBiH census thereby overrides the commonsense developed over decades in Yugoslavia while conforming to and objectifying the Dayton-born scheme.

The sociopolitical position of Others is as clear on the census as it is in the constitution. Rather than adhering to the alphabetical order of B-C-O-S, the

Ostali are listed last. They appear as an afterthought, a bothersome bunch of people who are necessarily citizens even as they fall outside the neatly ordered nations that constitute the tri-nation-state. Because they hold the potential to disturb the new, triangularly balanced scheme, it is in the interest of the state to keep their numbers small and their political impact weak.

We have already seen this process at work in census interviews. But even after Damir and Nebojša told me several times that ordinary people and not just state bureaucrats constantly push them to state who they "really" are, I was unconvinced that this was a commonplace practice, until it happened to me.

One cloudy day in March 2004, I bought a newspaper and a cheese *burek* (filo dough pastry) and settled down on a bench outside the Filozofski Fakultet of Sarajevo University to watch the students come and go. A young woman took a seat near me, opened her backpack, and rummaged around before fishing out her lunch of a chocolate bar and a bag of chips. She turned to me and asked the time. I hesitantly responded. "Thank you," she replied switching to English. Then she offered me some of her fare, explaining, "Americans like these foods." I smiled and showed her my burek, and we started talking.

She introduced herself as Samara, a name "from Arabic that means a girl with black hair and tanned skin. Centuries ago there was one group of Balkan Slavs; their tribes entered this region. Some of them took on the foreign religion of the Turks. Some of them took on the foreign religion of Orthodox Christianity." Then she declared that Tito is her hero. I asked if she considers herself a Bosniac. She replied, with a sigh, "Yes, I'm a Bosniac because I live now in Bosnia, but I prefer Yugoslavia." Then she asked about my background. I told her my first and last names. She told me that if I am Marković, I must be Catholic. No, I told her, I am Jewish. "Are you sure? You should check with your father about his family. They must be Croats and Catholics." No, I told her, they were from Hungary or Poland and Jewish. She continued to insist that I must "really" be a Croat, and I let her.

As a visitor to Bosnia, I found that incident amusing and insightful. Where else in Europe would anyone even imagine the possibility that a family would have converted from Christianity to Judaism? But for those natives who are daily reminded that it is far better to be a Bosniac, a Croat, or a Serb in their native country than a parenthetical Other, such encounters can be offensive and oppressive. Psychologist Nada Ler-Sofronić, who is an Ashkenazi Jew married to a Bosnian Serb, said that although they could have returned after the war to study at Sarajevo University, her two sons have opted to remain in Italy. "Here as children of a mixed marriage, they are Ostali. And they feel it. My sons say, 'Better to be a foreigner in a foreign country than an Other in your homeland.'"

It is estimated that during the 1992–95 war, well over a million people fled Bosnia to escape the siege of Sarajevo, bombings, sniper fire, and the threat of what was euphemistically called ethnic cleansing. Others left because they feared an end to the pluralistic Yugoslav society that enabled them to be who they were and where they wanted to be (see Stefansson 2004; Ugrešić 1998). For the most part, theirs was an uneasy, wait-and-see emigration; ordinary civilians became war refugees who arrived abroad not knowing if they were seeking temporary shelter or starting new lives (see Huseby-Darvas 2000; Markowitz 1996). Once the war ceased, some host countries, like Germany, expelled their Bosnian refugees (approximately 340,000), sending them to seek new places of refuge or forcing their return.

The process of homecoming in BiH has been riddled with problems from the start (Stefansson 2003, 2004), especially for those dubbed "minority returnees," that is, members of one B-C-S group seeking repatriation in an entity or canton dominated by another (Dahlman and Ó Tuathail 2005). According to the September 2001 position paper on Bosnia and Herzegovina by the United Nations High Commissioner for Refugees (UNHCR), along with minority returns, the Ostali, and in particular members of Roma communities and persons of mixed ethnicity, face severe discrimination and even bodily harm. Many are ambivalent about their return; some have officially repatriated; others return each year for a few weeks during the summer to test the waters, privatize their apartments, and visit relatives. Some who have received citizenship in other countries, after one return visit vow never again to set foot in Bosnia.

One day in May 2004, I met with Vesna and her daughter, Jasna, in the Marjindvor apartment of Vesna's recently deceased mother. Twenty-nine-year-old Jasna, her mother and father, and her two younger brothers have been living in Australia since 1996. Unlike Vesna, who had visited her elderly mother in Sarajevo on a yearly basis, this was Jasna's first return visit. Almost as soon as I entered their apartment, Jasna took the opportunity of my questions to declare how much she hates Sarajevo, Bosnia, and all of the former Yugoslavia. Vesna shifted uncomfortably in her chair as she heard her daughter's words and shook her head in disagreement. Surrounded by the furnishings of her childhood home, Vesna grew nostalgic about her youth: "My mother was Catholic. So too was my father. For me, for those of us who were raised in Yugoslavia, this didn't mean anything. For me there was only one line of difference: who were good people, who were bad people. We were all Yugoslavs. My husband is from a Muslim family. And we, we were Yugoslavs. That's how it was in Sarajevo. Until the war." Then they told me about their wartime experience.

Shortly after the war began, Vesna signed up for a convoy arranged by the Children's Embassy to bring mothers with small children to Croatia. Men were categorically excluded, so the family was forced to split.[3] Teenagers and young adults were not welcomed either, but Vesna would not leave without Jasna, who was then seventeen: "I couldn't leave her behind. The Četniks had already begun arrests and rapes of young women."

After they arrived and resettled in Zagreb, which was no easy task, Vesna found a job, and Jasna went to enroll in school. But she was turned away because she was not a Croat; "And I missed my last year of high school." Vesna jumped in to explain, "If you weren't born in Croatia, you had to prove that you were Catholic. And even if you were born in Croatia; I knew a family that couldn't get Croatian citizenship because they were Orthodox, and they had lived in Croatia all their lives. That's what things were like."

To change her children's status from Bosnian war refugees to Croats, Vesna appealed to the Catholic bishop of Zagreb, who contacted the Sarajevo bishopric, where her baptismal certificate was located. With that document, Vesna proved that although her nationality was recorded as Yugoslav, she was a Catholic Croat, and so too were her children. In a matter of weeks, they were all granted citizenship in the Republic of Croatia, and when the new school year began, Jasna returned to complete high school.

But all was not well, for as Jasna explained, when she and her brothers became Croats their Bosnian Muslim father, who was barely getting by in war-torn Sarajevo, was effectively erased from their lives: "In 1995 there was a ceasefire, and my father got out and came to Zagreb. And it was hard. We hadn't seen each other in almost four years. And he had lost some twenty kilos. He had been through hell, and it was hard for each of us to understand what had happened to the other. We entered into long discussions. I was sure that starting over, making a new beginning for the whole family was the only decision. My father wanted to leave, and I wanted to leave, but my mother wasn't sure." I asked about the possibility of remaining in Zagreb. Vesna jumped back in: "It would have been impossible. My husband is a Muslim, and he would not have gotten citizenship. No, starting over as a family in Australia was the only decision to make."

Throughout our conversation, Vesna moved back and forth between agreeing with her daughter that since Yugoslavia no longer exists there was no place for her ethnically mixed family in Sarajevo and thinking back wistfully to the wonderful prewar years. Jasna exploded in exasperation as her mother once more expressed longings for Yugoslav Sarajevo, a social space, she reminded her, that does not exist:

> We live in Melbourne, Australia, where people have respect for one another and themselves. You are always talking about "before the war." What I like about Australia is that people are looking forward, not backward. Here they talk about "before the war" and how the war destroyed them. The war, the war. Sometimes I think that is just an excuse to do nothing. Yes, there was a war and it was terrible. But get over it. I can't stand this place. . . . My home is there in Australia, 100 percent. I have no use for this place where all people do is sit around, drink coffee, smoke cigarettes, blame the war for all of their troubles, and look for someone else to save them.

Jasna, who would be Other in the city of her birth, emphasizes her attachments to Australia, where, as a self-motivated *person,* rather than an involuntary part of the B-C-S-(O) scheme, she is pursuing a degree in art and planning for the future. She tells her mother to stop complaining that she has one foot in two far-apart countries, to quit thinking of herself as a Bosnian refugee, and to embrace what Australia has to offer.

Vesna the mother and Jasna the daughter have lived different lives in Sarajevo. Standing in her childhood home decorated with lead-crystal chandeliers, dark wood armoires, and overstuffed armchairs, Vesna longs for the familiar comforts of Yugoslavia's Central European past. Jasna, who arrived in Australia as a young adult after having fled war-torn Sarajevo as a teenager to face ethnic discrimination in Zagreb, experiences everything in her former homeland with distaste. Although she could conform to the demands of state and claim belonging as a Bosniac or as a Croat, she rejects these forced choices and accepts the Otherness that goes with her mixed ethnic background. Similar sentiments by Others like Jasna may help to keep their numbers low in Bosnia.

A few weeks after meeting with Vesna and Jasna, my friend Klara, the daughter of a Sephardic Jewish father and a Croat mother, whose husband is a Bosniac, brought me to meet another mixed-ethnic family. In that household, the wife, a nurse who worked untiringly at Koševo hospital during the war, is a Bosniac, and the husband, a retired engineer, is a Serb. They have two sons. The younger son, Vedran, was injured by shrapnel during the last year of the war. Scared for his life, he sought a safe place outside Bosnia. He found a small college in the United States that offered him a basketball scholarship while he studied business administration. A few years later, his brother, Damir, did the same. Both young men earned their degrees and then returned to Sarajevo. Vedran now works for an international accounting firm, while Damir plays professional basketball for one of Bosnia's teams.

After hearing their parents identify as Muslim and Serb, I asked the twenty-five- and twenty-seven-year-old brothers how they define themselves. They looked at me as if I had asked a totally idiotic question and did not answer. I followed up: "Don't you have to choose a category like Serb, Croat, or Bosniac?" "White," answered the younger one, flashing a grin. "I just tell them I'm white." Klara and the boys' parents laughed uproariously at this answer. "And they accept it?" I asked, somewhat stunned. Everyone was laughing and ignoring my query, but I wanted to know: What about all the pressure to identify as Bosniac, Croat, or Serb? Were they treating me the same way that they deal with all those who ask, "But what are you really?"

Unlike Jasna, who found in Australia a homeland receptive to her mixed-ethnic family and a lifestyle that resonates with her notion of self, after several years in the United States, Damir and Vedran knew more than ever that Sarajevo is home. They were not about to let the Ostali category and intrusive people with impolite questions upset their sense of belonging to the place where they were born and raised. Their experiences in the United States gave them an alternate understanding of otherness as a racial category that they know has no relevance in Bosnia. By invoking their whiteness, they were telling everyone who wishes to know that the categories of state, particularly Ostali, hold no relevance for them. Damir and Vedran talked about the good times they had in college and their travels to several Midwestern cities; yet they both declared that they had never thought of staying in America. Never? No, they told me as they contrasted their daily routine in Sarajevo to the "terrible way of life in the States. Our people work all day every day just dreaming of their two-week summer vacation when they can come back to Bosnia." The brothers are hopeful, actually certain, that in time BiH will "truly become part of Europe," that is, the European Union, which will allow them to travel and work anywhere on the continent. Very optimistic and self-confident, Damir and Vedran defy otherness by making it irrelevant to their goals and to their lives.

Most Other people lack the skills, cultural capital, and self-confidence that these brothers possess. Parenthetical placement after B-C-S makes them an afterthought when it comes to jobs, mortgages, and university admissions. The UNHCR report of September 2001 chillingly notes that "the children of mixed marriages can encounter particular problems of re-integration, including the difficulty of being forced to choose their own [singular] 'ethnic' identity" (27). Damir and Vedran are exceptional.

But I cannot conclude the discussion on Ostali quite yet, for data from Centar Općina's marriage registration bureau tell a more nuanced story. Whereas in chapter 4 we saw quite a dramatic shift from Muslim to Bosniac in people's self-declared identities, the citizenry has not altogether acquiesced to state pressure to abandon now unnamed ethnicities. As table 4 indicates, while certainly most of those who married during the eight years following the signing of the DPA identified as Bosniacs, followed by Croats and Serbs, far more ethnonational categories were declared at the registry than the B-C-S triad. In 2002

Table 4. National Belonging in Centar Općina Marriage Registration Data by Percentages

Category	1996	1998	2000	2002	2003
Bosniacs[a]	73.9	67.0	66.0	62.0	67.0
Croats	5.2	3.6	4.6	5.6	6.0
Serbs	3.1	2.5	2.8	3.3	2.5
B-C-S subtotal[b]	82.2	73.1	73.4	70.9	75.5
Albanians	—	0.2	0.1	0.4	0.7
Czechs	—	—	—	0.1	0.1
Germans[c]*	0.6	0.5	1.6	2.5	2.1
Hungarians	0.1	—	—	0.2	—
Jews	0.1	0.1	—	0.1	—
Macedonians	0.1	—	0.2	0.1	0.1
Montenegrins	0.2	0.2	0.2	0.1	0.1
Roma	—	0.5	0.2	0.3	0.7
Slovenians	0.2	—	—	0.2	0.1
Turks	0.2	0.2	—	0.3	0.3
Yugoslavs	0.1	0.6	0.2	0.4	0.3
Other FN[d]*	1.3	1.8	2.0	2.4	1.8
Ostali	—	—	0.2	0.1	—
Ostali subtotal	2.9	4.1	4.7	7.2	6.3
Total	85.1	77.2	77.9	78.0	81.8

* It is impossible to tell from these data how many are members of the "international community" temporarily employed in Sarajevo, how many are BiH nationals, and how many are returnees to Sarajevo who are claiming the nationality of the country where they resided during the war and may have gained citizenship.

[a] "Bosniacs" here represents the sum total of Bosniacs + Bosniac-Muslims + Muslim-Bosniacs + Muslims (see table 3).

[b] Compare with the B+C+S total for the Centar Municipality in the FBiH 2002 census of 96.6%.

[c] Includes Austrians and Germans.

[d] Other foreign nationals, includes citizens of Anglo-American countries (United States, UK, Canada, Australia), Western Europe (EU plus Norway and Switzerland), Eastern Europe (including the states of the former Soviet Union), the Middle East (e.g., Egypt, Iran, Lebanon), and the Far East (e.g., Indonesia and the Philippines).

more than twice as many people in Centar registered as ethnic minorities (7.2 percent) than those counted in the census as Ostali (3.4 percent).

Although the proportions are small, the marriage registration data show that several hundreds of Sarajevans actively choose to declare their national affiliation with specifically named ethnic groups that the state, via the FBiH census, has unnamed. But as we saw in the previous chapter, those who act off-census at the county registry or in everyday life do not necessarily refuse to comply with census takers' demands to categorize them according to the B-C-S scheme. When they fill out their forms in the općina, no one asks them, "But what are you really?"

When census takers, university registrars, court clerks, and people on the street do ask, "But what are you really?" they are not probing for authenticity. Instead, they are demanding that those who call themselves Albanians, Bosnians, Macedonians, or some ethnic mix drop what the powers of state have determined to be insignificant and bothersome affiliations. Think again, they are told. Do you really want to be de jure citizens of the state, but without the national belonging that carries privileges reserved for the constituent peoples? As we have seen, some Ostali decide against living their lives in BiH precisely because of that ambivalent status. Like Jasna, they opt for citizenship in Australia or Canada, or, like the Sofronić brothers, prefer the position of a foreigner in a foreign land to being Other in the homeland. Other Others, like Damir and Vedran, who possess the resources to sustain such a stance, mock the B-C-S-(O) order of things and thereby render the state's categories irrelevant to their lives, while others shift back and forth in their feelings and stated affiliations. Still others insist on a place in the public domain, where they refuse to be ignored.

Constitutionally Unnamed, Noticed and Narrated Nonetheless

In her meticulously researched *Empire of Nations,* Francine Hirsch (2005) presents the Soviet Union as a work in progress where, toward the goal of modernizing "backward" peoples and accelerating their move forward toward socialism, ethnographers and state bureaucrats collaborated to forge nationalities from clans, tribes, villages, and culturally related small groups. Hirsch claims that after the census of 1926 and in preparation for the counts of 1937 and 1939, "Even rural and nomadic populations that previously had not exhibited 'national consciousness' were describing themselves as members of nationalities to argue for economic, administrative, and political rights.

Nationality had become a fundamental marker of identity, embedded not just in the administrative structure of the Soviet Union, but also in people's mentalities" (45).

The same claim can be made for Bosnia-Herzegovina. A shift away from the religious identities that characterized both the bureaucratic structure and the "mentalities" of Ottoman-era Bosnia began in the nineteenth century when Catholic and Orthodox Christians adopted the national labels of Croat and Serb. That switch reached its apex by the end of the twentieth century, when Muslims regularly began referring to themselves as members of the Bosniac nation. Subjectivities and administrative imperatives conjoined in the Dayton Peace Accords, in which the Bosniacs, the Croats, and the Serbs (along with others) were inscribed as BiH's constituent peoples.

Bosnia has always housed a wide ethnic variety of persons along with its Serbs, Croats, and Bosniacs. Turks, Jews, Gypsies, Albanians, and Vlachs are documented in Ottoman-era decrees, diaries, tax and court records, and in prose and song. During the nineteenth century, they were joined by German and Hungarian speakers, Czechs, Slovaks, and Slovenes from throughout the Habsburg Empire. And although twenty-first-century BiH may be succeeding in giving the B-C-S triad a monopoly over national affiliation, it has not (as yet) disciplined the population to dissolve the names of long-standing minorities into the Ostali category. Instead, Sarajevans continue to talk about these groups, and with that talk they maintain a public presence.

Some groups, such as the Jews, who will be discussed in the next chapter, retain visibility as a long-standing institutionally complete ethno-religious community; others do so through their ethnic niche in the economy. Albanians, for example, are known in Bosnia and throughout former Yugoslavia as owners of *slastičarnice,* or pastry shops. Bosnia's Albanians work in a variety of occupations, but they have not given up that niche. And although they were counted in the FBiH census as Bosniacs or Ostali, they have not disappeared into an undistinguished and indistinguishable bunch of others. Nor have the Gypsies.

THE ROMA

The Roma, as the Gypsies of Bosnia prefer to be called, have also carved out a niche in the urban economy. Within seconds of the first raindrops in Sarajevo, dark-haired, T-shirted young men and long-skirted women appear on major pedestrian thoroughfares crying: "*Kišobrani!*" (Umbrellas!). On bright summer days, they offer an array of sunglasses. Some stroll up and down the sidewalks of the city center hawking their wares; others set up stands near the bridges, where they also sell beach towels, cotton drawstring pants and T-shirts, pajamas and handbags. Still others hold a permanent place in local outdoor markets; I bought several cotton dresses from one woman and her family in a market near the Baščaršija and bed and bath linens from another woman who sits right outside the entrance to the market in the north of the Centar district.

Another way that some Gypsies eke out a living is through begging. Almost every summer evening in 2004 when I stopped into the convenience store on my corner, a young guy, really a boy, was hanging around asking passersby for spare change. Several times I saw him come into the store, where he asked the female cashier to change his coins into bills. Although he was usually dressed in unkempt clothing and sometimes shirtless, the cashier never chased him away. One night as I witnessed him coming in with his coins and going out with a 20 KM note, I asked the cashier about him, "Oh, he means no harm and doesn't bother anybody. We are used to him; he is ours." According to the Documentation of the Bosnian Section of the Society for Threatened Peoples, the Roma have been present in the Crni Vrh location of the Centar district of Sarajevo for some two hundred years, and "in that context Romani people have the status of legitimate citizens of the city."[4]

14. Gypsy children, a postcard distributed by the Sarajevo Post-Pessimist Club in 2003

15. Gypsy squatters

But most Bosnians are not nearly as generous to the Gypsies as my neighborhood store clerk. Jennifer Erickson (2003), who worked in an NGO in nearby Zenica, notes, "Both educated and uneducated people believe in the stereotype of Roma as dirty, lazy thieves . . . [and] asserted that the Roma deserve to be discriminated against because they choose their own lifestyle; they had only themselves to blame for their problems. Others said that Roma use their culture or music to gain sympathy. Some Bosnian teachers told me . . . that one solution to the 'Gypsy problem' would be to buy them soap."

A few days after I arrived in Sarajevo in March 2004, a young researcher very graciously showed me around. Almost as soon as we set foot on Tito Street, we passed some women clustered together in a small group. With their thick dark hair, brightly patterned shawls, the huge-eyed children tugging at their long skirts, and the swaddled babies they cradled, there was no doubt that they were Gypsies.[5] My companion took a look at them and then offered me advice: "Be very careful with them, especially on Ferhadija. One woman will come up to you and ask you to hold her baby. As you back away, it will seem to you that she is dropping the baby, and you will instinctively reach out to catch it. At the very moment that you take your hands off your purse, another woman will come up from behind and snatch your wallet."

Gypsies are known throughout Europe as thieves, fortune-tellers, con men, musicians, dancers, beggars, illiterates, and unfortunates. They are the freedom-loving vagabonds described by Lev Tolstoy and D. H. Lawrence, and the wretched of the earth (Trumpener 1995). Michael Stewart's *Time of the Gypsies* (1997) shows less variation among the Roma of Hungary, where they are unequivocally a despised group, and although by the 1980s the socialist regime had succeeded in making them part of the working proletariat, it did not provide the Gypsies with health care, social services, or education. Stewart's book ends ominously, hinting that prejudice and discrimination against the Roma in postsocialist Eastern Europe are not on the wane.

The 2001 UNHCR report "Categories of Persons from Bosnia and Herzegovina in Continued Need of International Protection" specifically mentions the Gypsies: "Roma constitute a large minority group in BiH and yet are often overlooked in all spheres of public life. The absence of 'national minority status' for Roma and a general lack of awareness that the Roma constitute a minority group add to the difficulties and prejudices encountered by Roma returnees" (26).

In the Federation, those Roma who want to assimilate, who strive to advance professionally and wish to educate their children, call themselves Bosniacs, and since they speak the Bosnian language in the local accent, they can often pass. Those who do not pass do what they have always done: work in the trades or as petty entrepreneurs, or as street musicians or beggars. Constitutionally unrepresented and overlooked as Ostali, Gypsies resist amalgamation by asserting their presence in Sarajevo's public spaces. On many a chilly evening, I have seen small groups of Romani men huddled around the centrally located eternal flame below the stone archway upon which is inscribed the names of all the peoples of Bosnia-Herzegovina who fought with the Partisans and gave their lives for a future of brotherhood and unity (see chapter 2).

In contrast to the "Golden Age for Roma," when they held constitutionally guaranteed minority rights in Tito's Yugoslavia, Gypsies throughout Bosnia face discrimination in the housing and labor markets and, like all Ostali, are prohibited from holding the country's highest political offices (European Roma Rights Center 2004). Refusing invisibility, they exert and perhaps exaggerate their presence through public performances of male sociability, female and child poverty, vending, begging, petty theft, and music. Although the fate of the Gypsies is difficult and uncertain, the Roma resist relegation to the Ostali by continuing to act according to stereotypes that defy the norms and boundaries demanded by nation-states. They thereby remain a salient cultural category and a tangible social and economic group. The Roma have been and continue to be Other in Bosnia-Herzegovina, but they are a specific type of other. By peddling umbrellas, pleading for spare change, singing bittersweet songs, and gathering alongside Sarajevo's eternal flame, they refuse to be dismissed or dissolved into a leftover category that ignores them for who they are.

SARAJEVO'S SLOVENES

I met a remarkable woman named Ljiljana in early April 2004 at the Jewish community's mini-seder for representatives of multiethnic, multiconfessional, and international Sarajevo (see chapter 6). When she introduced herself, Ljiljana was not yet forty years old and the president of Cankar, the Slovenian Cultural Association of Sarajevo, which was about to mark its seventieth anniversary. I was unable to attend the anniversary event, but three weeks later I met with Ljiljana to talk about Bosnian multiculturalism and the Ostali category and how she and Cankar fit into those schemes.

Cankar, the Slovenian Cultural Society, is located in a ground-floor apartment in a building across the way from the Viječnica, which is where we met. As we began our walk uphill, Ljiljana pointed to a small eighteenth- or nineteenth-century Bosnian-style house and asked me if I knew the story of that house. Its sign announces it as a restaurant called Inat Kuća. Ljiljana reminded me that *inat* means "spite," and then she told me its story.

I had read about Inat Kuća in my guidebooks, and just about everyone I met in Sarajevo had something to say about it. Sitting incongruously at the crossroads of the developed downtown, this little house was considered a physical reminder of a "typical Balkan character trait." As Ljiljana told me about the spite that accounts for the placement of that house, I thought to myself, "Too bad for me that cultural anthropology has moved beyond the culture and personality school" because I recalled another story of spite that I had heard over a decade ago, a popular *zlatna riba,* or golden fish folk tale, about two Bosnian peasants:

> Once there were two friends, and they went out fishing. One of them pulled up a golden fish. "Put me back, put me back, and I will grant you any wish!" exclaimed the fish. The man who caught the golden fish hesitated, but his friend urged him to throw the fish back into the river. He relented, and then the *zlatna riba* said, "Because you have been so kind I will grant you three wishes. And because your friend urged you to throw me back, everything I grant you I will give him twice."

> "All right," said the first man. "See that hill: Let there be the most magnificent house up there on my hill!"
>
> And poof! The most magnificent house ever built appeared on his hill. Just seconds later, poof! Two of those magnificent houses appeared on the hill of his friend.
>
> "What is your second wish?" asked the golden fish. The man thought a moment and said, "I want the most beautiful, wonderful wife to be waiting for me in front of my magnificent house." Poof! The most beautiful woman ever seen appeared in the doorway of his home. And just seconds later, poof! Two most beautiful women appeared on the next hill, one in front of each of the friend's homes.
>
> "And what is your third and final wish?" asked the golden fish. The man stroked his chin as he thought and thought. Then, suddenly, he blurted out: "Cut off one of my balls."

The drama of Inat Kuća is of another, milder sort, and unlike the friends of the golden fish tale, this one involves men of unequal power. The story goes that the Austro-Hungarian governor made plans to build Sarajevo's Town Hall at the foot of the Baščaršija. One house was in the way, and officials came to purchase the land from its owner. The owner replied that this was his home and he wanted no other. They offered him a good sum, more than the house and the property were worth. He insisted that he wanted no other house but his own. After a long series of negotiations, he agreed to allow government engineers to move his house across the river, wall by wall and stone by stone. And that is where it remains today as the Inat Kuća restaurant.

Ljiljana stopped the swirl of our Bosnian kaleidoscope as she ended the Spite House tale in front of a nondescript concrete-block apartment building. "And here is where we rent our space, in the same building as a dentist." The kaleidoscopic panorama of Sarajevo resumed as she pointed: "Up the hill is the Franciscan church, and yes"—she answered my question if this used to be the Latin Quarter, or Frenkluk mahala, which (as my *2003 Sarajevo Guide*, p. 19, states), "was in the Ottoman age, inhabited mostly by Dubrovnik people and other Catholics." From where we were standing, we could also see the white grave markers of the Alifakovac Muslim cemetery.

We entered the socialist-modern building and walked into the apartment that houses the Slovenian Cultural Center. It is divided into a main reception room, a library—Ljiljana was Cankar's librarian before becoming the organization's president—a classroom, and a kitchen with attached bathroom. I visited a Slovenian language class with some twenty students; half teenagers and young people in their twenties, and the rest women in their forties on up. I wondered aloud if the young people were preparing themselves for the possibility of studying in Slovenia. In response Ljiljana told me that during the 1990s, and especially during the war, there were two full beginners' classes and an advanced Slovenian class. Now the class I was viewing was the only one, except for the Saturday children's class. "Most of those students have left."

We moved into a corner of the reception area, where we settled down for a long conversation. I began by telling Ljiljana that the last time we spoke, she had told me that Slovenes had been in Sarajevo for centuries and had stated, "We never felt that we were anywhere but in our own country." She picked up that narrative thread:

> We came with the Austrian mandate, and we were all part of one country. In Slovenia those who went to school and worked in urban areas learned and communicated in German, but they retained their native Slavic language. So many people were recruited to come to Bosnia. My great-great-grandfather came as an engineer, and he stayed. . . . My other great-grandfather, my father's mother's father, came during the first Yugoslavia. Again, this was just moving across the country, not changing countries. In the 1930s, there were some three thousand Slovenians in Sarajevo, out of a city of fifty thousand. Cankar was not the first Slovenian cultural organization in Sarajevo. At the end of the nineteenth century, a group of intellectuals, say doctors, lawyers, professors, formed the Slovensko Omizije, or Slovenian Round Table. In 1934 a group of more-working-class Slovenes formed Cankar, [named] after the writer Ivan Cankar, which operated until 1941, when all these cultural organizations were eliminated. In 1944 [didn't she mean 1945?] in the second Yugoslavia, Cankar re-formed with the same people after the war who founded it before the war. Now that everyone in Yugoslavia was a "worker," there was no reason for any other [Slovenian] cultural organization. In the same year, also Preporod, Napredak, and Prosvjeta re-formed as well, and these all operated until 1951. In 1951 all these were closed, so that everyone should be all together, mixed. So they formed workers' cultural associations in every municipality. This was good, in my opinion, that all the citizens were mixed together, not separated by nationality.
>
> Then came the early nineties and democracy, and with that the nationalist parties. Preporod, Napredak, and Prosvjeta were then revived. Cankar was not renewed just then; we Slovenes [in Bosnia] had no need for nationalist parties. But then came the war, and there was some kind of need for gathering together. It was a very special time. People started to ask themselves, Who am I? I'm not a Serb, not a Croat, not a Muslim. I already knew who I was; that was not my point. In high school, I had always been very active in organizing environmental

> campaigns and conferences. And by the late 1980s—when Milošević came to power in Serbia—I began reading *Mladina*, a magazine out of Ljubljana.

Ljiljana continued to tell me about her interests in ecology and her political leanings that mirrored the Slovenian Republic's position during the last years of Yugoslavia and led to Slovenia's declaration of independence in 1991. Our conversation then returned to the revival of Cankar:

> I was not in the core, in the initial founding group of March 1993. My father was one of those first members who signed the registration application. I came and took Slovenian language lessons and began to attend some of the literary evenings. But mainly I was attracted by that magazine *Mladina* and the interesting things that were coming out of Slovenia. The membership was based on people with long-term relationships, friends, cousins, and then we published notice of our meetings in the newspapers and people came. We were given space by some offices—there were several Slovene companies here in Sarajevo, and they all closed their offices during the war, of course. We met mainly in Ljubljanska Banka when they pulled out during the war.

Although the representatives of Preporod, Napredak, and Prosvjeta stressed to me that their organizations were devoted exclusively to cultural activities (chapter 3), Ljiljana linked them implicitly to the B-C-S nationalist parties. While noting that Sarajevo's Slovenes had no need for such parties, Ljiljana connected her desire to investigate Cankar and her Slovenian heritage with the political changes under way in Ljubljana. As I have argued throughout this book, it is impossible to divorce "culture" from "politics" as people in Bosnia think about who they are, what they are doing, and why.

Warning me that she is "not typical," Ljiljana moved our conversation back to Cankar and away from her personal wartime experiences. She showed me pictures and press releases of the society's activities and the organization's budget. The largest amount of funding comes from the embassy of the Republic of Slovenia, followed by the Canton of Sarajevo. Then she described Cankar's main events: twice-yearly concerts that coincide with the Sarajevo Winter Festival and the Summer Fest, Baščaršija Nights, and a yearly tennis tournament held to honor the memory of Jan Doršner. Ljiljana describes Doršner, a young Sarajevo Slovene, as an excellent student and a versatile athlete whose favorite sport was tennis. He enlisted in the BiH army early in the war, and in December 1992 was killed on the front line of defense.

I asked Ljiljana how many Slovenes there are now in Sarajevo. She replied, "I can't tell because there has been no census, and even if there were, I wouldn't trust the results! From what I can see over the years, I'd say no more than three hundred families. But it is useful sometimes for people to be Slovenes, or anything else for that matter. I know of several politicians who have changed their nationality five times in the last ten years—from Yugoslav to Muslim to Croat to Serb to Bosniac!"

The evening turned to night, and the students had long left their language class before we parted from the premises of Cankar to head back downhill to catch a tram. En route Ljiljana told me that this, her second term as president of the organization, might well be her last. She added that she had heard talk about FBiH establishing an official Council of Minorities. As of the summer of 2009, that plan has not come to pass.

Although administratively dissolved into the Ostali, Sarajevo's Slovenes, through their Slovenian Cultural Organization and several streets named for distinguished Slovene literary figures, remain a distinguishable population in Sarajevo. Most, however, may be like Ljiljana, undeclared and unnoticed, until Cankar's concerts and tennis tournament remind everyone of the Slovenes in their midst, and that Bosnia and Slovenia were once part of a Yugoslav country and heritage that are slowly slipping into a mythical past.

As to the Ostali, some are so frustrated at being "other" in their homeland that they choose to emigrate; others mock that category, distance themselves from it, and use alternate terms to delineate their belongings. As I have shown, despite the B-C-S-(O) categories of the 2002 census, many former Yugoslavs, Albanians, Gypsies, and Slovenes are keeping alive their officially unnamed groups by persisting in specific social practices, through narratives of group identity, and by NGOs to advance their cause. Nonetheless, the gap in numbers between the 1991 census and FBiH's 2002 count forces again the question with which this chapter began: Where have all the Yugoslavs, Slovenes, and Gypsies gone? The ethnography offers a provocative answer: If not to Ostali, then to B-C-S, and reopens the still-unhealed wounds of ethnic cleansing. Only 1 percent of FBiH's population is Ostali because people have aligned with the census takers and decided that it would be best to count as Bosniacs, Croats, and Serbs. That would mean that all kinds of others—hybrids, tricksters, outsiders—have opted to become part of the constituent nations. Will the B-C-S groups simply overlook that inconvenience, or might internal cleansing eventually be demanded with the revelation that Czechs are counted as Croats, Macedonians as Serbs, and Gypsies as Bosniacs? Or might it be that the Serbs, Croats and Bosniacs will come to concede, as Bosnia's Roma, Slovenes, and Jews already know, that their groups are culturally and biologically hybrid, the results of historical circumstances, cultural dynamism, and personal choice?

6

Sarajevo's Jews

One Community among the Others

Most chroniclers of Sarajevo's Jewish community begin at the beginning by noting that Jews expelled from Spain at the end of the fifteenth century were greeted with tolerance and granted refuge when they arrived in Ottoman Bosnia (Levy 1996; Malcolm 1996; Schwartz 2005; Serotta 1994). A Sephardic Jewish community of merchants, artisans and laborers, and rabbis and physicians prospered in Sarajevo for over four hundred years, until their synagogues, businesses, homes, and lives were destroyed during the Nazi occupation of 1941–45.[1] Many of those who survived the camps, or fought as Partisans, or hid in the homes of Muslim and Christian neighbors left for the new Jewish state of Israel in 1948. The thousand or so Jews who resituated themselves in Sarajevo picked up the threads of their lives and wove them back into the multiply textured cultural pattern of Yugoslav Bosnia.

I will begin this chapter quite differently.

"Start with what you know best," said my colleague Olga Supek to me as she headed to the Adriatic coast after a day and a half together in bombed-out Sarajevo during August 1997. Remembering from my first visit in 1983 the bold Hebrew letters on the igloo-shaped tombstones on the hills of the Old Sephardic Cemetery, and the joys of finding a bustling lobby filled with my own folk in the pink brick neo-Moorish Ashkenazi synagogue, I made my way to the Sarajevo Jewish community on the northern bank of the Miljacka River. I hardly knew what to expect: Would there still be men engrossed in chess games surrounded by eager kibitzers? Would any gangly youths or parents with little children be there? Would my ears once again catch the strangely familiar phrases of Judeo-Spanish intermeshed with local Slavic syllables? Mindful of wartime evacuations and other losses from what I had read in the *New York Times* and the *Jerusalem Post*, I wondered, as I approached the building, if there would be anyone at all in the lobby.[2]

I entered the synagogue, and the lobby was quite full. It was early afternoon, and lots of older people were working their way toward the exit. I could smell the lingering odors of cooked meat and vegetables, and I saw some young men hauling out crates of apple peels and discarded cabbage leaves. I did not know what to make of the scene, but it bore no resemblance to those remnant communities of forgotten yet often feisty Jewish elderly documented by ethnographer colleagues (Kugelmass 1986; Myerhoff 1979).

I found my way to an office where framed photographs and certificates of appreciation covered the walls, and that was where Dragica Levi, the community's secretary general, explained to me that hot lunches, funded by the government of Germany and the American Jewish Joint Distribution Committee, were served daily to the mostly Muslim and Christian aged and poor of the neighborhood. But along with the elderly lunch crowd, I noticed some middle-aged and young people congregating in the building and blurted out that I had thought that the Jews of Sarajevo were evacuated during the first years of the war. Dragica gave me a long, cold stare, took a deep pull on her cigarette, and told me, as she slowly let out the smoke, that she and many others never did leave their city. They stayed to organize medical care, pharmacies, a short-wave radio communication station, hot lunches, and more. Didn't I know about the Jewish community's war efforts? Chastened and struggling for words, I told Dragica that she was very brave. She replied, "I don't know if it was brave or crazy." After a pause, she added, "Many did leave, and many returned—from Israel, from Spain, Switzerland, and Canada." And then she called in a young man named Alex, who had been to Israel and back again. We set a time to meet later that week, and when we sat together, he narrated to me the reasons for his family's decision to send him to Israel, and why, after six years there, he returned to Sarajevo. When I inquired about him again first in 2002 and then in 2004, Alex was long gone. But drifting in and out of the synagogue, living their lives and telling their tales were several other young people along with those at the peak of their adulthood.

The Jewish community of Sarajevo is as diverse as the city itself. It is comprised of so-called pure Jews (*čisti jevreji*) and those of mixed heritage; Sephardim and Ashkenazim;[3] those who spent their entire lives in Sarajevo, those who lived abroad and returned, and those, like me, whose peregrinations have not come to an end. Several are employed in the liberal professions within various businesses and governmental agencies; some hold jobs in the

Jewish community; most others are on pensions. Many participate in holiday services, social activities, and commemorative events, take their no-longer-free lunch in the restaurant, and drop by to see who is around and what is going on. No one is an Orthodox practitioner of Judaism.

This chapter, perhaps the most personal of the volume, is divided into three parts. The first gives an overview of the people who come and go in the Jewish community; the second focuses on ritual gatherings, highlighting the yearly festival of Passover; and the third considers how Jews are cognized and constituted in Sarajevo, from their own points of view, from the perspective of various Christians and Muslims, and from the dialogue that is produced by actions and interactions between the groups.

But before presenting my ethnography, I wish to note the work of two American journalists who recently offered their own observations of Sarajevo's Jews. Compelled by the fact that "for the first time during a modern European war, Jews have been actively saving and rescuing Christians and Muslims wherever, whenever they could," photojournalist Edward Serotta (1994, 10) spent several months during 1993 documenting the humanitarian efforts of the Sarajevo Jewish community. All the leaders of that community referred me to Serotta's volume when we discussed the war; they consider it to be a comprehensive and objective record of their work and accomplishments. The second book is Stephen Schwartz's *Sarajevo Rose* (2005), a postwar personal memoir that combines history with journalism, poetry with reports, and prayers and witnessing with self-reflection. Both authors' primary informants were the male, middle-aged officials of the Jewish community.

Although I certainly met and spent time with many of the same people, my closest friends in the Jewish community during 2004 were two women—Klara, a child psychologist in her midfifties, and Greta, a retired architecture professor who turned eighty that year—and several young people in their twenties. By including their voices and activities, my goal is to portray the internal variety of the Jewish community through its range of family patterns, individual experiences, and manifestations of group identity. In presenting the multiply refracting Jewish prism as part of the Bosnian kaleidoscope, this chapter offers a challenge to the state logic of the Ostali category, while revealing a competing but hitherto unrecognized logic of hybrid—or hybridizing—Bosnianness.

The Jevrejska Zajednica in Sarajevo and Beyond

Most days when I came to the community—also known as the *zajednica* (*zajedno* means "together") or *opština* in the local language,[4] or as the *kehillah* in Hebrew—for a meeting, an interview, or to lunch in the restaurant, business was brisk. During the summer, there are many returnees from abroad who meet up with friends over coffee. At other times, certain guests will visit: the Israeli ambassador makes a yearly call as does the European representative of the Jewish Joint Distribution Committee. Sometimes American rabbis and tourists will drop in; sometimes it is university students from Slovenia or Sweden; or staff from the shrinking array of humanitarian and political organizations that are collectively known as the international community. Less predictably, a stray traveler, journalist, or university professor will come by out of curiosity or to update his or her findings. Teams from the local television stations regularly arrive at the synagogue to chronicle holiday services; less frequently, film crews come from abroad to document the only operating synagogue in Sarajevo, which during the 1992–95 war served as a relief and communications station (see Serotta 1994).[5]

All that notwithstanding, most of the people who congregate in the synagogue's lobby are locals. In 2002, Ernest brought me there to meet Moric Albahari, who had as a teenager fought as a Partisan and then served as a pilot in the Yugoslav air force. He is also an official of the synagogue, but what Ernest told me en route was that Moric is a remarkably wise person with a great sense of humor and is thereby an example to the younger generations of Bosnian Jews.

When we arrived, Moric was sitting with a colleague who had served with him in the air force, and together they regaled me about how Yugoslavia had been a great country based on socialist humanism. Moric's friend then introduced himself: "I am a Muslim who has a Catholic wife. But what's the difference? All people are one under God; all people were one in Yugoslavia." He continued, "During the war, this place, the Jewish community, was the only place that gave food and medicine to anybody. Go to Merhamet [a Muslim charitable organization], and they ask your religion. If you're not Muslim, then go away. I wanted to change my religion to become Jewish because of the way that they treated everybody equally." He did not change his religion; he does not have to. He can sit in the synagogue lobby with his friend, drink coffee—with a shot of *rakija* [brandy] on the side—reminisce about the glory days of Yugoslavia, and share regrets about the ethnically divided aftermath of Bosnia's senseless war.

Most days two well-appointed women are on hand to meet and greet whoever comes into the synagogue. Both are named Nadja; one is the wife of the Jewish community's president. The other told me,

> I work here. Philanthropic work. There are old people who are sick, isolated, and cannot leave their houses. Their pensions are very small. We send a young woman to shop and to cook for them. From La Benevolencija [the charitable

> arm of the Jewish community]. And it doesn't matter what is their nationality. We offer services to all people. I myself am from a Muslim family. My husband was half-Jewish, half-Catholic. That's how I got here. I've been here since 1992. Before that, I was a biologist. I worked in one of those state enterprises. Oh yes, it closed. Nothing to talk about there. And, yes, I was in Sarajevo all during the war. We all were. Myself, my husband, my son, and my daughter. My husband has since died, and my son is in America.

Nadja's story of involvement in the Jewish community through intermarriage was but one of many. And reports of children living abroad repeat over and again.

In March 2004, I began to attend the meetings of La Bohoreta, the women's group that prepares the synagogue's social hall for Shabbat dinners and holiday feasts, arranges visits to the sick, makes condolence calls, keeps in phone and mail contact with members abroad, sends representatives to multiconfessional welfare organizations, and provides a reason to get together. The first meetings I attended were officiated by Zlata, who after living eight years in Israel returned to Sarajevo with her husband, although their married daughter remains there with her husband and twins. A few weeks later, after returning from a visit to her children and grandchildren in Canada, Neli, the group's president, resumed her duties. At the end of the business part of the meeting, photo albums showing smiling adults with their young children against the backdrop of broad Canadian vistas, London city scenes, and sun-drenched Israel changed hands.

At one of my first Bohoreta meetings, I met seventy-year-old Nada Levi, who, in her cheerful lavender, blue, and pink outfits, looks much younger than her years. She is the mother of four children but lives alone in Sarajevo. One of her sons is in Serbia, the other two went to Israel, and her daughter is an art teacher in Croatia. During the war, Nada volunteered at the synagogue, where everyday she oversaw the distribution of clothing, blankets, and foodstuffs. These days she spends most time in her favorite living-room corner, where she reads and writes essays and poems and sews for the rare client. When the weather is fine, Nada cultivates fruits and flowers in her garden. She tells me the amount of her meager monthly pension and shows me her household accounts book. "'How do we live?' you ask. *Moramo da živimo*—we must live."

Branko, a widower and the Jewish community's informal security guard, sits by the entrance to the synagogue and nods to all who come and go. I stopped to chat with him one day in May 2004, and Branko told me that he is the father of two grown children. His daughter, who that day turned thirty-eight, lives in the United States, in Fargo, North Dakota:

> She went there directly from Split in 1992, when she left Bosnia. She was alone then, and she is alone now. But she is content, very satisfied. She has a great job working for a company that makes discs, some kind of computerized road maps. She speaks English, and she carries an American passport. She's been back just once, for a visit, and she said that it was the first and last time. The war was very hard on her; she left in September; the war had begun in April. Everywhere there was sniper fire and shelling. It was dark inside the house; there was nothing to eat, and there were big problems with hygiene. She remembers that and wants to forget it. She has everything she wants—a good salary, a good job, vacation, a normal and good life.

"Have you ever been to visit?" I asked.

> No, I've never been there. I have no desire. There's nothing for me there, and I have no connection with that place. Now Israel is another thing. I like that country very much. It has its own soul, its spirit. There is always something going on there, something to do. My son lives there; he, his wife—she is also a Sarajevan—and their two sons. My eldest grandson is eight, the youngest is five and a half. . . . They are very happy there. No, none of them wants to return, except of course to visit. I've been there twice, and I'd go again. But to live there, no. It's too hot for me! Besides, I have my mother here. And my pension, and my job, and my community, my friends.

Unlike my experiences with Jewish parents in post-Soviet Russia (Markowitz 1994), I rarely if ever heard Bosnian parents complain of the hardships of life alone without their children. Most people told me matter-of-factly about their transnational families. They often added a positive note about their children's jobs and living conditions while stressing their own reasons for staying in Sarajevo. Perhaps Greta said it best: that the younger generation has the opportunity to lead good, happy, and productive lives abroad is something to celebrate. And she should know, for as a young woman no such opportunity had been offered to her.

Greta Weinfeld Ferušić was born and raised in Novi Sad in the Vojvodina region of Serbia, until that fateful autumn day in 1944 when the Nazis deported her and her entire family to Auschwitz.[6] After the war, Greta, the only survivor from that family, went to Belgrade, where she enrolled in the university and studied architecture. She also met the man who was to become her husband, a secular Bosnian Muslim. In 1952 they moved to his hometown of Sarajevo, where an engineering job awaited him at the promising new firm of Energoinvest along with an appointment at the university. Greta then entered a competition, and she too landed a position at Sarajevo University. When Sarajevo was shelled and war broke out in 1992, Greta and her husband resolved to stay put but insisted that their son, his wife, and their two children flee. She explained, "I left once with two suitcases and did not find anything when I came back. And I was twenty-one years old then. A second time, no. Not by my own will. I stayed here the whole time, with my husband, but the children we sent out. They have their own lives to live."

Several young people who were children or teenagers when they "were sent out" of Sarajevo told me that although they understand now that their parents acted to save their lives, or to give them lives to live, they remember feeling scared, alone, and abandoned as they rode the bus away from their city and their homes. But even prior to the outbreak of war in Bosnia, Jewish parents could and did extricate their children from difficult situations by sending them to Israel.

Alex was twenty-one years old that summer of 1997, when I met him after introducing myself to Dragica at the Jewish community. Seated on the synagogue's terrace overlooking the river, Alex told me of his sojourn in Israel. In Sarajevo, eager to make some money for his widowed mother, Alex had gotten involved in illegal business dealings when he was barely sixteen. These dealings proved profitable, but they were very dangerous, and his family feared for his life. To extricate him from that scene, Alex's uncle made arrangements through the Jewish community to send him for a year to Israel, and in November 1991, Alex headed for a kibbutz with his Yugoslav passport and a tourist visa. After two and a half months on that kibbutz, "where there were no classes and all [he] heard was Russian," Alex asked for and received placement in a boarding school near Tel Aviv: "I went to classes, but I didn't understand much. Each morning I had a one-hour private lesson; well, it was OK. And then three or four months later, a big group from Sarajevo arrived. I was the first [of the Bosnians] there, so I greeted everyone. What a great time that was! No one was serious; it was like a vacation because everyone thought the war would be over in two or three months and that's it, back to Sarajevo, back to our families. . . . But instead of two, three, four months, it was four years."

Renata was one of those children who arrived at the boarding school, but she did not remember a great time. In August 2002, within seconds of introducing ourselves, Renata, who was then twenty-four, narrated in one breath: "The war broke out in April 1992. I left in August 1993. I spent four years in Israel at a boarding school. Then I came back to Sarajevo."

Over the course of several meetings in 2004, Renata expanded on her story, confiding that the experience of being on her own was terribly difficult: "I cried and cried for three months. I was fourteen years old. What did I know? I had never been away from my parents. . . . At the end of my life, I'll say, 'Thanks Israel for everything. For four years of putting a roof over my head, an education, and so on.' But I'm afraid I didn't and wouldn't find myself there; to put it in short, from fourteen to eighteen I didn't find myself." After returning to her parents' home, Renata worked as a nanny for an American diplomat and then enrolled in the criminology program of Sarajevo University. She has made a few trips back to Israel and participated in the Walk for Life, which begins at Auschwitz and ends in Tel Aviv. Renata has also organized an intensive Hebrew class for the young adults of the community, and when Israeli delegations come to Sarajevo, she serves as a guide and translator. In May 2004, Renata was one of three young people who organized and presented the Holocaust Memorial Day commemoration service in the synagogue.

Jovan was another. When in 2002 I first met him, Jovan, known to everyone as Joja, was a twenty-two-year-old law student, volunteering at the Sarajevo Film Festival. Joja's mother is from a distinguished Sephardic Jewish family, but he carries the distinctly Serb first and last names of his deceased father. Here's how Jovan described his family:

> My father died in 1988. My mother is Jewish, but we were a communist, atheist Yugoslav family. My grandfather went to Prague in the 1930s, studied architecture, and joined the Communist Party. That was the end of our being Jewish as a religion! During the [Second World] War, grandfather was a Partisan, he and his brothers and uncles. Everyone else died in concentration camps—in Jasenovac, in Auschwitz. We grew up knowing we were Jewish: we went to the kehillah for celebrations, but we didn't do anything at home for Pesach or Hanukkah. We went to the Jewish community summer camps and winter camps. Since 1988 it's been me, Mother, her mother, and my little brother. My grandmother on my father's side was a diplomat for Yugoslavia all her life.

When the shelling of Sarajevo began, Jovan's paternal grandmother insisted that his mother send him and his younger brother to live with her. "To cut a long story short, we went to Belgrade on the last flight out of Sarajevo and lived there for two years with our two cousins." And here the story got murky. Joja was fidgety; he moved around a lot and chain-smoked as he talked. He told me in Hebrew that things were *dafuk* [screwed up] in Belgrade—

weapons and tanks in the streets, propaganda day and night. "But what did I know? I went to school, had a roof over my head, there were no bombings." He resumed the chronology:

> In 1994 our cousins took us to Budapest by car, where we met up with Mom. We thought that we were going to go back with Mom to Sarajevo, but we didn't really want to. At that time, it was not at all clear what was happening, but there was still a war. Belgrade was fine. We wanted to see Mom, but we didn't want to go to Sarajevo, and she definitely didn't want to go to Belgrade. So we went to Zagreb and stayed with friends, and thought about where to go next: Australia, the United States, England, Canada, and Israel. . . . It was one of those truce periods in the summer of '94, and finally we all decided to return to Sarajevo.
>
> In less than two weeks, I was out again. My name and my accent, both 100 percent Serbian, didn't promise me much here. We got in touch with the kehillah, and twenty hours later, I got out through the tunnel to Mostar, Split, and then Zagreb.[7] I spent a week in Zagreb, five days in Budapest, and then on to Israel. I was there in a boarding school until 1999, four years. . . . I've returned to Israel six times. I don't stay two months in one place! After all these years, I am very connected to Israel, very.

I saw Joja several times during my stay in 2004. He hopes to become a diplomat for Bosnia-Herzegovina so that he can continue traveling, especially to Israel and the Middle East. As Renata put it, "All of us who were in Israel, me, Goran, Jovan, Igor, Ernest, we see ourselves as the future of the Jewish community. We're a small community and we all need to join efforts to survive."

The members of Sarajevo's Jewish community live in various kinds of family arrangements that are sometimes transnational and sometimes local. Like Renata and Jovan, who rejoined their parents in Sarajevo, some families split generationally during the war; some spent all or part of the war years together in Israel; some stayed abroad; others made a collective decision to return; while still others have gone through a variety of splits and mergers. Lena, who owns a lovely gift shop in the city center, pointed to her mother's menorah (not for sale!) as she explained that her family, Hungarian Jews, came to Bosnia in the nineteenth century. Now Lena is the last of that family in Sarajevo because her children are thriving in North America. As the war came to an end, she and her husband joined them there. "Everything was fine," she told me. But after eighteen months, Lena simply missed hearing her native language and running into the people she knows. She and her husband decided that it was more important for them to return to their hometown than to live on the same continent with their children "who are already grown, who have their own lives."

One Friday evening after the Shabbat service, I met Sonja and Miroslav at the synagogue, and a few weeks later they invited me to their home. As we enjoyed tasty food, wine, and music, they told me about the good old days of Yugoslavia, the shock of the war years, why they left for Israel, and their decision to return four years later.

Miroslav, the son of two Sephardic Jews, and Sonja, the daughter of a Jewish father and a Croat mother, have known each other since they were children. They attended university, married, found good jobs, and raised a son. Miroslav worked as a government economist. As soon as the war began, he enlisted in the army of Bosnia-Herzegovina and served as a frontline soldier; "We were sure it would be a couple of months." Toward the end of 1993, he reassessed the situation and decided that the war would not be ending any time soon. He managed to get himself and his wife and son out of Sarajevo, and they resettled in Israel. Miroslav humorously tells about his four years as a forklift operator but grows dour when he explains that Sonja, who had been an English teacher, took an unskilled factory job. Sonja, though, credits her years in Israel, "where one needs to be rather aggressive to get anything done," for giving her the self-confidence to seek and find a new job when they returned to Sarajevo.

"And how did that go?" I asked. Again Miroslav made a joke out of a difficult situation. When he came to Sarajevo to get everything settled in advance of the return of his wife and son, he found a woman and her son living in the family's apartment, which they claimed as their own. Although Miroslav had the required ownership documents, since the occupants were internally displaced persons—Bosniacs who had fled their home under the threat of ethnic cleansing—it was just about impossible to evict them; "So we all lived together!" After months of filing claims and counterclaims, Miroslav received full title to his apartment, and the woman and her son finally left under a court order. Not all cases have ended so well, and Miroslav is certain that his favorable judgment, as well as getting (back) his job in the FBiH tax office, were due to his active service in the BiH army.[8] When Sonja returned to Sarajevo, she sought and found a position teaching English in a technical high school. Their son is studying business administration and hopes to find a job in an international firm after earning his degree.

My friend Klara's family decision to return to Sarajevo is a more complicated and ambiguous story than that of Sonja and Miroslav. Klara's children, her father, and his wife left Sarajevo on one of the early convoys organized by the Jewish community. In 1994, during a truce period, Klara joined a group of Sarajevo mothers for a visit to their children in Israel. Parting with her children for the second time was so painful that Klara resolved to reunite her family. Later that year, she and her Bosniac husband fled Sarajevo and joined the children in Israel. Klara became proficient in Hebrew in a remarkably short time, and with her master's degree and years of experience, she found employment as a school psychologist. Her husband, an architect, worked as a manual laborer. The children progressed in their studies.

As her son was completing high school and assessing various options for service in the Israeli Defense Force (IDF), family discussions began about returning to Sarajevo. Klara told me that she and her husband charged each member of the family to make an individual decision and then for each to investigate the viability of that decision:

> One of the reasons for returning is that my husband lost his job. He really suffered, a man sitting at home who was always a professional. He was out of a job six months, and it didn't look as if he would find something else. So in July '99, he was the first to come back to Sarajevo, and he wondered, "Will they accept me? Will they call me a traitor? Will there be work?" He found work in a week. Two months later, our son came to investigate, and in a week he too decided that he wanted to stay. He had his high school diploma, and he was accepted into the Sarajevo Art Institute. My daughter completed Bezalel Art Institute in Jerusalem, and by the beginning of October we were back here. Nataša found work, and I got my job back at the TV station. It was exactly five years for us.

Over the course of 2004, I met with Klara several times. "I am so overwhelmed by the goodness of Israel," she often repeated. "But all the same, I returned here. My heart is here. After all, this is our place." Although gratified that the entire family is back in their renovated downtown apartment, Klara was not sure that Sarajevo offers the best opportunities for her children. Echoing Greta, she said, "What they want to do they will do. Their decisions and lives are their own."

The Jews of Bosnia-Herzegovina are no strangers to dispersal and disruption. Nonetheless, from 1530 until 1941 they found there a haven and made it their home. And although their community was ravished and reduced in the Holocaust, Sarajevo's Jews rebounded in socialist Yugoslavia. During the 1992–95 war, many left, some to return, some to eke out new lives in different places. Families have separated and reunited, and separate and reunite again.

Although people come and go, the pink brick Ashkenazi synagogue on the northern bank of the Miljacka River remains solidly in place for the Jewish community of Bosnia-Herzegovina. It draws attention from students and scholars as a last repository of Judeo-Spanish texts and spoken Ladino and from journalists and novelists for its resolute and tough yet joyful and resilient individuals who triumphed over war. The synagogue endures as a mainstay of Jewish life in an unpredictable world and attracts people from all over to make a connection to their own Jewish heritage.

One Friday afternoon as I was leaving the synagogue with Greta, Moric joined up with us on his way to the market to buy something for the Shabbat meal. He was laughing out loud as he announced that he had just received another Kunta Kinte letter. Greta burst into laughter. "Kunta Kinte, do you know who that is?" Moric asked me. Kunta Kinte? Was I hearing right? "Kunta Kinte—the African who was enslaved from *Roots*?" I asked. Greta laughed some more, while Moric explained, "An American black man wrote this book, *Roots,* and now each time I get a letter from Israel or the United States or Canada telling me their name and asking if we are relatives, I say that they are writing to Kunta Kinte." So it is that Moric Albahari and Greta Weinfeld Ferušić, whose names carry the multiple heritage of the Jewish Diaspora, become Kunta Kinte in the Bosnian Jewish Community as its constituents, scattered all over the world, search for and remind themselves of their roots.

Rituals and Sociability

Once or twice a month on a Friday evening, I would go to the pink brick synagogue to welcome the Sabbath with David and Blanka Kamhi, Moric Albahari, Branko, Duško, Ella, and whoever else happened to stop by. Some Friday evenings there were more than enough people—that is, at least ten men—for a minyan, or prayer quorum. Sometimes there were not, but every week a stalwart group of men and women greeted the Sabbath in prayer and song, with a glass of wine, braided white bread, and some tasty morsels cooked up by white-haired, white-bearded, white-aproned Cicko, whose culinary skills took on new meaning when, during the 1992–95 Bosnian war, he made something from almost nothing everyday in the Jewish community's kitchen.

Greta is a member of the Jewish community's executive board, but I never saw her on a Friday evening. She participates in La Bohoreta meetings, social activities, and community events, but Greta does not attend religious services: "First of all, I am from a secular family. But more important, how can I participate in a religion that will take one thousand illiterate men and not one woman with a university diploma! No, I told them, I will serve my community, but I will not take part in these religious services."

Although I share Greta's outrage, I loved coming to the synagogue on Friday evenings, and at first I wrote no field notes of these events. I considered them my downtime, an hour or so at the end of the week among a group of coethnics/coreligionists before I went off to meet with someone else or to take in a concert or a movie. But after a while, I decided that I had to keep a record of the joyful irreverence that accompanied traditional observance. Most of the men would smoke after the festive meal, and sometimes they used the flame of the Sabbath candles to light their cigarettes—an absolute taboo, according to Jewish law. When I confronted David Kamhi, the community's lay religious leader, on the contradiction between allowing for the lighting of cigarettes; the use of the telephone, buses, and trams; and the exclusion of women from the minyan, he dismissed my complaint by reminding me that the Talmud exempts women from prayer obligations. The separation of the sexes for David is central to Jewish practice. As for the abrogation of Orthodox law that I noted, he just shrugged his shoulders as if to say that these are peripheral to the real reason for getting together on Friday evenings—to celebrate that we have made it through another week, to celebrate that we are Jews.

Passover is the yearly festival that commemorates the emancipation and perseverance of the Jewish people. It begins in the evening with a seder (*seder* means "order" in Hebrew), which is a special gathering and festive meal based on the ritual objects, prayers, stories, and songs detailed in the Haggadah, the Passover prayer book. Every year a community seder is held in the synagogue.

It was Passover eve, April 5, 2004, and I arrived at the Jevrejska Zajednica about fifteen minutes before the appointed hour of 7:00 P.M. David and Blanka Kamhi greeted me as soon as I crossed the threshold. Then I saw Renata for the first time since I had met with her in 2002. Standing with her was another young woman, as blonde as Renata is raven haired. That young woman, Berta, had also spent the war years at a boarding school in Israel. She had returned to Sarajevo some five years ago to look after the family's apartment, found a job in an American humanitarian organization as a translator, and stayed in Sarajevo, although her parents live in Israel. About a year ago, that humanitarian organization closed, and she was left without a job. But as she understands it, the situation is no better in Israel: "No work here, and no work there."

Renata told me that there are two halls for the seder: the one we were standing in is for the youth, and the other one across the way is for older people. And where should I go? Could I navigate between the two?

In the young people's hall, one long table was set for all. In the older people's hall, in addition to the head table, there were some twenty-five tables set for four to six people each. A young Sarajevo-born rabbi who came from Israel was to lead the general seder. Igor, otherwise known as Grga, was to officiate for the young people.

I did not introduce Grga in the previous section because his movements back and forth, with his sister (now married with two children in Israel), on his own, and with his parents proved too complicated for me to render into easily readable text. Suffice it to say that for the past few years, Igor, the holder of an Israeli high school diploma and a veteran of the IDF, had given in to his parents' pleas to "just try to be with us." Living with his parents after years of being on his own was "hard, very hard." He recalled, "In a week or two I called a family conference. I told them that seven years have passed, and you can't begin making a movie from where it paused. And we came to what is known as a compromise. Now I just have to call them and let them know when I'm coming home or if I'm not coming home. I have my space. But I would like in the near future to find some place of my own."

Grga, like the son of Miroslav and Sonja, is enrolled in a two-year business management program, but he talked about the program as a pragmatic, perhaps temporary arrangement, while he enjoys the attention of his friends and parents. "Studying in Israel is better than here, [but] I know that in Israel it will not be easy. . . . I like it now. I was alone enough. I won't have that there. It will be hard."

Grga keeps his link to Israel alive by active participation in the Jewish community. After the Passover seder, he told me about his role as the "vice rabbi" for the youth: "I'm not very religious, but I always do it. Among the youth, whenever there's a question of religion they come to me—there's Grga, he can do it! And I do it. If I don't do it, nobody will. And I prefer things to be done. I might go to Israel and study a bit of *hazanut* [cantorship], then return and be the hazan in the synagogue."

But now let's return to that synagogue where David the cantor and his wife, Blanka, were calling everyone to go upstairs into the sanctuary for evening prayers. From my field notes:

> Men in front, women in back; it's the evening holiday service. I counted some fifty men and about the same number of women—lots of gray or white heads,

but at least one-third of the congregants were much younger. Hardly any children, although there are some twenty to thirty people in their twenties. The last census of 1991 stated there were 426 Jews in the Republic of BiH, but no breakdown for Sarajevo.[9] I'd say that just about everyone who considers himself or herself Jewish in Sarajevo was there at the seder, over one hundred people. And just about all of the young ones had spent some time (during the war) in Israel. A young rabbi, as I understood it, who had gone from Sarajevo to Israel, was leading the service, with David Kamhi at his side as the cantor. The service was entirely in Hebrew, and no prayer books were distributed.

16. Detail, Sarajevo's Ashkenazi synagogue

> The sanctuary is beautiful—this is the 1902-built Ashkenazi synagogue, but it, like that of Budapest, is of neo-Moorish decor, so it evokes Sepharad Spain. TV cameras captured part of the service and panned the audience.

During the prayer service, I noticed behind me a woman about my age, standing with two younger women, one of whom had to be her daughter. She looked so familiar. Could she be Klara, whom I had met in 2002? After the service I approached her, and yes, indeed, it was Klara. She invited me to join her, her daughter, Nataša, and a friend of hers at their table. And that is how I ended up seated in the main hall for the community's Passover seder.

In the main hall, each of us had a seder plate meal. Ordinarily, a large porcelain or metal seder plate holding ritual food objects is placed in the center of the table for all to see. Participants' individual plates are empty until the festive meal is served at the halfway point of the seder. However, as we each took our places, a meal that replicated the items on the traditional seder plate was set before us. It included a roasted chicken leg and thigh, a sprig of parsley, a roasted egg, a dab of horseradish, and haroset—a special condiment made of apples, dates, wine, honey, and cinnamon—on a lettuce leaf, and a scoop of a savory potato salad. Each person also received three pieces of matzo, the yeastless bread of affliction; a cup holding salt water symbolizing the Israelites' tears; and a wineglass. There were no copies of the Haggadah on the tables.[10] Instead there were Xeroxed sheets of the joyful song "Dayenu" (It Would Have Been Enough), which is sung during the first quarter of the seder, and a Ladino version of "Ehad Mi Yodeya" (Who Knows One), which is sung toward the end.

Klara and I got reacquainted; I told her about my project of multicultural Sarajevo. She told me that if I wanted stories, there were plenty of them here, and then gave me some tidbits about people at nearby tables. Nataša reminded me that after returning to Bosnia, she left again for a year to earn an MA in architecture in Genoa, Italy. She is employed in Sarajevo's city planning bureau, but the job does not pay enough for her to live on her own. "And there's no possibility for anything else because of lack of political connections."

Meanwhile, the seder was under way, but ours was not the only table where hearty conversations were taking place. The young rabbi led the service in Hebrew and Bosnian and threw in a little English for the Jews of the international community, staff members of the American embassy, the U.S. Agency for International Development (USAID), and related projects, who were sitting up front. Most people followed along at the beginning; they drank the first cup of wine and sang the four questions that guide the stories and songs of the service, but when those seated at a table up front took up the rabbi's offer to read portions of the Haggadah in English, the Jews of Sarajevo increased talking among themselves. Nataša and her friend got up to check on the young people. They were back in a matter of minutes; "They are having a real seder there, very serious!" We drank the second glass of wine and then ate our meal as conversations become even more animated throughout the hall.

During the meal, Klara told me that here in Sarajevo

> We have our own—what's the name of that holiday? Oh yes, our own Purim story. Once, during the reign of the Ottomans, there was a very mean ruler here who for no reason hated the Jews. Maybe it was because they had some of the wealthiest shops in the Baščaršija. Like in the story of Purim that happened in Persia, he was planning to murder the Jews of Sarajevo. So he took his soldiers into the Baščaršija and asked all of the merchants and artisans to come out of their shops and line up. Then he commanded, "All the Jews, step forward!" And *every* one of the men—Jews and non-Jews—took a step forward. That way, he would have had to kill them all or none of them. That is the kind of tolerance and solidarity that Sarajevo is known for. And that is why it is still hard to understand how what happened here happened.[11]

The Americans up in front started singing "Had Gadya" (One Little Goat), which comes at the very end of the seder, right before everyone chants together, "Next Year in Jerusalem." None of the locals joined in the singing. There was a silent pause, and then several female and a few male voices joined together to sing "Ehad Mi Yodaya" in Ladino. It was lively and lovely.

The main hall dispersed, and many of us went into the young people's hall, where the serious seder had also ended. A tall young man was singing into the microphone; someone else was accompanying him on drums, Ernest was working a synthesizer board, and the room was heavy with smoke. Klara told me that the singer is a very talented boy. He was alone in Israel, and she got to know him well, as he and her son were friends. "Then he came back here and has been very successful, amazingly talented. He published a book. And do you know Joja?" I told her that, yes, I had met him in 2002, and he had told me then that he feels as if he has two homes, Sarajevo and Israel. "Yes," she said, "that often happens to children who lived through the war alone. All they are looking for is a place. These are wonderful children."

As the last stragglers left, I finally introduced myself to Jakob Finci, president of the Jewish community of BiH. "Do you want to see multicultural Sarajevo in action?" he asked. When I answered, "Of course!" he invited me to attend another seder, this time in miniature, on Wednesday at noon for diplomats, heads of Sarajevo's cultural societies, and clergy from the other faiths.

The next day, April 6, was the anniversary of the 1945 liberation of Sarajevo. In addition to the newspaper articles and the many placards announcing that event on Tito Street, some shops in the pedestrian mall had signs in their windows wishing חג שמח, *Sretan Pesah,* Happy Passover. In *Oslobodjenje* there were several such ads—from the FBiH, from the Canton of Sarajevo, from the Sarajevo airport, and from the newspaper itself.

On April 7, I attended the "mini-seder" staged by the Jewish community for the international and multicultural community. It was ten minutes before noon when I arrived, and uncharacteristically there was a police car on the street in front of the synagogue building. Standing by the entrance was a reception line of Jakob Finci, president of the Jewish community of BiH; Danilo Nikolić, president of the Jewish community of Sarajevo; and Zoran Mandlbaum, president of the Jewish community of Mostar. Each of the men wore a suit and tie—Zoran's was a bowtie—and a *kippah,* or skullcap. Many other men in suits entered the synagogue, along with at least one Orthodox priest in a long black robe, a Franciscan Catholic monk, and the Reis-ul-ulema, Bosnia's highest Muslim cleric in a cylindrical white fez. I talked with a woman who introduced herself as a representative of the EU, who had previously been a French diplomat. She repeated several times what a wonderful man Finci is and how much he has been doing for the city.

I entered the social hall where the community seder had been held two days earlier. Once again the room was set up with a long head table, where the Jewish community presidents, cantor David Kamhi, and the young rabbi who had come from Israel sit, and several smaller tables set for four or six. I saw a woman sitting alone at one table, so I went over and introduced myself as an American-Israeli anthropologist studying multicultural Sarajevo. She introduced herself as Ljiljana, the president of the Slovenian Cultural Center of Sarajevo. "We've been here in Sarajevo since at least the time of the Austrian Empire. We didn't leave because there was no reason to leave. We were all part of the same country, Yugoslavia. Today our organization is dedicated to preserving Slovenian culture in Sarajevo."

Another woman joined us; smartly dressed, nicely made up, lively, and eager to switch between Bosnian and English to help me. That was my first meeting with Greta Weinfeld Ferušić. In response to my introduction, she said that she had been to Israel twice, once in 1987 when she took a bus trip all across the country, and once two years ago while on a cruise that stopped in Haifa. After they disembarked, she had toured Haifa and Jerusalem.

Greta then told me briefly about her life and her determination to remain in Sarajevo during the recent war. Ljiljana had remained as well and commented, "They call us *promašen*; do you know what this means?" She continued without waiting for my reply. "It means missed, but it has another meaning, like losers. That means that anyone who could, left, and did something with their life. Those who stayed didn't." Greta argued with Ljiljana, pointing out how difficult it has been for those who left and then came back to apartments that were ruined. "And can you imagine if I had done that, starting over with a destroyed apartment at my age? I will be eighty in two months."

The model seder began with a "welcome to this celebration of Pesach in the year 5764" by Jakob Finci in Bosnian, then in English: "It is the world's oldest continually observed holiday." He explained that Pesach is a holiday of liberation. "The festival commemorates a historical event, the liberation of the Jews from slavery in Egypt, but freedom is not won once and for all. There is an ongoing process of self-liberation, not only for the Jews but for every human being to live out his freedom. This is a holiday with meaning not only for the Jews but for every citizen of Bosnia and Herzegovina." Jakob then introduced the young rabbi, Eliezer Papo, who took over, also in Bosnian and English, and began a shortened version of the seder.

As soon as he was introduced, Greta leaned over and told me that this rabbi wasn't originally Jewish.

> He's a Serbian boy from Sarajevo who before the war was coming to the synagogue. He got a scholarship and went to Israel, where he studied for the rabbinate, but he [also?] went to law school. He was supposed to come back to Sarajevo to be the rabbi here, but I guess he loves Israel too much. He works there not as a rabbi but as a lawyer. He comes here every year and performs the rabbi's role. There is no rabbi in Sarajevo. He was supposed to be it, but he didn't come back. They sent us someone last year, but I didn't like him. Nobody liked him. He wouldn't shake the hand of a woman [i.e., he was ultra-Orthodox]. That's not the kind of community that we are. He lasted three, maybe four months.

Meanwhile, the young rabbi was addressing the audience: "There is an old rabbinic saying: One should not do to others what you do not want done to yourself, and this later became known as the Christian golden rule.[12] I'm looking out into the audience, and I'm seeing many of the same faces I've seen over the years. But I'm not doing to you anything that we do not do to ourselves. Every year we read the Haggadah and explain every symbol on the table. In Bosnia and Herzegovina, every symbol of freedom is very important." He explained the meaning of three key symbols. "During the seder," the rabbi continued, "we drink four cups of wine to remind ourselves of the four verbs that come before salvation. But today we will drink only one." He recited in Hebrew the blessing over the wine, and then everyone ate lunch.

After Ljiljana left us, Greta and I continued to talk. We were joined by Zoran Mandlbaum, the president of the Mostar Jewish community. "You want multiethnicity—come to Mostar; we have it all!" Greta told me that there is a beautiful—but this is not really the right word—monument to the Jews from Mostar who were killed in World War II. They had also begun to build a new synagogue there, but all that has been erected is the foundation. Zoran, she told me, saved a Muslim woman during the 1990s war; by saying to the authorities that she was Jewish, he got her out of the Croat-Herzegovinian side, where she would have been killed. "No, no one did anything to the Jews, not in that war." Zoran insisted that I come to Mostar, and in June I did, with Greta and Michele, who works at the American Embassy, voluntarily teaches an English course to the women of La Bohoreta, and argues with David Kamhi about accepting women into the minyan. But right then the big event

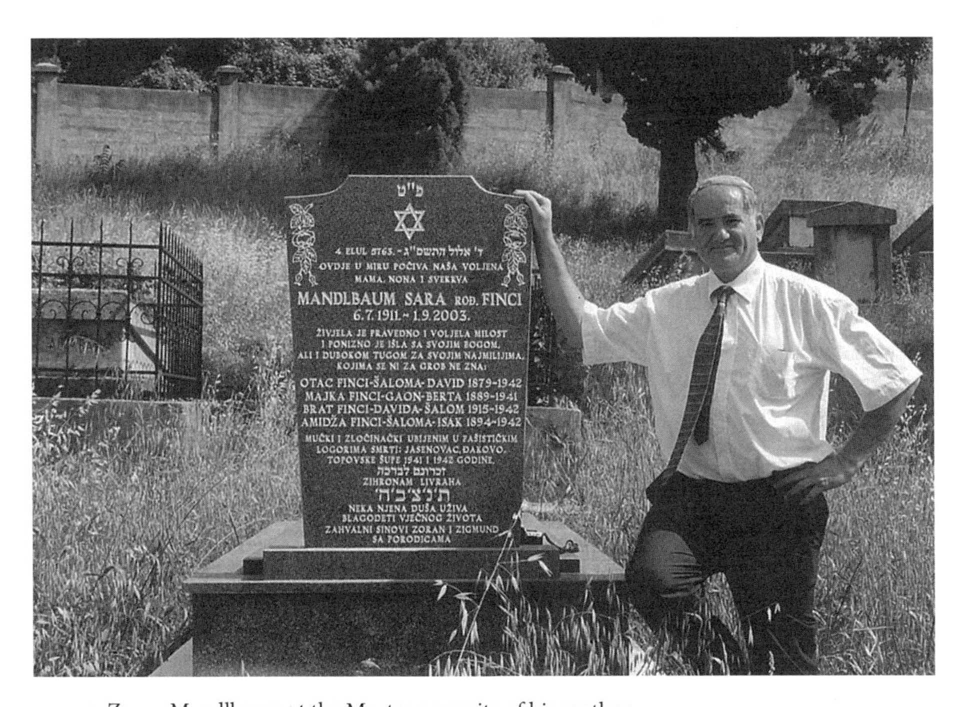

17. Zoran Mandlbaum at the Mostar gravesite of his mother

was winding down, and David joined us as we drank coffee and talked about this and that. Then Danilo Nikolić came over to shake hands—he had been going from table to table. I told him that this was a lovely event and then asked, "What's it like to be the president of the Sarajevo Jewish community these days?" He shrugged his shoulders. "Before the war," he said, "Sve mi smo bili zajedno—We were all together."

Now the Jews have become Ostali in the constitution and on the census. But through the rituals of Passover, they remind themselves of their ties to one another and show everyone in Sarajevo—including the Muslim, Catholic, and Orthodox clergy; presidents of cultural organizations; diplomats from the European Union, the Council of Europe, and many nations—their unique place in the city's history and the importance of freedom for the world.

Conceiving and Cognizing the Jews in Bosnia-Herzegovina

As the joyous hubbub of the mini-seder staged for multiethnic Sarajevo was winding down, I asked Danilo what it's like to head the city's Jewish community. His ambiguous answer echoed several replies I had already received to the more broadly framed question, "What's it like to be a Jew in Sarajevo these days?" which I often asked when I met with people in the Jewish community. In March 2004, Nadja Finci told me, "It used to be wonderful, but now, well, there's not much to look forward to," and closed the subject with a shrug of her shoulders. Branko's reply was somewhat more involved:

> Branko is a name that all groups in Yugoslavia name their children, except the Muslims. My mother is Jewish, Sephardic Jewish from an old Jewish family in Sarajevo. My father was Orthodox, but I did not know him; he died in 1941. All kinds of people come in here; our doors are open to all. During the war we had much to give, and we helped everyone—with food, medicine, convoys. And everyone loved us. Now we have nothing to give, and, let's put it like this, the love for us has declined. No anti-Semitic demonstrations or manifestations, no, not here, not against us. But without the interest, the love has declined.

One day in May, over a month after Passover 2004, I asked Dragica, who was deeply involved in a lawsuit waged on behalf of the community against the city to reopen its Jewish Museum,[13] "How are things going these days for Jews in Sarajevo?" She replied: "I'm afraid to say that they are not getting any better. I believe it is because of what is happening in the Middle East, yes, in Israel-Palestine. I heard on a TV program not long ago, 'No matter where they live, no matter where they are born, Jews are always the enemy of Islam.' No, not on a news program; I can't remember exactly, but nothing like this was ever before broadcast on TV." "Have you received any letters to that effect or seen such graffiti?" I asked. She replied:

> On the steps outside the Old Temple there was graffiti: Swastika = Magen David. There are not many of these, but I think it's because of the Middle East and all the influence of Saudi Arabia here. It's a different version of Islam, one that we've never had. Have you seen the young women in their long dresses and covering their heads? I think it's a little less now than immediately after the war. But I understand them. During the war, there were many humanitarian organizations that would only give help to those who went to the mosque, who grew their beards, who put on the dress. Those were desperate times, and I understand anybody who did that. And now there is still a strong influence from Saudi Arabia; have you seen those huge mosques built in the new sections of the town? Who knows what they are saying in there. . . .
>
> In general the situation is not so good. There are lots of people without work, including our young people. You see them all over, day after day sitting in the cafés. Coffee costs one mark, so for that one mark they can sit a few hours. But wouldn't it be better if they were studying?

"But many study and still cannot get jobs," I said, more as a question than as a statement. She responded, "Yes, that's true. Some of our young people have come back from Israel and are really studying, enrolled in our universities. Maybe it's because it's too expensive in Israel, that the tuition is too high for them to afford. We are having a seminar later this afternoon on small business initiatives. And then when they complete that seminar, you know that we have a micro-credit organization that can give them a small loan to get started."

I think that Dragica was relieved to have the opportunity to move the conversation away from what was a painful topic: anti-Jewish sentiments in a city where Jews had never been confined to ghettos, in a city known for its religious tolerance, a city that, although under siege, celebrated its Jews in "Sepharad 1992," the five-hundred-year anniversary of the Spanish expulsion. Yet Sarajevo is also a city where the Holocaust struck with all its venom and reduced the Jewish population from ten to twelve thousand to less than a thousand souls.

It was now Sunday evening, April 18, 2004, and the Yom ha-Shoah, or Holocaust Memorial Day, commemoration was about to begin. On a long table in the assembly hall, there were dozens of small white candles neatly lined up behind white cards with family names printed on them in black. On a raised platform behind the table stood six large white candles draped in black crepe. People came in and lit their family candles. Greta told me that it was easy to find her candle because her family name, Weinfeld, was at the end. She lit her candle and sat with me.

A disembodied voice was reading off name after name and their ages—from tiny children to the very old, with every age in between. People were talking in whispers among themselves as the names were read off. Most of the people in the audience were middle aged or older. Then four young people, Renata, Joja, Grga, and one other young man, entered and sat in the front row. Renata mounted the stage and said a few words to the audience. One of the young men led an opening prayer and then lit the six large candles. Danilo, the president of the congregation, rose and told us that Yom ha-Shoah commemorates the six million who perished during the Holocaust. "We and the Jewish people throughout the world remember the pogroms and the Holocaust that happened, and the anti-Semitism that takes place still throughout the world. We are here to remember the tragedy of six million civilians who suffered only because they were Jews." He then called for a moment of silence.

Renata resumed, "We are all obliged to tell about the Holocaust."[14] First Joja and then she read from documentary accounts of the deportation of the Jews of Sarajevo and their interment in camps. Grga then read from documents about the Partisans. I found it comforting—and I daresay most in the audience felt the same—to see and hear these lovely young Sarajevo Jews who had found sanctuary in Israel during a more recent war reading to the older generations, themselves World War II survivors or the children of survivors, about the Holocaust. During Renata's reading, an elderly couple was talking in the front row. "Shhhhh," came from many people in the audience. Greta told me that the woman who was talking is Neli's mother; she is eighty-nine years old. I asked Greta where the deported Sarajevo Jews were taken, to Jasenovac? She said she was not sure but to some place in Slavonia in central Croatia, reminding me again that she is not from here.

Jakob Finci, who certainly is, preferred not to dwell on the Holocaust. During a pleasant lunch in June, he told me how the community prepared for the 1992–95 war, and how he deflected rumors that "the Jews [were] leaving Sarajevo." With a smile, he told me that unlike most other places in Europe, for the last several decades the Jews of Bosnia have been objects of philo-Semitism:

> Many people have asked me why it is that the Jews were not bothered or singled out in this war, and I have put forth these two reasons: first, that because the Jews were slaughtered during World War II, we were too insignificant a number to bother with. . . . The other reason was that those three groups were spending so much time hating each other that they had no time to hate the Jews! But I have yet another reason: We have had here in Sarajevo not anti-Semitism but philo-Semitism. The Serbs say, Look, we are brothers. Both of us were victims during World War II of the Nazis and Ustaše, and today we are both victims of the Muslims. The Croats came to me and asked for a copy of the bylaws of the World Jewish Organization; they talk about their Diaspora and say that like the Jews, they have been persecuted and spread out all over the world. And the Muslims, they say, look, we have been living here together in Sarajevo for the last five hundred years. And every time I go on radio or TV, people call in to remember that our community gave them this or that medication, took their children out on the convoy, or provided them or their parents with food. No one has forgotten, and we still have our good name in Sarajevo.

But Jakob is not naïve, and after a pause, he adds:

> In the last two years, with the last Intifada, there are now bad feelings about Israel. I don't know how many times I've gone on TV and radio and explained that we Jews have been here in Sarajevo for five hundred years—that "ethnic cleansing" was invented not by the Serbs in the last war but five hundred years ago in Spain. That Israel was created in November 1947 by a UN vote that gave one part of the land for a Jewish state and another part for a Palestinian Arab state, but that the Palestinian part was controlled and occupied by Egypt and Jordan until 1967. Why did nobody talk about occupied Palestine then?

There is no Israeli embassy in Sarajevo. Through 2005 the Israeli ambassador to Hungary, stationed in Budapest, also held the title of ambassador to Bosnia-Herzegovina. During the last few years, one ambassador, who is based in Jerusalem, represents Israel in Albania, Bosnia-Herzegovina, Macedonia, and Montenegro. In 2008 that ambassador participated in the mini-seder for the multiconfessional and international community, where she delivered a celebratory speech about Israel's sixtieth anniversary. The "State of Palestine," however, is represented by an embassy and an ambassador in Sarajevo. Every evening on FBiH-TV, there is a report from the Middle East. Most of these reports show IDF soldiers firing on Palestinian civilians.

One evening Amila invited me, a native speaker, to attend her English conversation class and tell something about life in America. I thought I would talk about the vastness of the country, its different geographical regions, and the diversity of the population. But we never did get to that. As part of my introduction, I told the six women students and their teacher that I haven't been living full-time in America for a while because I teach at Ben-Gurion University in Israel. Suddenly the beautiful, blonde, blue-eyed teacher, Nuradžahan, interrupted, "And what do you think of the poor Palestinian people?" Before I could answer, she continued, "I see the facts on TV every night—and not just our BiH-TV, but BBC and CNN—of poor Palestinian people with no weapons, completely defenseless except for stones being attacked by the Israelis and supported by Bush. This reminds us of what we went through, and can you please tell me how the Israeli people react to this suffering?"

Just a little while earlier, when I told the class that I was an ethnographer researching ethnicity and multiculturalism in postwar Sarajevo, Nuradžahan had interrupted to tell her students that it isn't even worthwhile to speak about the war and their wartime experiences to anyone who wasn't here because they simply cannot understand what happened. I wanted to tell her the same thing about the situation in Israel, to bring her attention to the Qassam rockets shot from Gaza to explode on the civilians of Sderot and the innocent people—Jews, Christians, and Muslims—riding buses, food shopping, sipping coffee, and dancing in discotheques who were blown up by suicide bombers. And I did. But on that warm evening in 2004, Nuradžahan, who complimented me as the only foreigner who could pronounce her name, told me that she had never seen Palestinians with weapons on TV. She repeated her charges and attempted to rally her Bosniac students to discuss the equation that she had proposed: that the Palestinians fired on by the IDF are in the same abominable situation as Sarajevans had been in when their city was under siege and radical Serb aggressors fired down on them.

The students did not join with her, but I felt uneasy nonetheless. Is this what Dragica and Jakob were referring to when they intimated that things are not as they used to be? And is the logic that Nuradžahan proposed more widespread than this small group of polite female students refused to acknowledge? Might it be influencing government policy in the FBiH?

During that same month in 2004, Grga told me about his problems with the government:

> They want to get me into army service here. . . . I went there and told them that I did the IDF in Israel. A friend of mine in Mostar in the same situation was excused (from the BiH army). I didn't get the excuse, so see you in court!

> I'm twenty-five. By law they can take you into the army till age twenty-eight. When I went there, they were very arrogant. I said, "I did the army in Israel." They—it was a woman—asked me, "Did you kill any Palestinians?" I said, "136." It was the first number that popped into my mind.

Grga was a cook in the IDF and killed no one. He continued:

> She just looked at me. And I said, "You should organize a Jewish component of the Federation, and then you can call me to serve in that Jewish army. Look, there's the army of the Republika Srpska, and in the Federation you have two armies de facto, the Muslim one and the Croat one. If there was one army for the entire state of Bosnia-Herzegovina, then maybe I would serve. In the meantime, when you make a Jewish component, then you can call me." If they call me again, I don't know what to do. I can go to Israel and study . . . and return as clergy. They don't call those religious guys. And besides I'll tell them that they must provide me with kosher food and that I'm *shomer shabbes* [Sabbath observant].

Igor may have been overdoing the bravado when we discussed his experience. Ernest's older brother, also a veteran of the IDF who had returned from Israel to Sarajevo to complete a master's degree, fled in the middle of the night before he was arrested for refusing to serve in the BiH army.

It is not only among Bosniacs that the blurred boundary between (Bosnian) Jews and Israelis provokes reassessment of Sarajevo's philo-Semitism. If in the FBiH sympathies rest with Palestinian civilians and against the Israeli Defense Force, in the RS Serbs may express disappointment and anger that the Jews and the State of Israel did not rally to their support.

In 2002, in response to my question as to why she and her family left their Sarajevo apartment for the Republika Srpska, Gordana, the attorney turned café owner whom we met in chapter 3, told me of her fear of Muslim brutality and added, "You should know; it's the same as you in Israel." In June 2004, much the same thing happened when I met with two spokesmen from the SDS, the ruling Serbian Democratic Party in Pale. I began our conversation by asking R. and B. to explain their party's platform. They replied by describing the barbarism of the Muslims. Instead of describing their party's platform, they drew analogies between my people and theirs:

> R.: You're a Jew. You must know then that we Serbs and you Jews are very much alike. Your people lost six million during the Second World War. One and a half million Serbs were killed in the Second World War too. Serbs and Jews are very much alike; we have both

suffered a lot, and we are both European civilizations surrounded by enemies. Israel is in the same kind of problem as we are: a civilized, European nation with problems. Israel, Cyprus, Malta, and Lebanon, at least during the time of the French, have been civilized European nations, part of Europe, as are we Serbs.

F.M.: I suggest that the problems of the Serbs and Israel are not the same. Israel is a new state and an old nation, and the Jews faced a different population living on the land, using it and claiming it as their own when they returned, as some say, colonized, as others say, during the nineteenth and twentieth centuries. Serbs have always lived here along with other ethno-religious groups.

R.: You are an old people with a new state. We are an old state with new people: mixed languages, mixed peoples [here he grimaces]. And you have a strong Diaspora to help Israel. In America alone, there are 15 million Jews, the richest group in America.

F.M.: 15 million? 5 million!

R. and B.: 15 million, yes, 15 million. And the most influential. And the richest, Kissinger, Rockefeller.

F.M.: Rockefeller? He was Protestant!

Shut up, I silently tell myself: *This is an ethnographic moment!*

B.: Rockefeller, Kissinger, the richest and most powerful in America. A strong lobbying force with great influence. And the Greeks have 10 million beyond their borders to influence politics. There are only 3 million Serbs, and they don't help.

F.M.: Why don't they help?

B.: Here there was communism, state terrorism; they don't know how to help.

R.: We had the Turks here and then communism. There was a list of five people, and those were the five people who got elected. One party. We like this multiparty system, that everything will be clear and clean after Dayton, now the people can chose who they want with no *lopovi* [thieves; villains]. The people can see the names and they can choose.

F.M. (again): Would you now tell me about the party platform of SDS?

B. and/or R. (exasperated): How can it be that you as a Jew do not understand? How many we lost in the First World War and then in World War II, in Jasenovac during the fascist [Croat] state. The Ustaše, that's who killed these Serbs. In Jasenovac, 700,000 Serbs from BiH, and 50,000 of them children, children! And this was only fifty years ago. Serbs need the RS as our security, to protect ourselves. It is our only security against this aggression. You are a Jew. In 1940 there were 12,000 Jews in Sarajevo. And how many are there today?

F.M.: Maybe 1,000.

B./R.: And do you know who killed them? Croats and Muslims. This was a catastrophe. Our peoples have shared together in suffering.

And so, while there is truth to Jakob Finci's point that the Serbs invoke a common suffering with the Jews, they also—or at least these particular Serbs—express frustration that the wealthier, more powerful Jewish nation has not supported their side. This frustration can find expression in more traditional, anti-Semitic ways.

On April 9, 2004, Good Friday for Catholic and Orthodox Christians and the first Sabbath after the Passover seders, instead of starting the Shabbat service immediately, David Kamhi announced that on BiH Radio-1 he had heard an Orthodox priest state in his explanation of their Easter holiday that the Jews killed their God, Jesus Christ. David told his minyan, for there were more than ten men this evening, "We must not remain quiet! This is our public radio station of BiH. We must write a letter to send to the general editor of the radio station and to the minister of culture. We must not remain quiet!" Much discussion followed; agreeing that silence was out of the question, all the men told David to write the letter and they would sign. A white-haired man in front of me added that two years ago on a public BiH television program a discussion went like this: "During the 1930s, there was Catholic fascism in Spain and in the 1940s in Croatia. Our last war was due to the Orthodox fascism of those Serbs. And today Israel is an example of Jewish fascism." David ends the discussion by pounding his fist onto the table and telling his congregants, "Now we must pray!"

But the conversation resumed over dinner. David asked me if I had heard of the *Protocols of the Elders of Zion.*[15] "Do you know where this book was most recently published? In Belgrade, two years ago! The Catholics, no, they are not spreading this scandal anymore; their pope took care of that. But not the Serbian Orthodox." A few days later, I saw that libelous book in one of Sarajevo's leading bookstores, published, as David noted, in Belgrade, 2002.

In his latest book, Arjun Appadurai (2006) has delineated a seemingly universal "fear of small numbers." He claims that in contemporary nation-states, ethnic minorities' "movements, mixtures, cultural styles and media representations create profound doubts about who exactly are among the 'we' and who are among the 'they'" (5). Similarly, Zygmunt Bauman (1998) looks specifically at the uncertain position of European Jews. As strangers who came to stay, these Jews became part of the citizenry but remain excluded from the nation. The Jews thereby represent an irritating in-between-ness and provoke the question: Are they with us, or against us, and how do we know for sure?

During the 1992–95 Bosnian war, several Jewish men took up arms to fight on the side of independent Bosnia-Herzegovina. The official stance of the Jewish community, however, was neutrality and a commitment to assist everyone in need of food, medical care, medicines, and communication with the outside world. A decade after the war ended, that stance is being reassessed. Some, like Moric's Muslim friend, continue to laud the Jews for their humanitarianism. Others, however, may interpret their neutral stance as a statement of noninvolvement, a message that although they live in Sarajevo, they are not of Sarajevo and that their allegiance is elsewhere. Kemal Bakaršić, BiH's leading authority on the Sarajevo Haggadah and avid collector of Sephardic music, told me in 2004 that the Jewish community's biggest mistake was in declaring that "this war was not [their] concern." The Jews, he believed, ought to have declared their allegiance to independent, Bosniac-led Bosnia and publicly condemned the "bigger evil" of the other side.

The Jews' neutral stance, even in times of peace, can cause anxiety; it can be read not as neutrality at all but as an ingenious cover for their (innate or ultimate) duplicity. While Bosniacs, Croats, and Serbs each claim connections to Bosnia's Jews, the refusal of those Jews to stand exclusively with them provokes the question: What are you really? Are you indeed Ostali, beyond the pale of B-C-S categorization? And if so, whose Jews will you be if forced to choose?

And yet Sarajevo's Jews, as a people of history and as a contemporary community, can also provide a way out of the divisive obstacles plaguing the country. In their biological as well as cultural connections to all the groups that comprise Bosnia, the Jews symbolize and embody *bosanski način,* a distinctly Bosnian cosmopolitanism manifested in the overlapping heterogeneity and hybridity of its population, its architecture, and its traditions.

My young friend Amar voiced that very sentiment just about every time we got together. "What I don't like about the Jewish population is that almost all of them who left during the war stayed in Israel or went to the United States. There isn't even a rabbi in Sarajevo, and it shouldn't be like that. Jews have been a part of Sarajevo for five hundred years. Lots of Jews survived World War II, hidden by their Croatian and Muslim neighbors." One day, in the middle of these declarations, he interrupted himself to ask if I knew the story of the Sarajevo Haggadah.[16] "Go ahead and tell me," I responded, and this is what he said:

> I like this story very much because to me it is typical of everything good in Sarajevo. The Sarajevo Haggadah was not printed here in Sarajevo but was brought here from Spain by a Jewish family. For centuries it was in the home of a rich Jewish Sarajevo family. Somehow it ended up at the beginning of the twentieth century at the shop of a Muslim merchant in the Čaršija who did not know its value. The Austrians bought it up for a cheap price for the new museum that they were building in Sarajevo. They sent it off to Vienna to have its worth assessed. For years it went missing, misplaced somewhere among all the artifacts, until it was found years later in some cupboard where it had been placed when it was sent back to Sarajevo to the museum. Then the Nazis came, and they heard about the Haggadah, and they, who were stealing all valuables, wanted it. The director of the museum, who was a Croat, said to the Nazi who came demanding it that another German had already come for it and took it. Meanwhile, he had given it to a Muslim friend, who buried it under the floor of a mosque, and that's where it was all during World War II. Then it was returned to the museum. Two days before the bombardment of Sarajevo, it was put in the safe of the National Bank, you know, the place on Tito Street, and it spent all the war years there. Now it is back in the museum. I love that story because to me it expresses the spirit of the Balkans, the spirit of Bosnia.

With this story, Amar was saying that the Sarajevo Haggadah and the Jews of Sarajevo belong to all of us, to the entire city of Sarajevo, and to Bosnia-Herzegovina. All the people of the region are bound together through the Bosnian way, which involves mutual responsibility, a bit of trickery, a lot of tolerance, and respect. It seems that many Sarajevans agree with Amar because in advance of Passover 2008 the Radić publishing house brought out a new, beautiful version of the Sarajevo Haggadah with translation and commentary in Bosnian and English.

The story of the Haggadah meshes with the story of "Sarajevo Purim" told to me by Klara: In every age there are mean and powerful people who wish to bring harm on the Jews, but most Bosnians, be they Catholic, Muslim, or Orthodox, Bosniac, Croat, or Serb, will rally to protect the Jews who are part of the common heritage, who are part of "us."

But, I think to myself, over 90 percent of Sarajevo's Jews perished in the Holocaust or fled in its wake. Can the Jews trust Bosnia's constituent nations

18. The Sarajevo Haggadah

to include them as an integral part of the independent state? Doesn't the ambiguous Ostali status put them at risk?

I conclude this chapter by recounting one last incident, this time from a Friday evening toward the end of July 2004. That day was noteworthy because, finally, the Jewish Museum in the Old Temple reopened. There were more than enough congregants to form a minyan, and spirits were high. At the conclusion of the festive meal as I left the pink brick synagogue, one of the older men stopped me. He asked me if I speak Spanish. When I hesitated, he continued in Bosnian: "I just want you to know that I was here during the entire war. Bosnia is my homeland. Sarajevo is my homeland. The Bosnian people are my people. During the Second World War, Muslim neighbors hid me and my family and three other Jewish families as well. When the war came, I volunteered to serve in the BiH army. It's my land; it's my people. Yes, my children are in Austria, in Graz. It's better for them there. Not for me. This is my land, my people."

7

Insisting on Bosnia-Herzegovina

Bosnian Hybridity

Bosnia-Herzegovina has always been a contact zone. As we read in chapter 1, Noel Malcolm notes that "[t]he great religions and great powers of European history had overlapped and combined there: the empires of Rome, Charlemagne, the Ottomans and the Austro-Hungarians, and the faiths of Western Christianity, Eastern Christianity, Judaism and Islam" (1996, xix). Like other border regions, it was a place where people of varied religions and ethnic backgrounds lived together, sometimes as rivals, sometimes as friends; sometimes as equals, sometimes in relationships of dominance and subordination; sometimes in multicultural harmony, and sometimes in discord (Bringa 1995; Donia and Fine 1994; Lockwood 1975; cf. Ballinger 2003, 2004; Berdahl 1999; Green 2005; Rosaldo 1989; Wilson and Donnan 1998).

Accompanying this variety, the people(s) of Bosnia-Herzegovina have always been united linguistically through mutually intelligible South Slav dialects (Grubišić 2003; Okey 2004) and culturally in their common reliance on a system of meanings based on everyday encounters with one another (Bringa 1995; Karahasan 1993; Mahmutćehajić 2003; Pejanović 2004; Tanović-Miller 2001). Valuing the plurality of experience in a world where Catholic and Orthodox Christianity, Islam, Judaism, and socialist modernity all manifest themselves in the landscape, in family rituals and in public celebrations, in nuances of language, and in people's belongings is what many Sarajevans describe when they invoke the spirit of their city or the soul of Bosnia. To live the Bosnian way means being surrounded in one's personal environment by a range of human possibilities, respectful of differences and appreciative of their overlaps (Lovrenović 2001, 209; Weine 2000, 405). And although in

Yugoslavia it was never officially recognized as a category of national affiliation, an all-inclusive, pan-ethnic Bosnian identity was frequently expressed and experienced in daily practices, in anecdotes and conversation, and in song (Denich 2000, 40; Hayden 2000, 122; Woodward 1995, 36; cf. Kržišnik Bukić 1997; Magaš 2003).

A prime aim of the 1992–95 war was to purge the persons, artifacts, and records that attest to the region's crazy-quilt pattern of religions and ethnicities and to erase the biological and cultural results of their mergers. Targeted as more dangerous to the goals of ethnic cleansing than clearly defined members of opposing nations, the first war casualties were couples in mixed marriages who identified as Yugoslavs (Jansen 2005, 47; Nederveen Pieterse 2001, 234). In besieged Sarajevo, armed aggressors bombed centuries-old cultural landmarks and incinerated one-of-a-kind manuscripts in their attempt to blot out the city's vibrant history of diversity and overlaps: "The very pluralism of culture and religion which Bosnia had in its fairly simple way managed to achieve . . . had been used to undermine its specific identity" (Hastings 1997, 40).

At the same time, although their city was forcibly divided, shelled, and under siege, thousands of Sarajevans steadfastly went about their daily lives convinced that through these actions they would maintain the human dignity and respect for difference that had always characterized their lifestyle. They kept diaries, took photographs, attended the theater, held conferences and concerts, made films and wrote memoirs to document how the cosmopolitan spirit of Sarajevo united its residents in the face of divisive propaganda and unspeakable suffering (see, e.g., Dizdarević 1994; Filipovic 1994; Kurspahić 1997; Tanović-Miller 2001). Others published cultural histories (Lovrenović 2001) and philosophical essays attesting to the "pluriformity" of Sarajevo's overlapping ethno-religious groups (Karahasan 1993; Mahmutćehajić 2000, 2003) that shared an inclusive Bosnian identity (Kržišnik Bukić 1997). These books and essays, as well as public discussion forums provided proof that the violent hewing of three incommensurable nations from one population was not the inevitable result of history.[1] They suggested instead that the war was externally instigated and betrayed Bosnia's centuries-long tradition of heterogeneity and hybridity (see chapter 3).

With the signing of the Dayton Peace Accords and the constitution that derived from them, wartime goals of dividing the citizenry according to ethnicity became accomplished facts, which silenced the commonalities that had united the region's inhabitants. In its declaration that the BiH state is constituted of three incommensurable rights-vested nations, those mixed-ethnic, pan-ethnic, or nonethnic Bosnians who managed to survive the war were sidelined, if not written out of history. Lumped together with all the now unnamed minorities into the parenthetical, residual category of Others, Bosanci have been rendered invisible and just about unimaginable (Hayden 1996, 783).[2]

As we have seen in chapters 3 and 4, a decade of administrative practices deriving from the Dayton Accords has stifled expression of Bosnia's cosmopolitan histories and transcultural experiences by bolstering the popular historiographies that underlie the B-C-S scheme. Trinational divisions inform daily newspaper articles and guide the writing of school textbooks, the shaping of curricula, and the establishment of educational institutions; they drive the publication of mutually exclusive Bosnian, Croatian, and Serbian dictionaries, shape census categories, and determine citizens' identities. Their unremitting repetition—in government forms, in legal documents, in university bylaws, in the media, and in everyday conversations—reinforces an increasingly accepted and acceptable way of defining self and other. It sends one unwavering message throughout Bosnia-Herzegovina: although there may be an internationally recognized Bosnian state, there are no Bosnian people, and there is no Bosnian nation (Tanović-Miller 2001, 5).

Several commentators, within Bosnia as well as from without, have gone so far as to suggest that Sarajevans' cosmopolitanism and multiplicity of perspectives were demolished in the war's aftermath, if not by the war itself (Kampschror 2001; Lovrenović 2001, 210; Mertus 2000, 239; Simmons 2001). Noting the continuous, unchallenged electoral success of BiH's three major nationalist parties, most recently anthropologist Robert M. Hayden (2007) questioned whether there has ever been a "'Bosnian tradition' of tolerance."

Focusing on what Sarajevans do and say, I argue in this chapter that despite its hardening hegemony, in everyday activities an eclectic Bosnianness, as expressed in the words *Bosanci* (Bosnians) and *Bosanski/Bosanska* (Bosnian), emerges as a salient, but never simple, experiential challenge to the B-C-S scheme. By highlighting hybridity in Sarajevo, I seek to restore some ethnographic balance to the picture of Bosnia that has emerged since the signing of the Dayton Accords. That aim is neither naive nor morally neutral. It is motivated by the same sentiments that Paul Gilroy asserts in staking his place between camps, where he tries "to place a higher value upon the cosmopolitan histories and transcultural experiences whereby enlightenment aspirations might eventually mutate in the direction of greater inclusivity and thus greater authority" (2004, 7).

But let me be clear: in suggesting that invocations of Bosnian hybridity are not merely nostalgic longings but part of contemporary Sarajevans' practices, expressions, and identities, I am not denying that these are often quashed in

19. A display of "100% Bosnian" T-shirts for sale in the Baščaršija

their confrontations with an increasingly entrenched knowledge and power scheme that requires everyone and everything to be reduced to what they "really" are—Serb, Croat, or Bosniac.

I begin this chapter by presenting those Sarajevans who, despite the state's refusal to recognize their identity claims, insist that they are Bosanci. In that they receive no official recognition, self-declared Bosnians are embroiled in a highly asymmetrical dialogue with all those B-C-S persons who carry with them officially condoned histories, identities, and institutions. Yet it is from within that very imbalance that Bosanci send a provocative message that transcultural experiences and the transgressive vision of a hybrid nation-state are no less part of Bosnia-Herzegovina than the constitutionally sanctioned split of the country into three constituent nations.

That argument is extended in the next section as we explore what I call Sarajevo's practical hybridity. By "practical hybridity," I mean the enactment of a culturally mixed Bosnianness by Serbs, Croats, Bosniacs, and Others as they willingly or unwittingly create, participate in, and reinforce common spaces of shared experience, the *zajednički život,* or common life (Filipović 2007; Pejanović 2004). Sometimes Sarajevans overtly recognize and name certain persons and things as Bosnian. Sometimes hybridity is treated as part of the "natural" backdrop of their city, where it is ignored precisely because it is taken for granted (Nederveen Pieterse 2001). And sometimes, even when smelled, touched, and tasted, like a tiny cup of Bosnian coffee, or heard and pronounced, like the regional intonations that define (otherwise Serb, Croat, or Bosniac) speakers as Bosnians, it is disputed or denied.

Which leads to the third part of the chapter, in which, informed by a key assertion of Michael Herzfeld's *Cultural Intimacy* (1997a) that official nation-state discourse and popular, contradictory practices mutually reinforce the notion that "the nation must always be one and indivisible" (25), I ponder the (im)possibility of a modern, European state constituted by a hybrid nation. Slippery, flexible, and ever-changing, hybridity is both a threat and a promise that fuels, while it battles, state consolidation and the nation-building projects of Serbs, Croats, and Bosniacs in Bosnia-Herzegovina.

"Jesam Bosanac": Insisting on Bosnian Hybridity

Mehmet Zaimović, one of Sarajevo's most renowned artists, describes himself as a Bosnian. The curvaceous shapes and muted colors that make his artwork so remarkable derive, he says, from the landscapes of Bosnia, the green villages of his youth and the war-torn Sarajevo of his middle years. When we met in his atelier in June 2004, Zaimović was reconstructing a bullet-riddled painting that he had completed before the war, but my immediate reaction to that punctured canvas was that it depicted the war. "No," he told me after describing the sniper fire that had shattered his windows and ripped his pictures, "that is not my way. It is not the Bosnian way."[3]

Mehmet Zaimović's name tells those who wish to know that he is "really" a Bosniac, but Zaimović himself insists that he is "really" a Bosnian, a product of the region, its multiethnic history and intercultural blendings. The cupolas of Orthodox churches and the right-angled crosses of the Catholics are as integral to his artistic vision as the dome of a mosque and its towering minarets. Likewise the rivers, mountains, and valleys of Bosnia's countryside mesh with the cityscape of Sarajevo. One without the other leaves him incomplete, just as a Bosniac national affiliation fails to express the inclusiveness of how Zaimović relates to the people of the region and to the entirety of his country.

Such is also the case with Hasan and Mirzana, a middle-aged couple with deep roots in Sarajevo. During my visits, they described the reality of *bratstvo i jedinstvo* in socialist Yugoslavia, when their wide circle of friends and family once included—and still includes—people from all religions, ethnic groups, and walks of life, "all Yugoslavs, all Bosnians." They refuse to engage in nationalist politics and since the early 1990s have voted consistently for the Socialist Democratic Party (SDP). Considered the heir to the Yugoslav League of Communists, the SDP eschews ethnic nationalism and distributes a portrait of Tito with its yearly calendar. Hasan, who served all four years as a frontline soldier in the Bosnian army, and Mirzana describe that war as a tragedy: "Look, the same coalition of [nationalist] parties that brought us into that war in 1992 are in power today." For them the only logical solution to Bosnia's woes is to embrace the region's rich, culturally mixed past and build a BiH state of all its citizens.

That vision is at the heart of the tiny Citizens' Party, led by Ibrahim Spahić, who has directed the Sarajevo Winter Festival since its inception in 1984. In March 2004, Spahić described to me his early years "in the center of the city, among churches, mosques and synagogues," where he attended the First Gimnazija with all kinds of students, "Jews, Croats, Serbs, Muslims, intercultural." He told me that for its first one hundred years that school, which educated Nobel prize winner Ivo Andrić and other great Yugoslav writers, was taught neither in Croatian or Serbian but in the Bosnian language; "That was our history." Even now, after the war and under the dominance of the nationalist political parties, Spahić insists, "There are many, many people here who feel part of a broader Bosnian identity." But he adds that they have no way to express their unity because Bosnia is not yet a confident civil society. He has a plan for restoring the "spirit of Bosnia" by establishing five or six economic regions that will link cities with their hinterlands and cross ethnic divides. Although it is a ways off, Spahić insists that with BiH territorially united and "a united democratic citizenry, where all three peoples and minorities have the same rights, a tolerant and confident Bosnian identity will arise."

In 2004, Haris Silajdžić, whom we met in chapter 3, was not as sure, although the political party that he leads, Stranka za BiH, proclaims that very goal in its name. A year after the war's end, Silajdžić broke with Alija Izetbegović's governing party, the SDA, and formed his own Party for Bosnia-Herzegovina. When I asked him why, he replied that he did not want to live in an Islamic state (see Bougarel 2007 for a discussion of Islamicization in wartime Bosnia). But he did not leave it at that; Silajdžić explained in long and passionate detail that he is a Bosniac and that Bosniacs are Europeans who have always embraced a very tolerant, almost secular form of Islam. "I am a Bosniac, a Bosnian, and a European," he continued. "Could these identities be ranked or nested one inside the other?" I asked. Silajdžić rejected the idea of ranking, but he did agree that they could be viewed as increasingly large circles of belonging.

Silajdžić was not optimistic, however, about the chances of a unified Bosnia in the short run. Chastised by "the Americans" in 1996 for forming his Party for Bosnia-Herzegovina and advocating one state without the entities too soon after the hard-fought Dayton Accords, Silajdžić seems to have accepted as expedient the solution of an ethnically split Bosnia-Herzegovina. Several other not-nationalist politicians moved back and forth like Silajdžić in their use of the terms *Bošnjak* and *Bosanac* as they expressed longings for Bosnia as a unified state of all its citizens while accepting the current situation as the lesser of evils. That sentiment was voiced as well by an official spokesman for the SDA during our meeting in 2004. Responding to my surprise at hearing him use the inclusive *Bosanci* when describing the SDA's platform, he reminded me that the late Alija Izetbegović had always advocated one Bosnian state for all of Bosnia's multiethnic citizens.

In fact, at the last SDA congress before his death, Izetbegović and several supporters responded to the sentiments of part of their constituency by putting forth a motion to recognize Bosnians as a nation, that is, as an official rights-vested constituent group. The October 6, 2001, *Oslobodjenje* article describing this event captured the ambivalence surrounding such a move (Kalamujić 2001). It reported that while the initiative might call for a slight amendment of the DPA, recognition of the Bosnian nation would not change its basic terms or sabotage the national identities of Serbs, Croats, or Bosniacs. The rest of the article, however, presented comments from three prominent scholars whose names mark them as Bosniac, Serb, and Croat. Each warned that the establishment of what was provocatively called in the headline "Nadnacija Bosanaca," a supernation of Bosnians, was premature and dangerous. SDA leaders then rethought their position and agreed with other government decision makers not to nominate the *Bosanska nacija* into existence via the 2002 FBiH census or in any other way.

Lack of an inclusive Bosnian category leaves many Sarajevans frustrated, including those whose names lead others to define them as Serbs or Croats. Soon after the war began, Mirjana, who hails from a prominent Sarajevo merchant family, was dismissed from her position as a professor of dentistry at Sarajevo University for no reason other than her Serb name. Rather than accede to this discriminatory measure by moving to the Srpska Republika or leaving the country altogether, Mirjana became engaged in human rights work. She also launched a lawsuit to regain her position, which she ultimately won. Thinking over her refusal to capitulate to nationalism, Mirjana told me in July 2004 that Sarajevo is her only home. She described it as "not multicultural or multiethnic, but rather, interlaced and interlocked. That's what the aggression of this last war tried to destroy, this kind of tolerance and diversity." Her decision to remain with her family in Sarajevo, along with other Serbs, Croats, Bosniacs, and Others who once were and still can be intermixed as Bosnians demonstrates a lived-in hope that the city's intercommunal space and its eclectic Bosnianness have not been destroyed.

Twenty-six-year-old Asja M. is an art historian who is devoting her energies to establish an international museum of contemporary art in Sarajevo. She has taken a leading role in this project because she believes that by joining in a cosmopolitan conversation, her city has a chance to transcend regional politics, prod its citizens toward embracing their own transcultural creativity, and burst out of constricting ethnic entanglements. Yet as soon as she expressed optimism for the future, Asja returned to the frustrations of the present—obtaining funds and building permits for the museum and combating what she calls, "the making of truth from an untruth that Bosnia is comprised of three different peoples." She says of herself: "I'm Bosnian. . . . When that census interviewer came, I told her that I am Bosnian. Then she asked, 'But what are you really?' I told her that this is who I am. Really. 'And if you can't put me down as Bosnian, then list me as American—I lived there for six years. If I can't be Bosnian,' I told her, 'American is second best in saying who I am and what I stand for.' Just because my great-great-great-great grandparents came centuries ago from Serbia doesn't make me a Serb."

Rejecting "blood" or genealogy for the hybridity of place, Asja identifies with a history and territory that demonstrate the blending of traditions. Like Mehmet Zaimović, Asja insists that the origins or religion of her ancestors should not and will not determine her own belongings. And although these belongings are not recognized, she continues to assert them, even to representatives of the state.

The situation is somewhat different for people whose awareness of their mixed bloodlines, names, and proclivities places them outside the B-C-S scheme. Klara's daughter, Nataša, passionately maintains that she can only identify as Bosnian. "I am Bosnian: My mom's father was a Jew, and his wife was a Croatian Catholic who helped him when he was exiled during World War II to the island of Hvar. My father is a Bosniac. I am everything—and that's what Bosnia and the Bosnians are all about. I have some friends who ignore one side and just declare themselves Bosniac or Croat or Serb. How can they do that? It's betraying who you really are." Having returned to contribute the knowledge and experience she gained abroad to rebuild Sarajevo, Nataša is bothered that the Bosnianness that, as she puts it, pervades the air that she breathes, the language that she speaks, and how she thinks of herself is not officially recognized. In describing herself as much more than the sum of her parts, she claims that neither she nor her country can be reduced to the categorical demands of state.

On May 22, 2004, a letter to the editor of *Oslobodjenje* from Mladen of Canada said much the same thing. Published under the headline "Sarajlilja i Bosanac" (A Sarajevan and a Bosnian), it stated: "I support the theory that Bosnia is Bosnian, and that Bosnians are not only Bosniacs. I am Montenegrin through my father and a (Bosnian) Serb through my mother, but it is Bosnia that I view as mine, like all that I love, because I was born and raised there. . . . In this chaos over identity, I view myself as a Sarajevan and a Bosnian. I am now living in Canada, but Bosnia is and forever will be my homeland" (my translation).

This "chaos over identity," as we have seen in previous chapters, has driven many talented people out of Sarajevo, where they feel that their hybrid identity is incompatible with demands of nation and state. Nadja, who described her late husband as "half-Jewish, half-Catholic" and herself as "from a Muslim family," told me that despite surviving the siege of Sarajevo together as Bosnians, her son left abruptly within a year after the war's end. Why? "Because of a name." She explained, "His name is Igor. A Russian name. All of a sudden because of that name some friends stopped being his friends. His girlfriend stopped being his girlfriend. He said he could not live like that, and he left. Now he is married—to an American Korean girl. A lovely girl, beautiful, wonderful." Back in the 1970s, when Nadja and her husband named their two children, they believed that they had selected beautiful, international names. And they were not alone (Donia and Fine 1994, 185). Often, but not always, foreign or generic names were given to children of mixed marriages, who usually "thought of themselves as Yugoslavs or Bosnians without ethnic allegiances" (186).

In post-Dayton, Bosniac-majority Sarajevo, however, these names provoke new questions. Those with generic names like Asja, Damir, and Goran may be asked, "But what are you really?" to clarify their ethnic background (see chapter 4). Others, with Russian names, like the intermixed Bosnian children of Muslim Nadja and her Jewish-Catholic husband, may be perceived and treated negatively as Serb. Unable to accept those conditions, Igor left for the United States to recapture the respect for pluralism that he had once experienced in Sarajevo (cf. Sorabji 2006, 8–9). With his marriage and the birth of his first child, he has added to the hybrid mix.

Una is the daughter of a Serb mother and a Bosniac father, but both identified as Yugoslavs and lived their lives as such. As a child, Una spent summers at her Serb grandparents' beach house on the Montenegrin coast, and that is where she was with her cousins and an aunt during the first years of the Bosnian war. In 1994 during a truce period, Una's mother came to get her, and they left for Canada. Her father joined them there after the war. In Vancouver her parents built a large network of friends and were able to do what they believe is no longer possible in Sarajevo—be Bosnians or Yugoslavs and socialize with like-minded people guided by *bratstvo i jedinstvo.*

After completing her BA in 2001, Una returned to Sarajevo to pursue a master's degree. She was offered a job at the university and has stayed, but because she is troubled by the ethnic divisions in her family as well as throughout the country, Una did not know how much longer she will last. When I met with her in 2004, Una reminisced about huge holiday gatherings during her childhood when both sides of the family came together to eat, drink, and socialize. These events no longer take place. The relatives have scattered; on her mother's side, those who have not emigrated now live east of Sarajevo in the Srpska Republika. As regards her father:

> His family has always been of the Muslim faith, but both my parents identified as Yugoslav atheists. My dad never swerved from that view, and even now, two years ago when he came back and was dying, he asked me and my mom to promise that he would be buried in a mixed cemetery with no religious rites. "Make sure they don't make me a *hodža* [an Islamic cleric]," he said, if you know what I mean. And we buried him as he wished with a small family ceremony and a black marble slab on which only his name and the dates of his birth and death are written. . . . Both brothers changed, came closer to Islam. But not my father. He stayed a communist and an atheist.

Una paused, rhetorically asked, "And what identity am I?" and then answered:

> I have several at several different levels, and with each I am happy, and I don't have problems with any of them. I am from here—from Bosnia-Herzegovina-ex-Yugoslavia, and a Canadian, and a woman, first of all. . . . I was born here but then went to a small town in Herzegovina with my parents until age seven,

> when we came to Sarajevo. . . . I started grade 12 in Sarajevo, which I finished in Canada, which makes me Canadian. I don't have a strong Sarajevo identity or any kind of strong ethnic identity. When I have to fill in those forms that ask who you are, are you Bosniac, Croat, or Serb, I write BiH because I truly don't see myself in any other way. Sometimes now these forms also offer you Ostali, but they tell you that this category is reserved for Jews and Roma and others like that. None of these categories fits me. And I won't choose Ostali because I don't want to be other when I'm from here.

Una's mother refuses to leave Canada, where she has re-created a lifestyle and an identity that eludes her in her hometown. Una is unsure where her future lies, but she would certainly be more likely to remain in Sarajevo if BiH conferred recognition on Bosnians and switched its orientation away from collective national rights toward the individual human rights of all its citizens.

Una and Nataša, Asja and Mehmet, and all those whose brief stories we have heard are not alone in that vision of Bosnia-Herzegovina and their self-declarations as Bosanci. Over the course of the postwar years, some 20 percent of those who married in Sarajevo's Centar Općina refused to pinpoint any one ethnicity to describe their belongings. Instead, they left the *nacionalna pripadnost* space blank or drew in a slash. Others declared to the county registry that they were Bosnians or BiH. Smaller numbers maintained that they were of an "undetermined" ethnicity or modified the B-C-S designations with Bosnian or BiH. A few, signaling ironic acceptance of that insider/outsider category, wrote in their ethnic affiliation as Ostali, while a couple or two simply wrote "a-national" or "human being" (see table 5).

Table 5. Bosnian and Undeclared Affiliations in Centar Općina Marriage Registration Data by Percentages

Designation	1996	1997	1999	2000	2002	2003
Left blank or —	8.3	11.0	13.0	12.5	12.2	10.7
Bosnian or BiH	5.9	7.6	8.0	8.2	8.3	6.1
Bosnian/BiH + B-C-S	0.4	0.2	0.4	0.3	0.1	0.4
Undetermined	0.1	0.4	—	0.5	0.5	0.5
Other label	0.1	—	0.3	0.2	—	—
Ostali	—	—	—	0.2	0.1	—
Catholic	0.1	0.5	0.4	0.2	0.4	0.3
Orthodox	0.2	0.3	—	0.1	0.1	—
Other religion*	0.2	0.2	0.3	0.2	0.2	0.1
Totals	15.3	20.2	22.4	22.4	21.4	18.1

* The religions listed were Islam (indexing religion rather than ethnicity), Hinduism, Evangelism, Jehovah's Witnesses, and Adventists.

Since at least the 1960s, many men and women have identified with a particularly Bosnian way of being in the world, but the Yugoslav, and now the Bosnian state, never officially recognized that identity. Despite expressed sentiments for a unifying regional or citizenship-based category of affiliation, as this book goes to press no political party, member of the BiH presidency, or member of parliament has suggested amending the constitution of Bosnia-Herzegovina to include Bosnians as a constituent national group. Table 5 shows that the proportion of Sarajevans who rejected the B-C-S triad at the Centar marriage registry peaked in 2000 and declined thereafter. Offering a unifying Bosnian alternative to the tripartite division that ended the war could upset this increasingly accepted and acceptable social reality. Perhaps, though, all it would do is add one more national element to an already split citizenry. Or it just might pave the way out of the country's morass.

Despite the war, the ethno-territorial divides, and the barely functional state, there are those who insist on a united and inclusive Bosnia-Herzegovina. Combining and overcoming what seem to be intractable national boundaries, Bosanci, like the Yugoslavs of an earlier time, embody the threat and the promise of a Muslim-Christian-Jewish-Bosniac-Croat-Serb-Other point of convergence in the heart of Europe. Thus, they persist on the streets, in prose, and in song, even as they remain off-census and uncounted. In spite of administrative practices and constitutional decrees aimed at making trinational Bosniac-Croat-Serb BiH experientially real as well as politically viable, the people of Sarajevo continue to engage dialectically with state-defined population categories as they question their own subjectivities and enact practical hybridity in their daily lives.

Practicing Bosnian Hybridity

During our hour-long conversation in July 2004, the president of Preporod, a major Bosniac cultural and philanthropic organization, stressed that the Bosniac nation has existed for centuries. Repeating that it is his and all Bosniacs' cultural responsibility to ensure their nation's continuity, Professor F. observed that although they were named and misnamed differently over time, today's Bosniacs are the same people and practice the same traditions as Bosnian Muslims throughout history.[4] Toward the end of our conversation, when I advanced the idea of pan-Bosnian hybridity, he agreed that yes, there is much common culture among the B-C-S groups, but those minimal differences—in painting, in literature, in cuisine, in language—must be preserved. He repeated what I had been reading and hearing for months, that the Muslims' carefree way of being in the world had put them at risk from their expansionist Serb and Croat neighbors, and concluded our discussion by insisting that, like every other nation, the Bosniacs have the right to define themselves as they see fit, take every opportunity to proclaim that identity, and ensure it for future generations. Then Professor F. handed me a large picture book as a parting gift. Published by Preporod, the volume's title, *Bosanskohercegovačka grafika,* as well as the pictures displayed between its covers, testifies to the cultural overlaps and blendings that are manifested, at the very least, in the ideas and images of the ethnically varied artists of Bosnia-Herzegovina.

This incident is just one among many that illustrate how hegemony—the convergence of ideas, rules, and institutional practices that reinforces, indeed "naturalizes," social categories and cultural demands—complicates the relationships between people, their culture, and their identity (Williams 1977). Although Bosniacs, Croats, and Serbs throughout BiH may be doing the same things, speaking the same language, and harboring similar ambitions, many articulate an exclusive national identity by stressing intergroup differences over commonalities (Bose 2002, 194–200; Bringa 1995, 78–84; Ignatieff 1993, 22) and voting for nationalist parties (Donia 2006, 352; Hayden 2007). Nonetheless, a wide array of Sarajevans, including spokespersons for Bosniac, Croat, and Serb organizations, vividly described to me the circle of mixed ethnic friends to which they (once) belong(ed). Like Dubravko Horvat, the president of the Sarajevo branch of the Croatian nationalist party, whose first wife was a Muslim and whose current wife is a Serb, they commented, "Tako je kod nas." Hybridity, so what? An eclectic Bosnianness may be all around, in the most intimate regions of home and family; it might even be part of each of us. But as the recent war and international efforts to end it have shown, hybrid cultures, mixed populations, and flexible identities do not amount to much. Blurring or ignoring the differences that separate Bosniacs, Croats, and Serbs, they imply, is what caused the trouble in the first place.

Be that as it may, there are several "things," such as the graphic arts displayed in the volume published by Preporod, that Sarajevans, whether Bosniacs, Croats, Serbs, or Others, uniformly refer to as Bosnian. Four that come immediately to mind are Bosnian stew, Bosnian coffee, Bosnian houses, and the Bosnian way. None of these has a Bosniac, Croat, or Serb counterpart; they come only in hybrid form. Let us look at each in turn.

Bosnian stew is comprised of slow-simmered meats and roasted vegetables. It is prepared in a large, preferably ceramic vessel, which gives the stew its name, *bosanski lonac.* Variety is essential to the dish; any and every kind of meat, vegetable, and spice can go into the pot. Each ingredient contributes its juice to the dish's overall taste while retaining its own color, texture, and flavor.[5] Yet no one ingredient is mandatory, and the various stews made by people of varied means, persuasions, and preferences are all Bosnian. Pork, for example, may or may not be used; the same is true of beef, veal, or goat meat, eggplant, peppers, okra, or beans. In making use of the vegetables of the season and whatever meat is at hand, Bosanski lonac is always open to experimentation and difference. Listed as a "national specialty" on menus throughout BiH, Bosanski lonac is also a standard dish at Yugoslav restaurants worldwide.

Unlike Bosnian stew, which can differ from one preparation to the next depending on what is available and who is doing the cooking, Bosnian coffee has nothing to do with variety. It is uniformly prepared by stirring roughly ground coffee beans into a beaten metal beaker of boiling water called a *džezva*. Once the grounds settle, the coffee is poured into a tiny bowl-like porcelain cup (*findžan*) and sipped black with plenty of sugar. At many restaurants and in some homes, it is accompanied by a jellied sweet called *rahatlokum*, or Turkish delight. Some Sarajevans prefer to drink their coffee from demitasses nestled in saucers and with the cream cakes or strudel that entered BiH with the expansion of the Austro-Hungarian Empire. Others skip the sweets and smoke a cigarette. But no matter how it is accompanied or in what kind of cup it is served, the coffee, whether pronounced *kava*, *kafa*, *kahva*, or *kavica*, is always Bosnian. There is simply no such thing as Serbian, Croatian, or Bosniac coffee.

Bosnian coffee remains ubiquitous, the standard at every Sarajevo café and restaurant and, I daresay, in most homes. But at the supermarket, Bosanska kava vies with instant coffee produced in Germany or in the United States and at the cafés with pricier cups of espresso and *kapučino* (cappuccino) that come hissing out of imported machines. At the Baščaršija, pounded copper coffee sets are sold more as souvenirs than as everyday household implements. Some Sarajevans use plain metal or enamel-coated beakers to prepare their coffee. They place their handmade sets on display, as part of the home decor, and use them only on special occasions.

Bosnian houses, like the Inat Kuća (*kuća* means house) described in chapter 5, are characterized by a whitewashed plaster exterior that is trimmed, terraced, roofed, and fenced in dark wood. To Western European eyes, they look, perhaps, like a smaller, flatter version of a Swiss chalet with English Tudor details. Muslims traditionally preferred square-shaped houses, whereas Christians built theirs on a rectangular base, but both groups used the same whitewash and wood trim (Bringa 1995, 39; Lockwood 1975). Among the ornately sculpted facades of nineteenth-century Central European apartment buildings and the more massive late-twentieth-century high-rises, one can still find Bosnian houses in central Sarajevo and in the surrounding *mahalas* (neighborhoods). I lived in one for a few months. But nowadays when people renovate older homes or build new ones, they have just about abandoned the wood trim that had always marked a house as Bosnian, and the distinctive, shared architecture of the region is being relegated to history.

Svrzina Kuća, built in the eighteenth century and enlarged in the nineteenth, was continuously occupied until the Svrzo family sold it in 1952 to the Museum of the City of Sarajevo. Curator Amra Madžarević writes in the museum's guide, "This house is a cultural monument, and one of the most beautiful residential buildings of its period in the Balkans, but sadly, it is also one of the very few that have been preserved in Bosnia and Herzegovina." Most new houses under construction in the outskirts of Sarajevo are built on a concrete foundation. Like most residences in northern Europe, they are sided in brick, but then they are roofed in the terra-cotta shingles that can be found throughout the circum-Mediterranean area. Perhaps this contemporary architectural blend of north and south will become known as the new, twenty-first-century form of the bosanska kuća.

If it seems that things Bosnian are restricted to comestibles and the material culture of the domestic domain, then *bosanski način* explodes that hypothesis. Sarajevans invoke the "Bosnian way" to designate an intangible air, style, or approach to life in much the same way that many Europeans would declare something *à la française*. But unlike the consistently sophisticated haute couture, haute cuisine, and urbanity conjured by the French *je ne sais quois*, bosanski način is sometimes used to credit Bosnians for being urbane and clever and sometimes mocks them as dim-witted bumpkins. Most often it combines the two, and in so doing displays the twists and contradictions of what Michael Herzfeld (1997a) calls the "cultural intimacy" that constitutes a unified and unifying national character out of diversity and incongruities.

In recent years, Sarajevans have mentioned bosanski način to index a local cosmopolitanism, their heartfelt appreciation for varied religious practices and cultural traditions. Eso, the secretary general of the VKBI, put it to me like this: "Bosnia, how to explain this to you? Maybe it's easier to explain to you as an American than to a European, the English or the French. Bosnia was always a conglomeration of four different religious confessions. Tolerance, always." Melisa, a graduate student in pre-Slavic history, also stressed that being Bosnian is all about the region's compatibility of difference. She

20. A Bosnian house in Marjindvor, where I lived during March and April 2004

was eleven years old when the war broke out and recalled, "Horrible things happened during that war. People, can you believe it, even sold humanitarian aid! But there is one picture I keep remembering from that war: One day I came home, and on the stoop leading up to the apartment house were three women cooking outside. They had stacked up some bricks on those steps and made a kind of stove. And there they were cooking their lunch together: a Muslim, a Serb, and a Croat. That's the Bosnian way."

Sanjin remembers growing up in a large apartment building during the 1980s. He noted that most of the time no one in that building paid much attention to ethnicity; no one was a stranger, nor were neighbors overly familiar. But on Muslim holidays, Serbs and Croats were careful not to shake out their carpets over open windows or to hang out the wash. Instead, they would stop by to offer congratulations and accept a drink and a sweet. Sanjin's family reciprocated at Christmas and Easter by refraining from household chores and paying brief visits to their Croat and Serb neighbors. Living the Bosnian way meant participation in an inherently "pluralistic, polyphonous, dialogical" culture (Karahasan 1993, 66).

Although perhaps in attenuated form, this Bosnian way of valuing each of the city's religious traditions continues. In early April 2004, the Museum of the City of Sarajevo reopened with an exhibit of Easter traditions, featuring a wide variety of colored eggs. At the same time, the newspaper *Oslobodjenje* was filled with dozens of announcements from FBiH governmental agencies, commercial firms, cultural organizations, and private individuals wishing first a "Happy Passover" to the Jewish community and then a "Happy Easter" to Catholic and Orthodox Christians, who, for the first time in forty years, were celebrating the holiday on the same date. On Easter Sunday morning, FTV—the public television station of the Bosniac-majority Federation—broadcast the Sarajevo Serbian Orthodox cathedral's Easter service from 9:00 until 10:30 A.M., which was followed by the Easter mass at Sarajevo's Catholic cathedral from 10:30 until noon.

In addition to standing for a regionwide appreciation for religious and cultural diversity, Sarajevans invoke the Bosnian way to express in one phrase the incongruous, everyday social practices that pervade their lives. Although urbanism is known for its fast pace and goal orientation, in Sarajevo, even in the middle of a busy workday, it is the norm to take time out to duck into a café and join a friend for coffee. Nothing is so pressing that it cannot wait, and the pleasures of sociability often take precedence over the tasks at hand. Several young people who had spent time in the United States, northwestern Europe, Canada, and Australia commented ruefully that nothing gets done in Bosnia because of the Bosnian way of sitting around, drinking coffee, telling jokes, and putting off to tomorrow what should be done today. In the next breath, many of these same people confided that although they were proud of the long hours they spend abroad in work and at their studies striving to accomplish something in life, they hated the cold individualism there and the hard and fast line that separates home from work, and each person from all others. Mak, for example, told me that he returns from the Netherlands to Sarajevo during summer vacation to hear his own language, see the people he knows, and enjoy Sarajevo's relaxed sociability. Then he immediately added that he can stay in Sarajevo for only so long because he gets frustrated with the Bosnian way.

Perhaps at its fullest, the Bosnian way means living with contradictions, refusing to accept in its entirety any one path or creed. It means bending the rules while accepting the game and keeping an eye open to critique and modify everything. It is gentle irreverence, not cold cynicism or outright rejection, more Bourdieu's (1977) notion of habitus-grown heterodoxy or Certeau's (1984) tiny tactics of resistance than biting sarcasm or violent rebellion. In that they gather on Friday evenings to greet the Sabbath in song and prayer yet ignore religious injunctions by lighting cigarettes from the ritual candles, the Jews of Sarajevo are Jewish the Bosnian way. Those Bosniacs who identify with an Islamic heritage as they sip brandy or drink beer are Muslims the Bosnian way, while the Croats and the Serbs who celebrate Christmas and Easter but forego baptism and ignore Lent are Christians the Bosnian way.

Many Sarajevans point to the heretical Bogomils in support of what they view as their long tradition of dissent; it is the Bosnian way to oppose zealotry and single-mindedness. In homes, cafés, and on city streets, people can be heard calling attention to the cracks in seemingly impervious ideologies. Bosniacs are as critical as their non-Muslim neighbors of international funds diverted away from developing industry and reconstructing residences to build mega-mosques. People from diverse ethnicities and allegiances who voice fear of the day when NATO troops and OHR overseers leave BiH also criticize the large salaries paid to their personnel and the job that they assumed of "teaching democracy" to Bosnia, where Islam, Christianity, and Judaism had coexisted for centuries. The Bosnian way of living in and interpreting the world is reflexive and critical; it bends and changes; it is witty and worldly.

But not always. As Srdjan Vucetic (2004) has shown, legions of jokes and anecdotes from the former Yugoslavia circulate on the internet, as well as in face-to-face conversations, that portray Bosnians as provincial and stupid.[6] In many Bosnian jokes, the rural stock characters really do act as dolts, but in others their buffoonery serves as a buffer to harsh criticism. Here is a joke I remember from the mid-1980s at the peak of Yugoslavia's tourism industry:

> Haso is crouching behind a haystack.
> Mujo (incredulous): What the hell are you doing behind that haystack?
> Haso: The Germans are coming! The Germans are coming! Quick, come hide with me behind the haystack!

> Mujo (relieved): Yes, the Germans are coming. But there's no need to hide. This time we'll be frying their asses!

Although Haso certainly is ridiculous for hiding from tourists eager to spend their deutsche marks on an Adriatic vacation under the hot Yugoslav sun, his behavior calls attention to two troubling social issues: the hosting of former enemy occupiers, and the development of profitable, foreign-currency businesses in a socialist country. The seemingly stupid peasant is not as dumb or backward as he looks, nor is his Bosnian way.[7]

Bosanski način expresses an aesthetic that not only celebrates live and let live but also borrows from, incorporates, criticizes, and appreciates possibly contradictory elements that somehow fit together in a fluid, incongruous pattern that expresses the lived-in cultural understandings of its practitioners. At one and the same time, the Bosnian way places Bosnia and its Bosnians within the urbane orbit of modern Europe and in Europe's churlish backwaters; they are not one or the other, but both and in-between.

This always changing, never stable unifying potential of the Bosnian way is denied and derided by some Serbs and Croats who claim that there are specific Serb, Croat, and Bosniac traditions but no organic culture that can be called Bosnian.[8] They consider the "spirit of Bosnia" or the "Bosnian way" to be ideological maneuvers by Bosniac elites, whose concern it is to strengthen the legitimacy of the single Bosnian state. Dubravko Horvat of the HDZ commented, "*Bosanski duh* [the spirit of Bosnia]—this is a romantic, utopian view. It could be great. But if you would say such a thing in the RS, they would just kick you out. In [Croat-dominated] Herzegovina, they would not even talk to you. The Muslims, though, they would agree with you, and claim it as theirs. Just be careful of who is saying what to you." And so, although noted for decades throughout Yugoslavia, bosanski način may be refuted, even as it is enacted. The same contradiction is at the crux of the controversy over the Bosnian language.

To my list of things Bosnian—Bosnian stew, Bosnian coffee, Bosnian houses, and the Bosnian way—some might add the Bosnian language; after all, the citizenry of Bosnia-Herzegovina comprise one linguistic community (see, e.g., Okey 2004; Sucic 1996). Moreover, grammar books and dictionaries from the turn of the nineteenth to the twentieth century attest to Bosnian as the name of the language that was spoken and written throughout the region.[9] But after World War I when BiH was incorporated into the Kingdom of Serbs, Croats, and Slovenes, the Bosnian people and their Bosnian language disappeared from official records. Later in the twentieth century, when socialist Yugoslavia began to fracture along national lines, so too did Serbo-Croatian, the country's unifying language. As discussed in chapter 3, exclusively Croatian dictionaries and grammar books were being published in Zagreb, while in Sarajevo Alija Isaković compiled his weighty *Dictionary of Characteristic Words of the Bosnian Language* (1992). In the last Yugoslav census, over a third of Bosnia-Herzegovina's population named Bosnian as their native language.

In 2002 and 2004, I heard Sarajevans of varied ethnicities casually refer to their language as Bosnian. More times than not, however, when responding to my queries about language, friends and new acquaintances smiled and stated that they are multilingual and named themselves native speakers of Bosnian, Croatian, and Serbian; quite competent in Macedonian and Bulgarian; and able to get along in Slovenian. Some, like Greta and Jakob, told me that they simply call what is spoken in Sarajevo the local language. Others named it *Naški* (*naš* means "ours") or *Dobardanski,* for the greeting *dobar dan,* which means "good day" in all its versions. Of course, no dictionaries or grammar books carry such titles; they are Croatian, Serbian, or Bosnian.

In the preface to his dictionary, Isaković declares that Bosnian is "the language of all Bosnians and Herzegovinians of all religions and nationalities" (1992, 19) and urges his readers to (re)establish it as the language of the land. At the essay's end, however, this same "Bosnian language—both vernacular and literary" is described as the legacy of "the Bosnian Muslim people: their morality, their spirituality and their refuge" (27). Is Bosnian the eclectic unifying language of all Bosnians, or is it the specific South Slav dialect of the Bosnian Muslims? Can it be both?

On April 3, 2004, the Congress of Bosniac Intellectuals (VKBI) sponsored a public debate on these issues. Professor M. began by chastising the audience for not paying enough attention to their Bosnian language. He informed them that each people has its own language, and a people that disregards its language disregards its peoplehood.[10] Professor M. explained, "The Bosniacs, like any other people express their identity in their language, and they gain recognition as a nation through their language. They need to care about and manifest their history through their language; they need to fight for this language. Language is part of the political question for equal rights. But among us until recently, it has not been treated this way." He continued in this vein for several minutes, noting that just as the Croats take pride in the use of their language, and just as the Serbs take pride in the use of their language, "We Bosniacs must standardize our language and insist that our language is Bosnian, and it must be used exclusively in our media . . . and in our schools and universities."

His opponent, Professor V., opened her rebuttal by explaining that language is a social phenomenon and that most societies are strongly rooted in their languages. Then she asked the audience, "And what of the Bosnian language? What is it? Whose is it? Bosnia-Herzegovina's? Is the Bosnian language a national language? If so, then the language is not only that of the Bosniacs." Professor V. suggested that if the Bosnian language is the language of Bosniacs, so too is Croatian their language when they live in Croatia, or Serbian when they live in Serbia. "Having three national languages in a relatively small territory and population demands linguistic tolerance. And besides, we have more than three languages: It is really the case that within each of these languages there are a number of variants." She gave examples, and the audience laughed at each in turn. "Let's return to the Bosniacs and the importance of national language. For the Croats, language is very important to their national identity. For the Serbs, it occupies a middle level. For the Bosniacs, it has always been of lesser importance. We have a rich language and history, but we have no Bosnian belles lettres. These are hard times; this is a complicated question. To return to the beginning, language is a national symbol for its [national] members. Are they only Bosniacs? We need to be responsible, to take responsibility for the language and its politics and establish a general culture of communication."

The debate ended unresolved. Professor M. placed himself squarely in the B-C-S scheme, while Professor V. called attention to overlaps among the South Slav dialects and their speakers (see Bećerović 2004). Professor V.'s understanding of Bosnian as a hybrid regional language that is neither Serbian nor Croatian nor solely the language of the Bosniacs is highly contested, for even as people speak a united, albeit varied and flexible regional language, Professor M. and his like-minded Croat and Serb counterparts are demanding standards that will calcify porous linguistic boundaries and divide the one speech community into three.

Once again we are confronted by a practical hybridity that some Sarajevans refuse to name because of its perceived capacity to dissolve three equally rights-vested nations into one homogenized, Bosniac-dominated, Bosnian pool. And yet Bosnian, as the work of Russian theorist Mikhail Bakhtin (1981) has demonstrated, is like all languages. It is inherently double voiced; it holds the fundamental ability to be simultaneously same and different as it brings together the worlds in words of various speakers (and their ethnicities) while promoting the heterogeneity that makes linguistic hybridity possible. Bosniacs, as a rule, support the inclusive Bosnian term to name their regionwide language in all its variants. But the Turkish and Arabic words and expressions that dot Bosnian, as well as the religious background of those Bosniacs who claim it as their own, can serve as ominous reminders to Bosnian Serbs and Bosnian Croats that their ancestors once toiled under the Ottoman yoke, and that they might once again fall prey to the dominion of Muslims. Thus the daily practices that conjoin the B-C-S languages are repudiated by politically motivated Serb, Croat, and Bosniac linguists who emphasize the minute points of grammar, lexicon, and pronunciation that split it into three. The people of Bosnia-Herzegovina thereby end up rejecting as their unifying national language the very language that they speak.

Hybridity pervades Sarajevo. It is everywhere in the cityscape and in the sounds and rhythms of the streets. The faded roses of Sarajevo are a hybrid Bosnian strain that mark the spots where sniper fire from the last war killed civilians who insisted on going about their lives in a united, independent Bosnia-Herzegovina. Turning practical hybridity into positive articulation of an eclectic Bosnian identity, however, may not be possible, and not only because of postwar suspicions and the institutional entrenchment of national divides. If Yugoslavia, with its motto of brotherhood and unity and its so-what practical hybridity, failed to persist into the twenty-first century, is a viable future possible for Bosnia as a hybrid nation?

Hybrid Nation: Its Threats and Promises

Mitja Velikonja has declared:

> There can be no doubt that a specific Bosnian political, cultural, and religious identity did indeed exist in medieval Bosnia, a conscious sense of belonging shared by the majority of the population. It was an identity that was constantly being put to the test by Bosnia's trying neighbors, but it endured throughout the Middle Ages. The evolution of this singular Bosnian identity was encouraged by the region's specific judiciary system, currency, alphabet and customs. The people identified themselves as Bosnians (*Bošnjani*) in a geographic rather than an ethnic or religious sense—they served the Bosnian state, or identified themselves as subjects of the Bosnian king. (2003, 54; see also Donia and Fine 1994, 23; Hastings 1997, 130; Kržišnik Bukić 1997; Magaš 2003)

Bosnia lost its independence in 1463, and over the next four centuries, its regionwide identity yielded to the religious categories—Muslims, Catholics, Orthodox, Jews—that were used in the Ottoman Empire to count, classify, and tax its subjects. Over time Bosnia's porous religious boundaries solidified around four ethno-religious communities with distinct yet sometimes overlapping beliefs and practices. In the late nineteenth century, after the Ottomans ceded Bosnia-Herzegovina to Austria-Hungary, Benjamin Kallay actively attempted to revitalize the moribund sentiment of *bošnjatsvo.* This regional Bosnian identity, however, attracted few adherents from among the Catholics and the Orthodox, who had already begun to view themselves as Croats and Serbs. These national divisions were strengthened in the Yugoslav kingdom and were violently played out during the Second World War.

As the long list of census categories and the names of its republics attest, ethno-national groups were accepted as primordial and true in socialist Yugoslavia even as Tito instituted statewide practices that encouraged internalization of the slogan "brotherhood and unity" (see Ugrešić 1998; Wachtel 1998). By 1961, when the Yugoslav category first appeared on the decennial census, Yugoslavia had carved a position for itself in the United Nations as a sovereign state, a borderland-hybrid nation, and a leader of the world's nonaligned countries.

In Bosnia-Herzegovina, the most Yugoslav of all the Yugoslav republics, the Muslims demanded and ultimately received recognition as a constituent nation (see F. Friedman 1996; chapter 3 of this volume). At the same time, an unofficial counternarrative of a pan-ethnic *Bosanski* identity circulated in jokes and anecdotes and in the delineation of several practices as bosanski način. In 1975, Bjelo Dugme, Yugoslavia's premier multinational, Sarajevo-based rock group, recorded an exuberant song, "Tako ti je mala moja, kad' ljubi Bosanac!" Hitherto unrecognized Bosnians gained acclaim as radio stations throughout Yugoslavia broadcast its catchy tune and sassy lyrics, "That's the way it goes, my little one, when a Bosnian kisses!"

At around the same time, the poetry of Mak Dizdar (1917–71) was released in a volume titled *Kameni Spavač* (The Stone Sleeper). Evoking the uniquely carved tombstones from the Middle Ages found throughout the region, many of Dizdar's verses express a bold, collective vision for uniting BiH's multiple and variegated populace:

INSCRIPTION ABOUT A LAND

Thus once upon a time a brave questioner asked a man:

Well, pardon me, who is that one
Where is that one
Whence is that one
Which path is
That Bosnia
Tell me

And then the questioned man gave him the urgent response:
There is, pardon me, a land of Bosnia
She is, pardon me, both barren and barefoot
Both cold and hungry
And moreover
Pardon me
Defiant

Because
Of a Dream.[11]

In the 1980s, Yugoslav Bosnia seemed to be delivering on Dizdar's dream. The republic had experienced a steady rise in its standard of living; literary and artistic productions surged; and nine out of ten Bosnians lived in multiethnic municipalities (Bougarel 1996, 144, cited in Jansen 2005, 56). A palpable feeling of optimism accompanied the jubilant hosting of the 1984

21. A *stečak*, medieval tombstone unique to BiH, in the garden of the National Museum of Bosnia-Herzegovina

Winter Olympic Games. Yet not everyone shared the same dream. Nationalist divisiveness always competed with bosanski način (Donia 2006; Hayden 2007; Jansen 2005, 58–59), and different meanings of hybridity, developed over the decades of European modernity, vied for prominence in shaping particular perceptions of Bosnia's past and imagined futures.

Radovan Karadžić, who had grown up in semirural Montenegro, arrived with his parents as a teenager in Sarajevo. Like most Sarajevans, they settled into a high-rise apartment building in an ethnically mixed neighborhood. Karadžić studied neurology at Sarajevo University, where he was mentored by a Bosnian Muslim. Many Muslims participated in the intellectual and literary circles to which he aspired.

By all measures, Radovan Karadžić thrived in the welcoming, "multi-multi" atmosphere of Sarajevo. But years before his name became associated with radical, right-wing Bosnian Serb nationalism and the siege of Sarajevo, he wrote an ominous poem to his adopted city:

SARAJEVO

I can hear the disaster actually marching
transformed into a bug—when the moment arrives:
it will crush the bug as a worn-out singer
is crushed by the silence and transformed into a voice.

The city is burning like a lump of incense,
our conscience is twisting in the smoke, too.
Empty clothes glide through the city. The stone,
built into houses, is dying red. The plague!

Calm. A troop of armored poplar trees
in itself is marching upwards. Aggressor
air circulates in our souls,
—and now you're a man, now an aerial creature.

I know that all this is a preparation for wails:
what does black metal in the garage hold in store?
Look—fear transformed into a spider
Is searching for the answer in its computer.[12]

Sarajevo offends. Rather than seeing in Sarajevo an aesthetically pleasing entrepôt, Karadžić describes the city as a monstrosity, ambiguously straddling the line between human and nonhuman. The poem treats the city that dares to mix peoples, religions, and traditions as an outrage for overturning the "natural" order of nations: one people to one place. His 1971 poem predicts that it is only a matter of time before the dissonant blend that is Sarajevo will degenerate, and its humanity will ultimately be erased. Karadžić therefore prescribed that the city "burn like a piece of incense."

It has only been in the latter part of the twentieth century that optimistic postcolonial and/or postmodern scholars, such as Homi Bhabha, Paul Gilroy, Stuart Hall, and Renato Rosaldo, began to suggest that hybrid populations and their practices can lead to new, creative cultures and an antiauthoritarian politics (see Ballinger 2004, 31). For centuries Europeans viewed human hybridity as repugnant, particularly in the transgression of racial boundaries (R. J. C. Young 1995). By the middle of the nineteenth century, when much of Central Europe was in the throes of nation building and state formation, the *Mischling,* a person of ethnically or racially mixed parentage, came to represent social pathology (Herzog 1997, 2–3). According to common belief, even if the Mischling seemed at first glance to blend into the national body, in subsequent generations the traits of the Other—the African, the Asian, the Gypsy, or the Jew—would rematerialize in grotesquely exaggerated form, and take over. Hybridity was thus revealed to be a dangerous fraud; it was not a blend after all but a wolf temporarily disguised in sheep's clothing. The polluting blood, language, mannerisms, and mentality that seem to be submerged in the Mischling would reemerge with greater strength and determination. Only pure blood makes pure bodies, and only pure bodies make pure nations (see Linke 1999; cf. Bunzl 2004).

This fearful belief seems to be at the root of Karadžić's monstrous image of Sarajevo. The delicate pastels used by Tatjana Neidhart to illustrate mosques, churches, and government sites in her lovely book, *Sarajevo Kroz Vrejeme* (2004), and the gorgeous vistas of Haris Pasović's film *Apropos de Sarajevo* (2004) are not what all people see when they find themselves amid the diversity of Sarajevo's built environment. Those influenced by the now repudiated yet still circulating degenerative theory of hybridity are likely to perceive the crazy-quilt pattern of Bosnia's ethnicities, religions, and styles as grating, threatening, and unnatural. Some people like Jelena, whom we met in chapter 3, do not even recognize the buildings that give substance to Christianity and European modernity but focus instead on Sarajevo's Turkish past and its possible future of Muslim dominance (cf. Spangler 1983, 80). Radical nationalists like Karadžić view Sarajevo as a ghastly scene of threatening, clashing traditions.

I have shown in this chapter that the denial of hybridity and the nonrecognition of hybrids in present-day Bosnia-Herzegovina have nothing to do with the nature of hybridity but everything to do with how hybrids have come to be defined through the workings of power and history. There is nothing inherent in hybridity that defies categorization; any scheme—including the periodic table of elements and the "great chain of being"—can be and have been amended to account for compounds and multiplicity. Humans have recognized the in-betweenness of the platypus and the mule, yet gave them both a name and a place in the animal kingdom. In the former Yugoslavia, people who crossed, blurred, or disregarded national boundaries called themselves and gained official recognition as Yugoslavs.

Embracing Bosnian hybridity beyond the tangibles of coffee, stew, graphic arts, and houses demands a radical cultural overturn, a new way to relate to self and others. The hybrid tradition of bosanski način offers BiH its own way out of the ethno-national glitch. But like nonaligned Yugoslavia, which belonged neither to Europe's East nor to its West but straddled both worlds, it is risky for Bosnia-Herzegovina to go it alone. In European realpolitik, it is not just that nations are good to think; they are the only way to think. Stuart Hall (1995, 186) has noted that "there are powerful reasons why people persist in trying to retreat defensively from the fact of cultural hybridity and difference into closed definitions of culture." So too are there powerful reasons for avoiding hybrid persons and hybrid nations: in its official disregard of Bosanci and BiH, Bosnia now resembles most other European countries.

But the story does not end here. Even after following the European convention of setting territorial boundaries congruent with the claims of its nations, Bosnia-Herzegovina is still viewed as an unsteady state of mixed-up peoples who need to be disciplined to avoid erupting into another war. Although recognized as a member state of the United Nations, BiH remains a protectorate of the European Union, which is backed militarily by NATO. The unitary republic is more spectral than operational, and the strange-bedfellows coalition of the nationalist parties that has been reelected since the first multiparty elections in 1990 is not eager for that situation to change.

For many Serbs and Croats, it is not difficult to imagine that the present trinational balance can turn into the unequal multiconfessionalism of Ottoman rule. Yes, there has always been a place for Christians and Jews in Sarajevo, but until the last decades of the nineteenth century, they were subjects of Muslim leaders and subjected to the priority of Islamic law. A century and a half after the end of Ottoman rule, to keep the peace in politically shaky, postwar Bosnia, the population has been legally divided into three separate nations, each vested with equal and inalienable rights to self-governance.

There is no room for hyphenated individuals or hybrid traditions in this juridico-moral scheme (see Werbner 1997, 239; Markowitz 2004).

Contemporary Sarajevo's actually existing hybridity (cf. Robbins 1998) has its own history. It developed from the heterogeneity of the region and has long been imbricated in the constellations of power grouped around the privileged notion of the nation. Bosnian hybridity is nothing new; officially naming it and opting for a cosmopolitanism that embraces cultural blends along with distinct ethnic traditions would be a revolution indeed.

Conclusion

8

After Yugoslavia, after War, after All

Sarajevo's Cultural Legacies

Almost six years after the events of 1989 that turned it from an ordinary year into the *annus mirabilis* that ushered in postsocialism, the war in Bosnia-Herzegovina was losing its momentum. The cease-fire declared in late 1994 between the mainly Bosniac Army of Bosnia-Herzegovina and the Croat Defense Force of Herceg-Bosna had stabilized into a wary peace, and during the spring of 1995 the United States increased pressure on Serbian president Slobodan Milošević to rein in the armies and militias of the Republika Srpska. It would still take the atrocities of Srebrenica and a gruesome massacre at Sarajevo's main market to jolt the United States and NATO into direct military action and terminate the war. Nonetheless, by April 1995 many Sarajevans felt for the first time in three years that an end to the violence was in sight. And they began to look ahead to the difficult but peaceful transitions that would return them to Europe.

In more westerly parts of the world, journalists, historians, and political pundits were recovering from their shock at the downfall of communism by pondering and celebrating that unexpected turn of events. Some conceded that things might be messy for a time while transitioning governments maneuvered for stability. Nonetheless, many in Western Europe and North America expressed optimism that even if history had not come to an end (Fukayama 1989), Eastern Europe's postsocialist countries would sooner, rather than later, move into the free market and adopt democracy.

Yugoslavia's violent dissolution, as well as the extended instability of many Soviet successor states, caused some to rethink that stance. Early on, Benedict Anderson cynically dubbed the dramatic changes that began with the fall of the Berlin Wall "the new world disorder" (1992). During the last spring of the Bosnian wars, political scientist Valerie Bunce (1995) provocatively asked, "Should transitologists be grounded?" Noting that the linear transitology model derived from political changes that had occurred years earlier in Latin America and southwestern Europe and might not be relevant to the diverse and complex conditions of postsocialism, Bunce warned that it offered little predictive value for developments in the former Soviet Union and Yugoslavia's successor states. Four years later, as NATO-led troops were enforcing the stability necessary for post-Dayton Bosnia-Herzegovina to forge ahead in its EU-mandated "transitions toward democracy," Michael Burawoy and Katherine Verdery asserted much the same thing. Emphasizing that the changes of postsocialism are multifaceted processes laden with unintended consequences, novel adaptations, creativity, and resistance, their ethnographic approach to Eastern Europe's unstable political environments and uncertain economies sharpened the transitology critique (1999, 2).

To a large extent, these criticisms were right on target. Far from following a neat, incremental path, Eastern Europe's postsocialist experiences have been dizzyingly diverse (Berdahl, Bunzl, and Lampland 2000; Burawoy and Verdery 1999b; Hann 2002; Svašek 2006), seldom triumphant, and often painful (Kideckel 2008). Czechoslovakia and Yugoslavia, both born at Versailles in 1918, dissolved in the early 1990s; but while one split peacefully, the other blew up in bloodshed. Russia, the largest postsocialist state, lost political clout and monetary strength in the early 1990s, but after riding an economic seesaw in the latter part of that decade, by the early twenty-first century, it had reclaimed its place as an oil-rich, rearmed global power, eager to exert influence over its neighbors. One of those neighbors, Belarus, has retreated into a near-dictatorship, while Ukraine has been working hard to implement its democratic Orange Revolution. In Central Europe, reunited Germany ditched its deutsche mark and went the way of the euro. But post-Soviet Moldova, Europe's poorest country, has made no overtures to merge with Romania.

In 2007, Romania and Bulgaria followed the path of Estonia, Latvia, and Lithuania, and the Czech Republic, Hungary, Poland, Slovakia, and Slovenia and joined the European Union. Despite the variety among them, the growing number of postsocialist countries striving to become candidates for membership in the EU refutes, in its turn, rejection of the transitology model. Many informed observers agree that European integration offers the most desirable future for Europe's postsocialist states, and EU accession has become the critical benchmark for measuring success in postsocialist transitions.

Normalization of the EU route, however, ignores or marginalizes those states that are seeking their own way or are weighing the option of tying their fate to Russia instead of struggling with the uncomfortable fit of the West. Worse yet, it neglects consideration of what is in store for countries like Bosnia-Herzegovina that fail to live up to Europe's stringent and sometimes contradictory demands, even as they accept that EU integration may very well be their only viable option.

So it goes for kaleidoscopic Bosnia and its post-Yugoslav, postwar, and postmodern capital, Sarajevo, whose political prospects and cultural legacies continue to expand and constrict as this book draws to a close. Finding it impossible to conclude with a definitive, modernist happy end, I am returning now in the book's final chapter to the question posed at the beginning: How is Bosnia's mixed heritage of colonialism, cosmopolitanism, and Yugoslavism, and the ethnic identities that developed along with it being interpreted, accepted, challenged, and co-opted by contemporary Sarajevans? Reconsideration of this question leads me to assess the various "afterological" scenarios that ordinary people, powerful politicians, and international institutions are suggesting for, if not imposing on, twenty-first-century Bosnia.[1]

W(h)ither the State: Ethnic Overdeterminism and Neocolonialism

Bosnia-Herzegovina is where it has always been: betwixt and between opposing empires, filled with a diverse population, and vulnerable to power plays within and beyond its borders. As then-president Bill Clinton explained in his November 27, 1995, "Why We're Sending Troops to Bosnia" Address to the Nation, "Securing the peace in Bosnia will also help build a free and stable Europe. Bosnia lies at the very heart of Europe, next door to many of its fragile new democracies and some of our closest allies."

Socialism and armed conflict are now things of the past, but their scars, visions, and legacies remain. The post-Dayton governing structure of BiH is top heavy and overly bureaucratic (Deets 2006; F. Friedman 2004; Gilbert 2006), and the country is nowhere near the end of its transitions. Over a decade after its wars, Bosnia seems stuck in a maddening state (Arextaga 2003).

Since early in 1996, BiH citizens have been bombarded by messages imploring them to change their nationalistic, undemocratic ways. "*Put u Evropu,*" they were reminded again and again, "*zavisi od Vas*": The way into Europe depends on you (Coles 2002). According to top EU officials, however, these messages have fallen on deaf ears. In January 2004, the third high representative, Paddy Ashdown, told a reporter from the Croatian newspaper *Vjesnik*, "This country is not a state yet. Neither was Germany in 1945, however, Bosnia and Herzegovina is on the road to statehood. . . . There are some in BiH, not exclusively but mostly among Bosniaks-Muslims, who believe that a great International Community archangel will descend upon Bosnia and Herzegovina on a shining cloud, grab the Dayton Agreement from their hands, fly off to some American airbase tens of thousands of miles away and re-write it for them. That will not happen. The BiH Constitution must be rewritten by the people of this country, making hard compromises."[2]

If citizens of Bosnia-Herzegovina harbor fantasies that the great international community will resolve their woes, it should be recognized that presidents and prime ministers of powerful countries contribute to these pipedreams. Bosnians, along with millions of people worldwide, looked on as dozens of new postsocialist states were welcomed into the United Nations, including their own. Some of these countries, like little Slovenia, which was once an integral part of Yugoslavia, turned westward early on, averted warfare, and prospered.[3] BiH had no such luck. Lately, while still stuck in the morass of their Dayton-born constitution, Bosnians witnessed the formation of two more nation-states from what was once Yugoslavia. In June 2006, Montenegro left Serbia without incident and became a state of its own. Less than two years later, following recurrent verbal and military violence, Kosovo, which in Yugoslavia was an autonomous province in the Socialist Republic of Serbia, declared its independence. Immediately thereafter, the Republic of Kosovo received recognition as a sovereign state from the United States and most European Union members.

Spurred by Kosovo's decisive action in February 2008, politicos and their followers in the Republika Srpska stopped waiting passively for the "great International Community archangel" and staged demonstrations while also planning a democratic referendum in favor of secession from Bosnia-Herzegovina. The fifth high representative, Miroslav Lajčak, took immediate action. Secession, he told Bosnia's Serbs, is unconstitutional. None of BiH's constituent nations possesses the right of self-determination, and even discussion of secessionist plans is illegal. Lajčak made that position clear in the Banja Luka newspaper *Glas Srpske*: "Bosnia-Herzegovina is an internationally recognized sovereign state and its territorial integrity is guaranteed by the Dayton Peace Agreement. The Constitution of Bosnia-Herzegovina stipulates that BiH is a state consisting of two entities and that Serbs, Bosniaks and Croats are its constituent peoples."[4]

What are we, to say nothing of the people of Bosnia-Herzegovina, to make of this situation? On one hand, Bosnians have been chided for their passivity, for refusing to exert pressure on their leaders to change the country's governing structure. On the other hand, they have been given the distinct message that their country's three constituent groups are legally bound to each other in the unwieldy Dayton scheme of things. That demand for BiH to remain as a two-entity, trinational, yet insufficient state flies in the face of international support for the independence of Montenegro and Kosovo. The irony is further heightened by increased feelings in Belgium, a founding member of the European Community and host of the EU's headquarters, that after almost two hundred years together the time has come for Flemings and Walloons to part ways.[5] All these events have reinforced the Euro-modern wisdom that ethnically homogeneous (read: nation) states stand a far better chance for autonomy, peace, and prosperity than those that are heterogeneous and hybrid (cf. Munasinghe 2002).

During the course of my research in 2004, everyone I met in Sarajevo supported the internationally sanctioned decision for Bosnia-Herzegovina to remain one state, even with its internal divisions.[6] Pointing to Bosnia's centuries-long unity, they declared that its Bosniacs, Croats, and Serbs, or Muslims, Catholics, and Orthodox, have always lived together and should continue to do so. Moreover, as Elvir, a veteran of three and a half years of frontline service in the Army of Bosnia-Herzegovina, stated, "No one should be rewarded for his or her aggression. It would be a political mistake and morally wrong to reward wartime aggressors with their own state. So I say, *No* to the secession of Republika Srpska."

During April 2008, however, several other Bosniacs surprised me by taking a different stance. Concluding that not much has changed for the better during the postwar years, they sidelined the morality invoked by Elvir and declared that for the larger good of peace and economic reconstruction it might be better if the Federation and the Serbian Republic went their separate ways. My friend Melisa, who in 2004 had insisted that Bosnia-Herzegovina carries a historical mandate to remain united, told me, "I can honestly say that I would have no problem with the RS seceding. But they would have a problem: Serbia doesn't want them. Russia is investing, buying all kinds of businesses. Sorry to say, it looks like we are stuck with each other." Mustafa, a carpet vendor in the Baščaršija, offered a solution for getting unstuck: "I am a Bosniac, and I must say that I think now that the best thing to do, the best thing for the people, is to split Bosnia-Herzegovina and be done with it. Then Europe will have finished her work. Give the Federation to Croatia, which will join the EU soon enough, and the RS to Serbia, which is being supported by Russia."

Throughout February 2008, High Representative Miroslav Lajčak held a series of town meetings across Bosnia-Herzegovina, once again urging citizens to remember that the "way to Europe depends on you." In September 2008, Lajčak expressed his frustration that the people of Bosnia-Herzegovina have not made a "sea-change" in their political attitudes; instead of coming together, they remain "dominated by the nationalist agenda." Rather than making yet another appeal to the deaf ears of the country's Serbs, Croats, and Bosniacs, he then asked the European Union to be "ready to take the lead role in BiH."[7] How, if at all, will that "lead role" change the policies and practices established by the EU during its thirteen- year supervision of Bosnia? More important, what has been and what will be the continuing effect of the European Union's involvement?

As we sat together in the social hall of the Ashkenazi synagogue and enjoyed the April 2008 mini-seder for Sarajevo's diplomatic and multicultural communities (see chapter 6), the Italian ambassador to BiH assured me that Europe has always acted and will continue to act in Bosnia's best interests. "The EU," he said, "is the only way for Bosnia-Herzegovina. It will take some time, but it will come about. People will see what EU membership did for Ireland and Portugal, and they will pressure their government to make a change." Many Sarajevans agree with that line of reasoning. "The big reward for serving in the army," Elvir said, "will be for the country to remain together and get better. If I could, I would outlaw nationalist parties." Echoing the Italian ambassador, he added, "I think it will take a long time, but people must change their mentality, and then we can enter Europe as a united country."

Not everyone, however, thinks that it is Bosnians who must change. As Yugoslavs, Sarajevans freely traveled and worked throughout Europe. The war and its unsettled aftermath put an end to that. In order for them to enter EU countries, a special visa is required, and as Renata discovered when she was planning a honeymoon in Greece, "you have to prove that you have at least three hundred euros in your bank account" (see Bideleux and Jeffries 2007, 593).Bosnians want to be reconnected to the continent of which they are part. Some are suggesting that it is the policies and goals of Europe that keeps them adrift. As my friend Melisa, who is a graduate student in Bosnian prehistory, observed, "Why is Bosnia in such a mess? It must be good for the EU to have us this way. They can point to us as a problem and that takes the problem away from them. It must be good for someone to have us as a place of dirty laundry—trade in crime, drugs, and women. I'm sorry to say, someone is profiting from this—the higher up in government you go, the higher up in corruption."

Down in the Baščaršija, Mustafa the carpet vendor, who belongs to no political party and advocates splitting BiH, voiced his opinion:

> Who is responsible for the situation here in Bosnia? I'll tell you who, my dear lady: Europe! And when will things get better? When Europe finishes her work here and leaves. . . . Europe is no friend of the Bosniac people. A unified Europe is what they want, a *Christian* unified Europe. Europe is a *stara kurva* [an old whore] and a very smart and wily one. Europe could have ended our war, and now they could just lay down the law and be done with it. Why haven't they found [indicted war criminals] Karadžić or Mladić? I could find them in five days. . . . Only America understood that the Bosniacs are not Muslim fundamentalists, and President Bill Clinton stepped in to end the war. A few years earlier, remember, French President Mitterrand came here to Sarajevo and said there was no war. Understand that there was genocide here, in Srebrenica and on the streets of Sarajevo. Innocent people were killed and injured, many of them children. Europe doesn't want to think of us, and our own politicians are just getting rich without building industry or creating jobs.

Ever hopeful that the EU countries would rally to support them when their city was under siege and then take an active role in Bosnia's economic reconstruction at the war's end, during the 1990s Sarajevans kept their criticism of Europe to a minimum. But in August 2002, I had an eye-opening conversation with a Baščaršija coppersmith. Pointing to the new products he had developed for the international community, he declared,

> I have a ridiculous business—souvenir plates for the SFOR soldiers! Now the bases order them from me. When the soldiers finish their tour of duty, they get a plate with a map of Bosnia-Herzegovina, their country's flag, their name, and the dates of their service.
>
> This shop is a family tradition, handed down for hundreds of years. This is my country, my city. I have this business after how many people were killed and injured? Three years of war and no one did anything to stop it. Srebrenica—that was a real holocaust. The Dutch troops went off to drink wine! They—the generals of the UN so-called Peace Force and the leaders of the European Community—should all be tried in The Hague as war criminals together with Milošević!

To Melisa, Mustafa, and Samir, although Saudi Arabia or Iran would be far, far worse, the European Union is not Bosnia's best patron. They would prefer the United States. But because the United States has insisted that the EU take the lead problem-solving role for a country "at the very heart of Europe," and since there is no going back to Tito's Yugoslavia, EU supervision might just be the country's only option. Because the high representative insists on compliance with the terms of the Dayton Peace Agreement even though these have resulted in an ethnically overdetermined, unmanageable government, Sarajevans have conformed to this arrangement, sometimes enthusiastically, sometimes reluctantly, by voting for nationalist parties.

For over a decade since postwar Bosnia began its "transition to democracy," Sarajevans have had to be inventive and use their well-honed wit and wisdom to find jobs, earn a steady wage, privatize their apartments, and ensure their children's future. Some have had the great fortune of landing long-term employment in a humanitarian organization, an international business, or with USAID, the EU, or the UN.[8] Nebojša, who works for a Norwegian NGO, told me several times that one international salary supports an entire extended family; his supplements his parents' meager pension and the minuscule teacher's salary earned by his wife and makes possible the artistic pursuits of his brother. Likewise Damir, who by 2004 had risen through the ranks from a field worker in a de-mining organization to an administrative position, used his salary to buy himself a car and a small apartment, contribute to his parents' household, and pay his sister's university tuition. In 2008 I called his Sarajevo mobile phone number and was delighted when he answered. But Damir told me that it would be impossible to meet for coffee because he was talking to me from Jordan, where he has been stationed since August 2007, when his Sarajevo office closed. He has returned to his old job of locating and detonating mines; "It's well paid, and you're part of the international community. But there is a lack of people to do this dangerous job, so they are even taking Bosnians!" Damir would certainly have preferred to remain in Sarajevo, but family obligations and his own desire to do something more important than sitting around in a café all day have taken him to a very different part of the world.

The third high representative Paddy Ashdown and the fifth high representative Miroslav Lajčak (2007–09) complained that with their votes for the Bosniac SDA, the Croat HDZ, and the Serb SDS in election after election, the citizens of Bosnia-Herzegovina continue their destructive allegiance to nationalism.[9] These voting patterns, however, might reflect something other than ethnic chauvinism. Good-paying and interesting work is scarce. So too is affordable housing. Just as I demonstrated in chapter 4 that census statistics are not absolute representations of the ethnic distribution of the population, votes for nationalist parties might have more to do with the governing structure of BiH and its attached distribution of resources than with radical nationalism.

In 1990 people throughout Bosnia cast their ballots for the new nationalist parties for several reasons; some did so as a protest vote against the increasingly ineffective Yugoslav League of Communists. With good cause to be distrustful of other groups, in the immediate aftermath of the war they may well have voted the nationalist linc. But in the early twenty-first century, many BiH citizens, including Sarajevans, have been making a rational choice to vote for the SDA, the HDZ, or the SDS because these are the parties that have delivered the goods and seem best poised to continue to do so. Pointing to "my own Bosniac people" who resettled in Sarajevo during the war, Mustafa declared, "They are villagers, and they are primitive people. And they got everything—jobs, apartments, money. And they only think one thing: SDA. They don't think about more than that because the party supplies them with everything." Nataša, an architect in Sarajevo's city-planning bureau, agreed: "You have to belong to a party to get ahead, and the strongest parties are the nationalist parties. If I wanted to make a career, to become a manager or department head I would have to join a party, just to have them behind me." The taxi driver who brought me to the airport at the end of my April 2008 stay offered a slightly different take: "*Narod je ovci*," he began. "The people are sheep. The politicians steal and manipulate, and the people only follow. They are scared that something worse will happen, so they follow the leaders, the nationalist parties, and hope that things will get better."

By 2008 ideological messages, optimistic or apocalyptic, no longer offered much appeal to the people of Sarajevo, if they ever did. Their concerns are to have interesting work that pays a decent wage, and a privatized apartment; they want to enjoy the companionship of friends and kin and educate their children to thrive in twenty-first-century Europe. Due to the trinational structure adopted in Dayton and inscribed as the law of the land, the nationalist parties that superceded the Yugoslav League of Communists have become major routes toward achieving those life goals.

The B-C-S structure of the Republic of Bosnia-Herzegovina exerts its influence in yet another way. As I have shown throughout this book, Sarajevans are not only unique individuals; whether they like it or not, they are also ethnically marked and marking actors who know full well how dangerous unchecked group rivalries can be. During our most recent meeting in 2008, Amila told me about a discussion she recently led at Sarajevo University: "Many of my students said they were first Bosniacs and then Bosnians. I asked, 'Why not simply Bosnians?' They said that because Serbs and Croats always put the nation before the whole state, if they didn't insist on their Bosniac identity they would be ignored, overlooked, and exploited. So they vote for the SDA." Even some of my not-nationalist, ethnically mixed Sarajevo friends who ordinarily vote for the Social Democrats consider casting their ballot for the SDA or for Silajdžić's increasingly Bosniac-leaning Party for BiH. They are doing so to counter nationalist votes by Serbs and Croats. If the European Union is seeking a sea change in Bosnian political attitudes and voting behavior, it would be wise to entertain the idea of a sea change in the governmental structure of Bosnia-Herzegovina.

On October 22, 2004, the *Radio Free Europe/Radio Liberty Balkan Report* published an article reporting that many people inside and outside Bosnia now believe that the 1995 Dayton Agreement has outlived its usefulness (cf. Bideleux and Jeffries 2007, 403–4; Chandler 2000, 43, 174). Four alternative models were listed:

1. Strengthen the OHR, which would "break the power of the nationalists."
2. Reduce and eliminate the role of the OHR, which would thereby entrench the nationalists.
3. Scrap Dayton and call for a new constitutional convention.
4. Partition BiH along ethnic lines because "Bosnia is unlikely to ever be a truly multiethnic society again in the foreseeable future."[10]

As of the middle of 2009, it appeared that only the first option had won the endorsement of the Office of the High Representative. But if the OHR continues to insist on the terms of Dayton, it is highly doubtful that the power of the nationalists will be broken (Bilefsky 2008).

Because "no-go areas, unrest and disobedience, collapse of law and order" (Bauman 1991, 8) are not tolerated in contemporary Europe, when Bosnia-Herzegovina came within a hair's breadth of annihilation the Euro-American world interceded and forced an end to the war. With this intervention, they also concluded that the country could only prove itself worthy of self-rule by completing the disentanglement of its intermixed population. The Dayton-born governmental structure then clarified and hardened each of the B-C-S groups while also making them interdependent. Statewide unity, however, has been thwarted, and with each passing year intergroup divides grow wider. The European Union, in the person of the unelected high representative, has become increasingly frustrated that Bosnia's "transition to democracy" is leading nowhere. In September 2008, with no happy end in sight, the OHR shifted its appeal from the people of Bosnia-Herzegovina to ask the EU to take matters even more firmly into its own hands. Only when the Federation's cantons, BiH's entities, and the unitary state conform to the demands of Dayton will EU overseers decolonize Bosnia and accept it as part of Europe (see Bilefsky 2009).

Heterogeneity and Hybridity in Twenty-first-Century Sarajevo

As the twentieth century turned to the twenty-first, as-if-unchangingness and even the unidirectional change known as progress failed as metanarratives. In Eastern Europe, the promise of socialism's bright future came to naught, and for two decades postsocialism has come to feel like a permanent condition of unpredictable transitions. In Western Europe, that most modernized part of the world, once-exotic black and brown people have become visible everywhere, transgressing colored boundaries of place and disrupting a centuries-old geography of nation, culture, and civilization (Hall 1997; Markowitz 2004, 330). Some experience this diversity as threatening; it seems an unwanted and uninvited multiculturalism in their own backyards (Stolcke 1995; Wright 1998) that can destroy the national project (Bowen 2007; Gilroy 1987) and a united vision for Europe (Borneman and Fowler 1997). Others, particularly ethnic and sexual minorities and big-city cosmopolites, relish the opportunities of an inclusive European identity and postnational citizenship (Bunzl 2004; Soysal 1994). The afterology of Europe is far from clear or unitary.

In Sarajevo people out for an evening stroll continue to delight in their city's kaleidoscopic offerings. Literature, art, music, theater, and dance are flourishing, and various cultural societies, mountaineering groups, sports clubs, and discussion circles provide Sarajevans with a wide range of activities. The city's diverse stimuli remind them that they once were and must again be vitally connected to the wide world.

Despite the naysayers, Sarajevo's "multi-multi" character and extravagant cosmopolitanism have not been destroyed. Young people are finding employment, getting married, and having children. Amila, now the mother of a baby girl, married a fellow graduate student in 2006. His family practices Islam. Her parents are adamantly secular. Welcoming me into her new home, she explained, "He asked me, and we decided to live an Islamic lifestyle." Amila's mother, who comes to help out a few times a week, shook her head and said she could not understand how her own daughter could make such a change. Nataša, however, has followed in her parents' footsteps. She married a man whose father is a Catholic Croat and whose mother is a Bosniac. Nataša said that mixed marriages like hers are "typical, at least among [her] group." FBiH statistics reveal that the practice of marrying across the ethnic divide is not typical, but it certainly has not come to an end (Federacija Bosne i Hercegovine 2008, 121–22).[11] And yet, while it, along with the rest of Bosnia-Herzegovina, remains separate from Europe, Sarajevo's mirth and mixity are overshadowed by the melancholy of its ethnic strife (Bilefsky 2008).

Throughout history Bosnia was an acutely hybrid space, first in an internally divided Christian world, then on the western margins of the Ottoman Empire, then as part of ethnically diverse Habsburg Central Europe, and finally, as the only republic in Yugoslavia without a majority nation. By the beginning of the twenty-first century, Bosnians' preferences for monoethnicity have become normal and natural. But these are not completely entrenched. Even as governmental practices and cultural hegemony combine to reinforce national purity as morally right and politically desirable, Sarajevans continue to encounter and enact practical hybridity in their daily lives. Just as important, thousands of citizens like Mak and Damir, Vedran and Goran, Davor, Klara, and Renata are the 100 percent Bosnian products of parents who crossed and dissolved ethnic divides. Despite their muted voices, they offer living proof of a counterhegemony that piques the social imaginary and vexes the political order. In that way, Bosnia-Herzegovina remains unsettled in its B-C-S-(O) national divisions, and the truth that accompanies them is not uncontested or static, at least not yet.

Nestor Garcia Canclini has noted that "hybridization does not by itself guarantee democratic multicultural politics. By being not only the sum of the contributions that converge in it but 'the third space that makes the emergence of the other positions possible' (Bhabha 1994:21), hybridization is more than a simple overcoming that denies and conserves . . . it is a field of energy and sociocultural innovation" (2000, 49). *Tako je u Sarajevu.* And so it goes in Sarajevo, where the kaleidoscopic panoply of possible patterns makes it difficult to predict what will emerge and when. Sarajevo's history of heterogeneity and hybridity has bequeathed the city with a diversity of vistas, people, places, and things, making it intriguing even as it offers hospitality. Twice that variegated capital came close to destruction; first toward the end of the seventeenth century and then in the final decade of the twentieth. One can only hope that the Bosnian ways of resilience and tolerance will cause Sarajevo to thrive again as an energetic and innovative urban field, absorbing and withstanding Europe's twists, shakes, and turns throughout the twenty-first century and beyond.

Glossary

B-C-S	Bosniacs-Croats-Serbs; Bosnia-Herzegovina's three constituent nations
BiH	Bosna i Hercegovina, the Republic of Bosnia-Herzegovina
Bosanac, Bosanka, Bosanci	A pan-ethnic Bosnian man; a pan-ethnic Bosnian woman; Bosnians
Bošnjak, Bošnjanka, Bošnjaci	A Bosniac man; a Bosniac woman; Bosniacs; formerly referred to as the Muslimanska nacija, or Muslims
Bošnjastvo	A regionwide Bosnian identity, or Bosnianness, fostered by BiH's Austro-Hungarian rulers (1878–1918)
bratstvo i jedinstvo	Brotherhood and unity, the central slogan of socialist Yugoslavia (1945–91)
DPA	The General Framework Agreement for Peace in Bosnia-Herzegovina, also known as the Dayton Peace Accords and the Dayton Peace Agreement, which ended the 1992–95 wars in BiH, signed in Paris on December 14, 1995
FBiH	The Bosniac-Croat Federation of Bosnia-Herzegovina, 51 percent of BiH's territory
HDZ	Hrvatska Demokratska Zajednica; the Croat national party
Hrvat, Hrvatica, Hrvati	A Croat man; a Croat woman; Croats
Hrvatska	Croatia
IFOR	NATO-led Implementation Force (1995–96)
Jugoslaveni	Those citizens of the Socialist Federation of Yugoslavia (1945–91) who identified and declared themselves as nonethnic, pan-ethnic, or mixed ethnic Yugoslavs

KM	Konvertibilni mark (convertible mark), the currency of the Republic of Bosnia-Herzegovina, which is tied to the euro; 1 KM = 0.5 euro
nacionalna pripadnost	National or ethnic belonging
OHR	Office of the High Representative; created under the DPA, the OHR is an unelected governing superstructure responsible for overseeing the implementation of the civilian aspects of the DPA
Ostali	Others; those citizens of BiH who cannot or will not be counted as members of the B-C-S constituent nations
RS	Republika Srpska, the Serbian Republic of BiH, covering 49 percent of the state's territory (it actually covers 48.5 percent of the territory because the Brčko District remains under international supervision, part of neither FBiH nor RS)
Sarajlije	Sarajevans, the people of Sarajevo
SDA	Stranka za Demokratsku Akciju, the Bosniac national party
SDP	Social Democratic Party
SDS	Srpska Demokratska Stranka, the Serb national party
šehid	Martyr (from Arabic); Muslim soldier in the Army of Bosnia-Herzegovina who died defending his country during the 1992–95 war
SFOR	NATO-led Stabilization Force (1996–December 2005)
Srb, Srbinka, Srbi	A Serb man; a Serb woman; Serbs
Srbija	Serbia
Stranka za BiH	The Party for Bosnia-Herzegovina, designed as a pan-Bosnian party advocating one state without the entities
VKBI	Vijeće Kongresa Bošnjaških Intelektualca, the Congress of Bosniac Intellectuals
zajednički život	The "common life"; a term used by Sarajevans to convey the everyday practices of Bosnia's heterogeneity and hybridity

Notes

Chapter 1. Meeting and Greeting the City

1. Recognized as independent by the European Community and the United States on April 6, 1992, Bosnia-Herzegovina is called Bosna i Hercegovina in the Bosnian-Croatian-Serbian language(s), which is abbreviated to BiH (pronounced *Bikh*).

2. The title I originally proposed for this book was *Kaleidoscopic Bosnia: Heterogeneity and Hybridity in Sarajevo.* To avoid confusion with Tanya Richardson's (2008) *Kaleidoscopic Odessa,* I have renamed the volume *Sarajevo: A Bosnian Kaleidoscope.*

3. In July 2007, the Web site of OHR, http://www.ohr.int, declared: "The Office of the High Representative (OHR) is an *ad hoc* international institution responsible for overseeing implementation of civilian aspects of the accord ending the war in Bosnia and Herzegovina. The position of High Representative was created under the General Framework Agreement for Peace in BiH, usually referred to as the Dayton Peace Agreement, that was negotiated in Dayton, Ohio, and signed in Paris on 14 December 1995."

4. The third high representative, Paddy Ashdown (2002–5), demanded that the separate Bosniac, Croat, and Serb police forces and armies integrate into statewide institutions, and only with the achievement of that goal was SFOR disbanded. The OHR aimed to close by the end of June 2008, but as this book goes to press that goal has not been achieved.

5. Prior to 1992, Latin and Cyrillic scripts could be seen almost equally dispersed throughout Sarajevo, on street signs, public buildings, and newspapers. Although both scripts hold official status in the Republic of Bosnia-Herzegovina, in the Bosniac-Croat Federation it is rare indeed to see Cyrillic lettering on billboards, street signs, or public buildings. Official state offices display signs announcing Bosnia-Herzegovina in Latin and Cyrillic, but Cyrillic lettering, associated with the Serbs, is rarely seen

on the streets of Sarajevo. By way of contrast, in the Srpska Republika, street signs are written in Cyrillic. See chapter 3.

6. The Jewish community of Bosnia-Herzegovina maintained an official policy of neutrality and provided communication services and humanitarian aid to one and all. Chapter 6 explores the continuing ramifications of this policy.

7. These peoples are variously known as Illyrians, Avars, Thracians, Dacians, and Vlachs. Remains of Roman baths with mosaic floors have been found near the sulfur springs of Ilidža, but very little material culture has survived from the pre-Slavic period.

8. The first written mention of Bosnia dates from a 958 handbook of the Byzantine emperor Porphyrogenitus (Malcolm 1996, 10).

9. The 1189 Charter of Ban Kulin, written in the Bosnian vernacular with a distinctive local script, grants trade privileges to Dubrovnik merchants while delineating Bosnia's borders and asserting its autonomy.

10. Lovrenović (2001, 93) states unequivocally that although "the Ottoman Empire used various methods to achieve the integration of the countries it conquered [it] did not force them into linguistic, religious and ethnic assimilation" (see also Malcolm 1996, 56–63). Albania and parts of Macedonia were also fertile ground for conversions to Islam.

11. After Tito's break with Stalin (or Stalin's break with Tito) in 1948, the name of the organization was changed to the Yugoslav League of Communists. For histories of Yugoslavia, see Cohen 1995; Djilas 1991; Lampe 2000; Lane 2004; P. Ramet 1984; Wachtel 1998.

12. The original plan was to resettle these Bosnian Muslims in Arab villages in the Galilee, but the Israelis quickly realized that such a decision would be inappropriate for sophisticated, secular urbanites. They were first given temporary quarters in Kibbutz Michal Magen, where they took an intensive Hebrew course, and then moved to Kibbutz Beit Oren, near the city of Haifa.

13. This fact of Yugoslav academia is yet another indicator of BiH's betwixt-and-between (post?) colonial position. Ethnographers from neighboring Croatia and Serbia, as well as those from more-distant Slovenia—in addition to those from the United Kingdom and the United States—would come to Bosnia for fieldwork, but aside from the tiny ethnology division at the Zemaljski Muzej, no academic Department of Cultural Anthropology was ever established in Bosnia-Herzegovina.

14. Unbeknown to me at the time, Anders H. Stefansson was conducting doctoral research on the cultural dynamics of refugee return and (re)integration in postwar Sarajevo (Stefansson 2003).

Chapter 2. Practices of Place

1. Sarajevo also became what Donia has called "the center of antinationalist repression in Yugoslavia during the 1980s [where] prosecutors . . . conducted two prosecutions in hopes of discouraging such public expressions" (2006, 245). One trial was

against thirteen members of the Young Muslims, including future BiH president Alija Izetbegović; the other was against Vojislav Šešelj, a Sarajevo-born Serb who advocated Serb nationalism in his academic writings and eventually made a political career as a hard-line nationalist.

2. http://www.olympic.org (accessed July 2009), the official Web site of the Olympic Movement, notes, "In 1984, the Winter Games took place in a Socialist country for the first and only time. The people of Sarajevo gained high marks for their hospitality, and there was no indication of the tragic war that would engulf the city only a few years later."

3. The phrase "common life" is repeated frequently in the literature and will be used throughout this text. Speakers of Bosnian-Croatian-Serbian call it *zajednički život* (*zajedno* means "together"). Filipović (2007, 25) offers a one-sentence description, which I am presenting here in translation: "That common life was constructed as a form of mutual relations in which each could live according to his or her internal identity, which above all means that of customs and religion, but one to which [all] people were connected by living and working together, one with another in their connections and contents, dialectically uniting the same overall civilizational and cultural values and regional historical life."

4. It was on this date that the European Community and the United States recognized Bosnia-Herzegovina as an independent state. April 6, 1992, was also the forty-seventh anniversary of the liberation of Sarajevo from fascist occupation.

5. The Bosnian inscription reads as follows:

> Na ovum su mjestu Srpski zločinci
> u noći 25/26 8 1992. godine zapalili
> Nacionalnu i
> Univerzitetsku Biblioteku
> Bosne i Hercegovine
> U plamenu je nestalo više od 2 miliona
> kniga, časopisa i dokumenata.
> *Ne zaboravile,*
> *Pamite i opomnijite!*

6. There are no regular sightseeing companies offering Sarajevo city tours, except perhaps during the summer months. I joined a tour that Zijad had already scheduled for two women from Washington, D.C., consultants from the World Bank who had just completed their assignment in Sarajevo.

Chapter 3. National Legibility

1. In her prescient article about nationality categories in multicultural Bosnia, Tone Bringa (1993, 81) distinguishes between ethnicity as "mainly related to self-definition" and nationality, which "is about to which group the state decides one belongs." The present endeavor shows, however, that such a self-state distinction is far from dichotomous.

2. The Srebrenica Research Group's July 11, 2005, report cites the Red Cross figure as 7,300 murdered civilians (http://www.srebrenica-report.com/numbers.htm, accessed July 2009).

3. When I visited Lebiba, an ethnology staff member, in April 2008, she told me that conditions had changed radically for the better since 2006, when the acting director was appointed director. Under Ajša Softić's leadership, the museum has received a reasonable budget; it has been offering new temporary exhibits that complement the permanent collection; and on a mid-morning tour of the museum, I saw quite a few people of all ages. Since 2006 the staff has been paid on time, and their 1,000 KM (500 euros) monthly salaries are quite good by local standards.

4. http://www.hercegbosna.org/engleski/dummies.html (accessed April 27, 2006).

5. Čolović (2004) contends that among Croats as well as Serbs the "evocative *hayduk* (highwayman) tradition played a role . . . [as] legendary folk avengers and protectors" especially against the Turks.

6. http://www.srpska-mreza.com/library/facts/srbi_bih.html, last revised: March 20, 1997 (accessed July 2008).

7. Silajdžić broke with the SDA in 1996 to form his Party for Bosnia-Herzegovina (see chapter 7). Since October 2006, he has served as the Bosniac member of BiH's trinational presidency.

8. Mašović (1998, 145) asserts that, "to the end of the eighteenth century, they were all called '*Bosantsi*' [Bosnians, or in Turkish *Bosnevi*]" but there seems to be some disagreement among other sources as to whether the generic term was Bosanci or Bošnjaci (see Malcolm 1996, 148; Magaš 2003, 19). According to Skok (1971, 191), the form *Bošnjak* is attested from the fifteenth century, while *Bošnjanin* appeared in the fourteenth.

9. The borders of the medieval Bosnian kingdom expanded in the fourteenth century under its two strongest kings: Stjepan (Stephen) Kotromanić (d. 1353), who was born Orthodox (Fine 1975, 168; Malcolm 1996, 18), and his nephew, Tvrtko I (d. 1391), a practicing Catholic. Although these facts are almost indisputable, their ramifications and the circumstances surrounding them give rise to many questions.

10. On March 2, 1992, the newspaper *Oslobodjenje* published a story on page 6 under the headline "Nezapamćen zloćin na Baščaršiji: Krvana Svadba" (An Unforgettable Crime in Baščaršija: A Bloody Wedding). An attack on a Serbian Orthodox wedding party ended in the death of the bride's father and injuries to a cleric. In the days that followed, police investigators arrested a petty criminal with a Muslim name who had a history of mental illness. Ioannis Armakolas (2007, 87) notes that this incident was used as a scare tactic by radical Serb nationalists to spur Sarajevo Serbs to flee their city and resettle in the RS.

11. In Serbia many on the (radical) left prefer to use the Latin alphabet, as does the distinguished publishing house Biblioteka XX Veka.

12. http://www.sarajevo-tourism.com (accessed July 2009).

13. The first secular classical high school, or *gimnazija*, was established in Sarajevo toward the end of the nineteenth century under Austro-Hungarian rule. The University of Sarajevo was established in fits and starts during the 1940s and inaugurated its first rector in 1949. If Bosnians wished to attend a university prior to that date, they needed to study abroad.

Chapter 4. Census and Sensibility

1. Unlike the 1994 decision taken by the Council of Europe and the European Union to fund an extraordinary census in Macedonia (see V. Friedman 1996), these institutions did not insist on a statewide enumeration in BiH, nor did the OHR. See "No Population Census for Bosnia and Herzegovina in 2005," http://archive.oneworld.net/article/view/96351 (accessed July 2009).

2. Thanks to Mr. Mirko Popović, FBiH statistical librarian.

3. *Općina* can be glossed as "community" or "county," and the city of Sarajevo is divided into five of these. According to the 2002 census, Centar is home to 17 percent of Sarajevo's residents. Thanks to Amira Hađziosmanović, Jasna Beba, and Amer Ahmić for their kind hospitality and assistance.

4. See http://www.gfbv-sa.com.ba/romabihe.html, "Roma of Bosnia and Herzegovina" (accessed July 2009). The Roma of BiH are certainly citizens of the state, but they are outside its constituent nations. The report also notes, "Before the war, Roma in B&H lived just like other Roma in Yugoslavia with their minority rights respected. They describe the period of Tito's rule as the 'Golden Age' for Roma."

Chapter 5. Where Have All the Yugoslavs, Slovenes, and Gypsies Gone?

1. They are listed in Serbo-Croatian alphabetical order. See table 1.

2. These are also listed in Serbo-Croatian alphabetical order. Albanians and Hungarians were accorded a Yugoslav homeland in the Serbian autonomous provinces of Kosovo and Vojvodina, respectively. Jews and Gypsies did not qualify as nations according to Marxist-Leninist doctrines of the self-determination of nations and were not granted a national territory in Yugoslavia. The remaining national groups represent the legacy of earlier colonialism (Germans and Turks), propinquity (Italians), and/or movement among the Slavic peoples of Eastern Europe. But it is noteworthy that neither Bulgarians nor Greeks appear in the 1991 Yugoslav census. See Karakasidou 1997.

3. This is neither the time nor place to delve into the issue, but I must point out that those like Swanee Hunt (2004) who proclaim that the war in BiH was a male-only affair should reassess that assertion. Men throughout Bosnia-Herzegovina were forced into the war and had no escape hatches. Most convoys and refugee camps refused them. Some of my male Bosnian acquaintances in Israel told me they hid out near the Pula refugee camp in Croatia to be near their wives and daughters, although

they were subject to arrest and conscription. All this is to say that "This was not our war" applies as much to the men who objected to ultranationalist politics as to the women. Women, however, were given a legitimate way out of the war, whereas men had no such option (see Žarkov 2007).

4. See http://www.gfbv-sa.com.ba/romabihe.html.

5. Interestingly, during my 1997 visit to Sarajevo only eighteen months after the end of the war, when I noted to one of my hosts that Gypsy beggars were ubiquitous on the city streets, he responded that most of these so-called Gypsies were Bosniacs or Albanians who had fled their villages in Serb-dominant parts of Bosnia and were penniless immigrants. But their (ethnic) pride would not allow them to beg as they were, so they dressed up as Roma, for whom begging is just one of several occupational options.

Chapter 6. Sarajevo's Jews

1. My thanks go to Michele Sumka, who in 2002–6 participated in the Sarajevo Jewish community, for her comments on this chapter. Michele suggested that I eliminate the word "prosper" and use instead "exist" because most of Bosnia's Jews were quite poor. I have decided not to amend my text because even if they were not a wealthy community, the Jews of Sarajevo lived free of anti-Semitism and their community did indeed thrive.

2. The following are the dates and headlines of several *Jerusalem Post* articles from 1992: April 14, 1992, "Two Hundred More Jews Flown Out of Sarajevo"; August 18, 1992, "Last Group of Jewish Children Flees Sarajevo"; October 18, 1992, "Seventy-five Jews evacuated from Sarajevo"; October 22, 1992, "Forty More Jews from Sarajevo Are Expected Here Today."

3. Ashkenazim, or Jews from German and Eastern European lands, began settling in Sarajevo in the nineteenth century. Their numbers increased after 1878, when the Ottomans ceded Bosnia-Herzegovina to the Austro-Hungarian Empire. Ashkenazim, in the main, spoke Yiddish, a German-based language with many Hebrew, some Latin, and some Slavic words. Sephardic Jews' vernacular is Ladino, a Spanish-based language with many Hebrew and some Latin words. Both languages use the Hebrew alphabet. Synagogue liturgy and melodies and the pronunciation of Hebrew differ between Sephardim and Ashkenazim. The Ashkenazi synagogue is home to the Jewish community of Sarajevo, which since 1941 is the only operating Jewish house of worship. It has no rabbi. David Kamhi, the lay cantor, adheres to the Sephardic liturgy.

4. In earlier chapters the word *opština* was written as *općina*, which is the spelling used by the FBiH Bureau of Statistics. But several Sarajevans insist that *općina* is the Croatian variant, and *opština* the correct form in Bosnian. See chapter 7 for a longer discussion of the Bosnian language.

5. By the late 1930s, Sarajevo's Jewish population was estimated at ten to twelve thousand and constituted 10–15 percent of the city's population. The Sephardic com-

munity had completed its grand, bronze-domed new temple in 1930. The Nazis razed that building and confiscated or destroyed its contents. In the 1950s, the site of that building was donated by the Jewish community to the Socialist Republic of Bosnia-Herzegovina, and it is now home to the Bosnian Cultural Center.

6. A brief portrait of Greta appears in Swanee Hunt's *This Was Not Our War* (2004, 101–3 and 216–17). Greta is also the subject of a 1997 film by that name by Bosnian director Haris Pasović.

7. From January 1993 through July 30 of that year, men worked in three shifts to dig and reinforce an underground tunnel, which became the only route into and out of besieged Sarajevo.

8. In August 2002, Ernest's father, Mladen, regaled me with a long, horrible story about the family who took over his apartment during the war. During the same visit, Davor, the son of a Croat-Serb couple, whose brother was badly injured during the war, and Serbian Novica, who had served in the BiH army, were struggling to document claims to their apartments. Implicitly or explicitly conversations revolved around the suspicion that non-Muslims, especially Serbs, were given a harder time than anyone else in privatizing their apartments. A 2001 UNHCR report notes "discriminatory dismissal or recruitment based on ethnicity [and] political affiliation" as well as property repossessions (23).

9. As we will see in the next chapter, many in Sarajevo's Jewish community declared themselves Yugoslav in the census.

10. This struck me as odd because one of Sarajevo's central symbols, often invoked as a treasure of the city's multicultural heritage, is the Sarajevo Haggadah. Housed in the National Museum of Bosnia-Herzegovina, it has been described as "a masterpiece of Spanish illumination art from the 14th century[,] brought to Bosnia in the 16th century" (Bakaršić 2001, 268).

11. Here's Noel Malcolm's (1996, 112) version: "One intriguing story from the early nineteenth century involves the fate of a Jew from Travnik, Moses Chavijo, who converted to Islam, took the name of Derviš Ahmed, and began to rouse the local Muslims against the Jews. In 1817 the leaders of the Bosnian Jews complained to the next governor of Bosnia, Ruždi-paša, who seized the opportunity to squeeze some money out of the Jews: he commanded that they pay a recompense of 500,000 *groschen*, and seized ten leading Sarajevo Jews, including the rabbi, threatening to kill them if the payment were not made. The end of the story, however, is that a crowd of 3,000 Muslims took up arms and demanded the Jews' release—which was promptly done."

12. Actually, the golden rule is phrased positively, "Do unto others as you would have them do unto you." That is also Rabbi Hillel's oft-quoted answer to the question of how to summarize the Torah while standing on one foot.

13. During the war, and for a decade afterward, the Museum of the City of Sarajevo stored its artifacts in the Old Temple, property that belongs to the Jewish community. The city and the community agreed that once hostilities ceased the City Museum would remove its artifacts, and the Jewish Museum would reopen. Due to severe

budgetary problems, it took the City Museum years to vacate. Finally the Jewish community initiated a lawsuit. That course of action proved effective, and the Jewish Museum of Bosnia-Herzegovina reopened at the end of July 2004 to much fanfare.

14. This phrasing echoes that of Passover; Jews are obliged to tell the story of their liberation from generation to generation.

15. This notorious forgery was originally published in Russia by Professor Sergei Nilus in 1905 as an authoritative document that describes the meetings of Jewish elders conspiring to take over the world.

16. See Bakaršić 2001 for the most assiduously researched version of the story.

Chapter 7. Insisting on Bosnia-Herzegovina

1. The most notable of these forums are the Congress of Bosniac Intellectuals (VKBI) and the interdenominational, nonpartisan Krug/Circle 99. Yet we should keep in mind that intellectuals are not necessarily open to fluid or hybrid views of history. As Aleksandar Bošković (2005) has convincingly argued, historians and ethnographers throughout the former Yugoslavia were instrumental in framing and legitimizing nationalist narratives.

2. I have modified Hayden's definitive remark about the unimaginability of alternatives for several reasons that I hope will become clear as the chapter unfolds.

3. Sniper fire tragically killed his twenty-four-year old son, Karim, one of the last civilian casualties of the war. But Zaimović did not mention that death during our conversations.

4. As we have seen in chapter 3, although the ethnic designations and everyday practices of Bosnia's Catholics = Croats, Orthodox = Serbs, and Muslims = Bosniacs have changed over time, their historical narratives stress continuity (see Herzfeld 1997a, 39).

5. There are similar sorts of national dishes in several mixed-ethnic countries. See Munasinghe's *Callaloo or Tossed Salad* (2001) as an example from Trinidad.

6. Vucetic adds, "In addition to being portrayed as stupid, Bosnians come out as sexually promiscuous, omnisexual, and alcoholic" (2004, 17). From the sources he cites, it is impossible to tell if this unflattering portrayal comes from within Bosnia or from neighboring countries of the former Yugoslavia.

7. I heard that joke the same time that I first I heard mention of bosanski način during a 1983 visit to a Muslim family in rural Bosnia. Describing their lifestyle in a patrilineal, extended family, where everyone held age- and gender-specific tasks and pooled resources, they told me, "We are living the Bosnian way." Later I learned that this family form, the *zadruga,* was not unique to Bosnia (see St. Ehrlich 1966), but in modernizing twentieth-century Yugoslavia, the zadruga as a Bosnian way of life was deemed traditional and backward. At the same time, however, residents of the republic's capital boasted that their Bosnian way of warmth and hospitality, coupled with the beauty and efficiency of their city, made Sarajevo the world's choice for the 1984 Winter Olympic Games.

8. I never heard Bosniacs dismiss as romantic or inauthentic the idea of a unifying regionwide Bosnian culture. This does not mean, however, that there are no Bosniacs who harbor such sentiments.

9. See, for example, Ibrahim E. Berbić's *Bosansko-Turski Ućitelj* (Istanbul, 1895), and the *Gramatika Bosanskoga Jezika za Srednje Škole* (Sarajevo, 1903).

10. I gloss the word he used, *narod*, as "people," although it could also be translated as "nation."

11. From his collection *Kameni Spavač / Stone Sleeper* (1966–71), first published in Yugoslavia in 1966 and then republished in 1973. The English translation of the poem included here can be found at http://www.humanityquest.com/themes/inspiration/Languages/Croation/index.asp. The latest edition of *Stone Sleeper*, translated by Francis R. Jones, is scheduled for publication by Anvil Press in 2009.

12. Published in Sarajevo by Svjetlost in 1971. This version has been translated and printed by Branimir Anzulović, who notes, "Some of the terrifying images in the poem . . . were transformed into reality by the author some twenty years later" (1999, 129). A somewhat different translation can be found in *Under the Left Breast of the Century*, Karadžić's new (2005) book of not necessarily new poetry.

Chapter 8. After Yugoslavia, after War, after All

1. I alter somewhat the meaning, while remaining true to the spirit of this neologism offered by Marshall Sahlins, who collectively calls, "postmodernism, poststructuralism, postcolonialism and the like" "afterology" (1999, 404). Here I use "afterology" to signify the multiple conditions of the time of the "post(s)," that is, the unexpected and the expected, the creative and the mechanistic, the constrained and the freewheeling multidirectional transitions of postsocialism.

2. See Interview: Paddy Ashdown, High Representative: "Mostar will become a single city again," OHR Press Office, Vjesnik, January 27, 2004.

3. See the *Guardian*'s "Special Report: May 1, 2004: Slovenia Joins the EU": http://www.guardian.co.uk/eu/country/0,14489,1199966,00.html (accessed July 2009).

4. See "Interview: Miroslav Lajčak, EU Special Representative/High Representative in BiH," http://www.ohr.int/print/?content_id=41439 (accessed July 2009).

5. Despite Stroscheim's insistence in 2003 that Belgium is a model "divided house state," in the fall of 2007 lively discussions were under way about the future of the country after the Flemish language newspaper *Het Loatste Nieuws* revealed its September 18 poll results: 46.1 percent of Belgium's Flemish community advocated splitting the country now, while about two-thirds of the respondents said that they believe the country will split sooner or later.

6. In 2004 most, but not all, of my interlocutors in the RS were in favor of splitting the country. If BiH must remain together, they advocated maintenance of the Dayton decision that established the Serbian Republic on 49 percent of its territory and vested the constituent nations with governing power.

7. See the September 11, 2008, OHR Press Release, http://www.ohr.int/print/?content_id=42272 (accessed July 2009).

8. I am quite sure that most Sarajevans with good-paying jobs in international organizations consider themselves lucky, but sometimes those jobs make stringent demands. In August 2002, I met a professional musician who had resigned from his job in the Sarajevo Symphony Orchestra, which paid close to nothing, to become a Bosnian-English/English-Bosnian translator for the International Red Cross. He spoke of this decision with great enthusiasm, but I cannot help wondering if he regrets sidelining his music.

9. Citing frustration with the post, Lajčak resigned as high representative in February 2009. According to the March 12, 2009, *RFE/RL Balkan Report,* his replacement, Valentin Inzko, "is likely to be the last high representative appointed."

10. "Bosnia-Herzegovina: The Dayton Debate Revisited," *RFE/RL Balkan Report* 8 (39) (October 22, 2004), http://www.rferl.org/content/article/1341000.html (accessed July 2009).

11. Bulletin 110, published in May 2008 by the Federation's Statistical Bureau, shows that ethnically mixed marriages throughout Bosnia-Herzegovina peaked in 1983 with 12.8% of all marriages. In the Federation, 6.9% of all marriages were mixed in 1998; by 2006 that percentage had fallen to 4.7. The figures are somewhat higher for Sarajevo, and the downward trend is not steady: 9.8% (2001), 9.1% (2002), 7.7% (2003), 5.8% (2004), 6.8% (2005), 6.3% (2006).

References

Amin, Ash, and Nigel Thrift. 2002. *Cities: Reimagining the Urban.* London: Polity.

Anderson, Benedict. 1991. *Imagined Communities.* London: Verso.

———. 1992. "The New World Disorder." *New Left Review* 193:3–14.

Andreas, Peter. 2008. *Blue Helmets and Black Markets: The Business of Survival in the Siege of Sarajevo.* Ithaca, N.Y.: Cornell University Press.

Andrić, Ivo. [1945] 1961. *The Bridge on the Drina.* New York: Macmillan.

———. 1970. "A View of Sarajevo." In Tahmiščić 1970, 8–12.

Anzulovic, Branimir. 1999. *Heavenly Serbia: From Myth to Genocide.* New York: New York University Press.

Appadurai, Arjun. 1996. *Modernity at Large.* Minneapolis: University of Minnesota Press.

———. 2006. *Fear of Small Numbers: An Essay on the Geography of Anger.* Durham, N.C.: Duke University Press.

Arextaga, Begoña. 2003. "Maddening States." *Annual Review of Anthropology* 32:393–410.

Armakolas, Ioannis. 2007. "Sarajevo No More? Identity and the Experience of Place among Bosnian Serb Sarajevans in Republika Srpska." In Bougarel, Helms, and Duijzings 2007b, 79–99.

Bakaršić, Kemal. 1994. "The Libraries of Sarajevo and the Book That Saved Our Lives." The New Combat. New York. http://www.newcombat.net/article_thelibraries.html (accessed August 2007).

———. 2001. "The Never-Ending Story of C-4436 A.K.A. Sarajevo's Haggada Codex." *Wiener Slawistischer Almanach* 52:267–89.

Bakhtin, Mikhail. 1981. *The Dialogic Imagination.* Translated by Carol Emerson and J. Michael Holmquist. Austin: University of Texas Press.

Bakić-Hayden, Milica. 1996. "Nesting Orientalisms: The Case of Former Yugoslavia." *Slavic Review* 54:917–31.

Ballard, Roger. 1996. "Islam and the Construction of Europe." In *Muslims in the Margins: Political Responses to the Presence of Islam in Western Europe,* edited by W. A. R. Shadid and P. S. Van Konigsveld, 15–51. Kampen, Netherlands: Kok Pharos.
Ballinger, Pamela. 2003. *History in Exile: Memory and Identity at the Borders of the Balkans.* Princeton, N.J.: Princeton University Press.
———. 2004. "'Authentic Hybrids' in the Balkan Borderlands." *Current Anthropology* 45 (1): 31–60 (including comments).
Banac, Ivo. 1984. *The National Question in Yugoslavia: Origins, History, Politics.* Ithaca, N.Y.: Cornell University Press.
Bauman, Zygmunt. 1991. *Modernity and Ambivalence.* Cambridge: Polity.
———. 1996. *From Pilgrim to Tourist—or a Short History of Identity.* In *Questions of Cultural Identity,* edited by Stuart Hall and Paul du Gay, 18–36. London: Sage.
———. 1998. "Allosemitism: Premodern, Modern, Postmodern." In *Modernity, Culture and "the Jews,"* 143–56. London: Polity.
Baumann, Gerd. 1996. *Contesting Culture: Discourses of Identity in Multi-Ethnic London.* Cambridge: Cambridge University Press.
Bećirović, A. 2004. "Tribina VKBI: Jezik u medijama; Svega, a najmanje bosanskog jezika!" *Oslobodjenje,* April 4.
Beck, Ulrich. 2002. "The Cosmopolitan Perspective: Sociology in the Second Age of Modernity." In *Conceiving Cosmopolitanism: Theory, Context and Practice,* edited by Steven Vertovec and Robin Cohen, 61 85. Oxford: Oxford University Press.
Benjamin, Walter. 1979. *One Way Street and Other Essays.* London: NLB.
Berdahl, Daphne. 1999. *Where the World Ended: Re-Unification and Identity in the German Borderland.* Berkeley: University of California Press.
Berdahl, Daphne, Matti Bunzl, and Martha Lampland, eds. 2000. *Altering States: Ethnographies of Transition in Eastern Europe and the Former Soviet Union.* Ann Arbor: University of Michigan Press.
Bhabha, Homi. 1990. "The Third Space." In *Identity, Community, Culture, Difference,* edited by Jonathan Rutherford, 207–20. London: Lawrence and Wishart.
———. 1994. *The Location of Culture.* London: Routledge.
Bideleux, Robert, and Ian Jeffries. 2007. *The Balkans: A Post-Communist History.* London: Routledge.
Bilefsky, Dan. 2008. "Fears of New Ethnic Conflict in Bosnia." *New York Times,* December 14.
———. 2009. "Bosnia Serbs and Envoy Are at Odds on Powers." *New York Times,* June 20.
Blu, Karen. 1996. "'Where Do You Stay At?' Home Place and Community among the Lumbee." In Feld and Basso 1996, 197–227.
Boon, James A. 1999. *Verging on Extra-Vagance: Anthropology, History, Religion, Literature, Arts . . . Showbiz.* Princeton, N.J.: Princeton University Press.
Borneman, John, and Nick Fowler. 1997. "Europeanization." *Annual Reviews in Anthropology* 26: 487–514.

Bose, Sumantra. 2002. *Bosnia after Dayton: Nationalist Partition and International Intervention.* London: Hurst.

Bošković, Aleksandar. 2005. "Distinguishing 'Self' and 'Other': Anthropology and National Identity in Former Yugoslavia." *Anthropology Today* 21 (1): 8–13.

Bougarel, Xavier. 1996. *Bosnie, anatomie d'un conflit.* Paris: La Découverte.

———. 2007. "Death and the Nationalist: Martyrdom, War Memory and Veteran Identity among Bosnian Muslims." In Bougarel, Helms, and Duijzings 2007b, 167–91.

Bougarel, Xavier, Elissa Helms, and Ger Duijzings. 2007a. "Introduction." In Bougarel, Helms, and Duijzings 2007b, 1–35.

———, eds. 2007b. *The New Bosnian Mosaic.* Aldershot, England: Ashgate.

Bourdieu, Pierre. 1977. *Outline of a Theory of Practice.* Cambridge: Cambridge University Press.

———. 1984. *Distinction: A Social Critique of the Judgement of Taste.* Cambridge, Mass.: Harvard University Press.

Bowen, John R. 2007. *Why the French Don't Like Headscarves: Islam, the State and Public Space.* Princeton, N.J.: Princeton University Press.

Bozic, Gordana. 2006. "Reeducating the Hearts of Bosnian Students: An Essay on Some Aspects of Education in Bosnia and Herzegovina." *East European Politics and Society* 20 (2): 319–42.

Bringa, Tone. 1993. "Nationality Categories, National Identification and Identity Formation in 'Multinational' Bosnia." *Anthropology of East Europe Review* 11 (1–2): 80–88.

———. 1995. *Being Muslim the Bosnian Way.* Princeton, N.J.: Princeton University Press.

Brubaker, Rogers. 2004. *Ethnicity without Groups.* Cambridge, Mass.: Harvard University Press.

Bulgakov, Mikhail. 1996. *The Master and Margarita.* Translated by Diana Burgin and Katherine Tiernan O'Connor. London: Vintage.

Bunce, Valerie. 1995. "Should Transitologists Be Grounded?" *Slavic Review* 54 (1): 111–27.

Bunzl, Matti. 2004. *Symptoms of Modernity: Jews and Queers in Late-Twentieth-Century Vienna.* Berkeley: University of California Press.

Burawoy, Michael, and Katherine Verdery. 1999a. "Introduction." In Burawoy and Verdery 1999b, 1–17.

———, eds. 1999b. *Uncertain Transition: Ethnographies of Change in the Postsocialist World.* Lanham, Md.: Rowman and Littlefield.

Burns, John F. 1992. "Bosnia Loss Hints at Croat-Serb Deal." *New York Times,* October 11.

Bushnell, John. 1988. "Urban Leisure in Post-Stalin Russia: Stability as a Social Problem?" In *Soviet Society and Culture: Essays in Honor of Vera S. Dunham,* edited by Terry E. Thompson and Richard Sheldon, 58–86. Boulder, Colo.: Westview.

Campbell, David. 1999. "Violence, Justice, and Identity in the Bosnian Conflict." In *Sovereignty and Subjectivity,* edited by J. Edkins, N. Persram, and V. Pin-Fat, 21–37. Boulder, Colo.: Lynne Rienner.

Canclini, Nestor Garcia. 2000. "The State of War and the State of Hybridization." In *Without Guarantees: In Honour of Stuart Hall,* edited by Paul Gilroy, Lawrence Grossberg, and Angela McRobbie, 38–52. London: Verso.

Cattaruzza, Amael. 2001. "Sarajevo, capitale incertaine." *Balkanologie* 5 (1–2): 67–78.

Certeau, Michel de. 1984. *The Practice of Everyday Life.* Translated by Steven Rendall. Berkeley: University of California Press.

Chandler, David. 2000. *Bosnia: Faking Democracy after Dayton.* 2nd ed. London: Pluto.

Chaveneau-Lebrun, Emmanuelle. 2001. "La Ligne Frontiere inter-entites: Nouvelle frontiere, nouveau pays?" *Balkanologie* 5 (1–2): 79–91.

Cohen, Lenard. 1995. *Broken Bonds: Yugoslavia's Disintegration and Balkan Politics in Transition.* 2nd ed. Boulder, Colo.: Westview.

Cohn, Bernard S. 1990. "The Census, Social Structure and Objectification in South Asia." In *An Anthropologist among the Historians and Other Essays,* by Bernard S. Cohen, 224–54. New Delhi: Oxford University Press.

Coles, Kimberley A. 2002. "Ambivalent Builders: Europeanization, the Production of Difference, and Internationals in Bosnia-Herzegovina." *PoLar* 25 (1): 1–15.

Čolović, Ivan. 2004. "A Criminal-National Hero? But Who Else?" In *Balkan Identities: Nation and Memory,* edited by Maria Todorova, 253–68. New York: New York University Press.

Crane, Susan A. 1997. "Writing the Individual Back into Collective Memory." *American Historical Review* 102 (5): 1372–85.

Dahlman, Carl, and Gearóid ÓTuathail. 2005. "Broken Bosnia: The Localized Geopolitics of Displacement and Return in Two Bosnian Places." *Annals of the Association of American Geographers* 95 (3): 644–62.

Deets, Stephen. 2006. "Public Policy in the Passive-Aggressive State: Health Care Reform in Bosnia-Hercegovina, 1995–2001." *Europe-Asia Studies* 58 (1): 57–80.

Deleuze, Gilles. 1990. *The Logic of Sense.* New York: Columbia University Press.

Del Negro, Giovanna. 2004. *The Passeggiata and Popular Culture in an Italian Town.* Montreal: McGill-Queen's University Press.

Denich, Bette. 2000. "Unmaking Multiethnicity in Yugoslavia: Media and Metamorphosis." In Halpern and Kideckel 2000, 39–55.

Derrida, Jacques. 2001. *On Cosmopolitanism and Forgiveness.* London: Routledge.

Dizdar, Mak. 2009. *Stone Sleeper.* Translated by Francis R. Jones. London: Anvil.

Dizdarević, Zlatko. 1994. *Portraits of Sarajevo.* New York: Fromm International.

Djilas, Aleksa. 1991. *The Contested Country: Yugoslav Unity and Communist Revolution, 1919–1953.* Cambridge, Mass.: Harvard University Press.

Donia, Robert J. 2006. *Sarajevo: A Biography*. Ann Arbor: University of Michigan Press.

Donia, Robert J., and John V. A. Fine Jr. 1994. *Bosnia-Hercegovina: A Tradition Betrayed*. London: Hurst.

Durkheim, Emile. 1964. *The Division of Labor in Society*. Translated by George Simpson. New York: Free Press.

Ekmecic, Milorad. 2000. "Historiography by the Garb Only." Response to Malcolm. http://www.kosovo.net/nmalk2.html (accessed August 2008).

Erickson, Jennifer. 2003. "Reflections of Fieldwork with Romani Women: Race, Class, and Feminism in Bosnia-Herzegovina." *Anthropology of East Europe Review* 21 (2): 113–17.

European Roma Rights Center. 2004. "ERRC Country Report: The Non-Constituents; Rights Deprivation of Roma in Post-Genocide Bosnia and Herzegovina." http://www.errc.org/cikk.php?cikk=112 (accessed July 2009).

Farmer, Paul. 2004. *Pathologies of Power: Health, Human Rights, and the New War on the Poor*. Berkeley: University of California Press.

Federacija Bosne i Hercegovine. 2003a. *Bosansko-Podrinjski Kanton u brojkama; Hercegbosanski Kanton u brojkama; Hercegovačko-Neretvanski Kanton u brojkama; Kanton Sarajevo u brojkama; Kanton Tuzla u brojkama; Posavski Kanton u brojkama; Srednjobosanski Kanton u brojkama; Unsko-Sanski Kanton u brojkama; Zapadno-Hercegovački Kanton u brojkama; Zeničko-Dobojski Kanton u brojkama*. Sarajevo: Federalni Zavod za Statistiku.

———. 2003b. *Statistički godišnjak/Ljetopis Federacije Bosne i Hercegovine*. Sarajevo: Federalni Zavod za Statistiku.

———. 2008. *Stanovništva Federacije Bosne i Hercegovine 1996–2006 / Population of the Federation of Bosnia and Herzegovina 1996–2006*. Statistički Bilten / Statistical Bulletin 110. Sarajevo: Federalni Zavod za Statistiku.

Feld, Steven, and Keith Basso, eds. 1996. *Senses of Place*. Santa Fe: School of American Research Press.

Ferguson, James, and Akhil Gupta. 2002. "Spatializing States." *American Ethnologist* 29 (4): 981–1002.

Filipović, Muhamed. 2007. *Ko smo mi Bošnjaci?* Sarajevo: Prosperitet.

Filipovic, Zlata. 1994. *Zlata's Diary*. New York: Viking.

Fine, John V. A., Jr. 1975. *The Bosnian Church: A New Interpretation*. New York: Columbia University Press.

Foucault, Michel. 1973. *The Order of Things*. New York: Vantage Books.

———. 1991. "Governmentality." In *The Foucault Effect: Studies in Governmentality*, edited by Graham Burchell, Colin Gordon, and Peter Miller, 87–104. Chicago: University of Chicago Press.

Friedman, Francine. 1996. *The Bosnian Muslims: Denial of a Nation*. Boulder, Colo.: Westview.

———. 2004. *Bosnia: A Polity on the Brink.* New York: Routledge.

Friedman, Victor A. 1996. "Observing the Observed: Language, Ethnicity, and Power in the1994 Macedonian Census and Beyond." *New Balkan Politics—Journal of Politics* 3. http://www.newbalkanpolitics.org.mk/OldSite/Issue_3/friedman.eng.asp (accessed July 2009).

Fukuyama, Francis. 1989. "The End of History?" *National Interest* 16:3–18.

Gagnon, V. P., Jr. 2004. *The Myth of Ethnic War: Serbia and Croatia in the 1990s.* Ithaca, N.Y.: Cornell University Press.

Gellner, Ernest. 1983. *Nations and Nationalism.* Oxford: Basil Blackwell.

Gilbert, Andrew. 2006. "Reifying Orders: Problems of State-Building and State Authority in Post-war Bosnia-Herzegovina." Paper presented at the 105th Annual Meeting of the American Anthropological Association, San Jose, California.

Gilloch, Graeme. 1996. *Myth and Metropolis: Walter Benjamin and the City.* Cambridge: Polity.

Gilroy, Paul. 1987. *There Ain't No Black in the Union Jack.* London: Routledge.

———. 2000. *Beyond Race: Imagining Political Culture beyond the Color Line.* Cambridge, Mass.: Harvard University Press.

———. 2004. *Between Camps: Nations, Cultures and the Allure of Race.* London: Routledge.

Glenny, Misha. 2001. *The Balkans: Nationalism, War, and the Great Powers.* New York: Penguin.

Goldberg, David. 1997. *Racial Subjects.* New York: Routledge.

Gottdiener, Mark. 1985. *The Social Production of Urban Space.* Austin: University of Texas Press.

Gozdziak, Elzbieta M. 1995. "Needy Guests, Reluctant Hosts: The Plight of Rumanians in Poland." *Anthropology of East Europe Review* 13 (1): 9–14.

Grandits, Hannes, and Christian Promitzer. 2000. "'Former Comrades' at War: Historical Perspectives on 'Ethnic Cleansing' in Croatia." In Halpern and Kideckel 2000, 123–42.

Green, Sarah. 2005. *Notes from the Balkans.* Princeton, N.J.: Princeton University Press.

Grubišić, Vinko. 2003. "The Language Situation in Post-Dayton Bosnia and Herzegovina." *Toronto Slavic Quarterly: University of Toronto Academic Electronic Journal in Slavic Studies.* http://www.utoronto.ca/tsq/03/vinko/shtml (accessed July 2008).

Hall, Stuart. 1995. "New Cultures for Old." In *A Place in the World? Places, Cultures and Globalization,* edited by Doreen Massey and Pat Jess, 175–213. Oxford: Oxford University Press.

———. 1996. "Introduction: Who Needs Identity?" In *Questions of Cultural Identity,* edited by Stuart Hall and Paul du Gay, 1–17. London: Sage.

———. 1997. "The Local and the Global: Globalization and Ethnicity." In *Dangerous*

Liaisons, edited by A. McClintock, A. Mufti, and Ella Shohat, 173–87. Minneapolis: University of Minnesota Press.

Halpern, Joel, and David Kideckel, eds. *Neighbors at War: Anthropological Perspectives on Yugoslav Ethnicity, Culture, and History*. University Park: Pennsylvania State University Press.

Hanak, Peter. 1998. *The Garden and the Workshop: Essays on the Cultural History of Vienna and Budapest*. Princeton, N.J.: Princeton University Press.

Hann, C. M., ed. 2002. *Postsocialism: Ideas, Ideologies and Practices in Eurasia*. London: Routledge.

Hannerz, Ulf. 1980. *Exploring the City*. New York: Columbia University Press.

———. 1996. *Transnational Connections: Culture, People, Places*. London: Routledge.

Hastings, Adrian. 1997. *The Construction of Nationhood: Ethnicity, Religion and Nationalism*. Cambridge: Cambridge University Press.

Hayden, Robert M. 1996. "Imagined Communities and Real Victims: Self-Determination and Ethnic Cleansing in Yugoslavia." *American Ethnologist* 23 (4): 783–801.

———. 2000. "Muslims as 'Others' in Serbian and Croatian Politics." In Halpern and Kideckel 2000, 116–24.

———. 2007. "Moral Vision and Impaired Insight: The Imagining of Other Peoples' Communities in Bosnia." *Current Anthropology* 48 (1): 105–31 (including comments).

Henkel, Heiko. 2007. "The Location of Islam: Inhabiting Istanbul in a Muslim Way." *American Ethnologist* 34 (1): 57–70.

Herberg, Will. 1955. *Protestant-Catholic-Jew*. Chicago: University of Chicago Press.

Herzfeld, Michael. 1997a. *Cultural Intimacy: Social Poetics in the Nation-State*. New York: Routledge.

———. 1997b. "Theorizing Europe: Persuasive Paradoxes." *American Anthropologist* 99 (4): 713–15.

Herzog, Todd. 1997. "Hybrids and *Mischlinge*: Translating Anglo-American Cultural Theory into German." *German Quarterly* 70 (1): 1–17.

Heywood, Colin. 1996. "Bosnia under Ottoman Rule, 1463–1800." In Pinson 1996, 22–53.

Hirsch, Eric. 1995. "Introduction." In *The Anthropology of Landscape: Perspectives on Place and Space*, edited by Eric Hirsch and Michael O'Hanlon, 1–30. Oxford: Clarendon.

Hirsch, Francine. 2005. *Empire of Nations: Ethnographic Knowledge and the Making of the Soviet Union*. Ithaca, N.Y.: Cornell University Press.

Holbrooke, Richard. 1999. *To End a War*. New York: Random House.

Holston, James, and Arjun Appadurai. 1999. "Introduction: Cities and Citizenship." In *Cities and Citizenship*, edited by James Holston, 1–18. Durham, N.C.: Duke University Press.

Hunt, Swanee. 2004. *This Was Not Our War: Bosnian Women Reclaiming the Peace.* Durham, N.C.: Duke University Press.

Huseby-Darvas, Éva V. 2000. "Refugee Women from Former Yugoslavia in the Camps of Rural Hungary." In Halpern and Kideckel 2000, 339–56.

Huyssen, Andreas. 1997. "The Voids of Berlin." *Critical Inquiry* 24:57–81.

Ignatieff, Michael. 1993. *Blood and Belonging.* New York: Farrar, Strauss and Giroux.

Imamović, Mustafa. 2000. *Bošnjaci / Bosniaks.* Sarajevo: Vijeće Kongresa Bošnjačkih Intelektualaca.

Isaković, Alija. 1992. "A Word about the Bosnian Language." Preface to *Dictionary of Characteristic Words of the Bosnian Language.* Wuppertal: Bambi.

Jansen, Stef. 2001. "The Streets of Beograd: Urban Space and Protest Identities in Serbia." *Political Geography* 20 (1): 35–55.

———. 2005. "National Numbers in Context: Maps and Stats in Representations of the Post-Yugoslav Wars." *Identities: Global Studies in Culture and Power* 12:45–68.

Judah, Tim. 2000. *Kosovo: War and Revenge.* New Haven, Conn.: Yale University Press.

Kalamujic, Azhar. 2001. "Izetbegoviceva Kongresna Inicijativa: Nadnacija Bosanaca." *Oslobodjenje—internet izdanje,* October 6, 2001.

Kampschror, Beth. 2001. "Multi-cultural Bosnia?" *Central European Review* 3 (17). http://www.ce-review.org/01/17/kampschror17.html (accessed July 2009).

Kaplan, Robert D. 1994. *Balkan Ghosts: A Journey through History.* New York: Vintage Books.

Karahasan, Dzevad. 1993. *Sarajevo: Exodus of a City.* Translated by Slobodan Drakulić. New York: Kodansha International.

Karakasidou, Anastasia N. 1997. *Fields of Wheat, Hills of Blood: Passages to Nationhood in Greek Macedonia, 1870–1990.* Chicago: University of Chicago Press.

Kennedy, Ruby Jo Reeves. 1944. "Single or Triple Melting Pot? Intermarriage Trends in New Haven, 1870–1940." *American Journal of Sociology* 49 (4): 331–39.

Kenny, Michael, and David I. Kertzer, eds. 1983. *Urban Life in Mediterranean Europe: Anthropological Perspectives.* Urbana: University of Illinois Press.

Kertzer, David I., and Dominique Arel. 2002. "Consensus, Identity Formation, and the Struggle for Political Power." In *Census and Identity: The Politics of Race, Ethnicity, and Language in National Censuses,* edited by David I. Kertzer and Dominique Arel, 1–42. Cambridge: Cambridge University Press.

Kideckel, David A. 2008. *Getting By in Postsocialist Romania.* Bloomington: University of Indiana Press.

Koštović, Nijazija. 2001. *Sarajevo: Evropski Jeruzalem.* Sarajevo: Bravo Public Team.

Kržišnik Busić, Vera. 1997. *Bosanski identitet: Između prošlosti i budućnosti.* Sarajevo: Bosanska Kniga.

Kugelmass, Jack. 1986. *The Miracle of Intervale Avenue.* New York: Schocken Books.

Kurspahić, Kemal. 1997. *As Long as Sarajevo Exists.* Stony Creek, Conn.: Pamphleteer's Press.

Lampe, John R. 2000. *Yugoslavia as History: Twice There Was a Country.* 2nd ed. Cambridge: Cambridge University Press.

Lane, Ann. 2004. *Yugoslavia: When Ideals Collide.* New York: Palgrave-Macmillan.

Lefebvre, Henri. 1996. "Right to the City." In *Writings on Cities: Henri Lefebvre,* translated and edited by Eleanore Kofman and Elizabeth Lebas, 61–181. Oxford: Blackwell.

Levy, Moric. 1996. *Sefardi u Bosni.* Sarajevo: Bosanska Biblioteka.

Linke, Ulli. 1999. *Blood and Nation: The European Aesthetics of Race.* Philadelphia: University of Pennsylvania Press.

Lockwood, William G. 1975. *European Moslems: Economy and Ethnicity in West Bosnia.* New York: Academic Press.

Lovrenović, Ivan. 2001. *Bosnia: A Cultural History.* London: Saqi Books in association with the Bosnian Institute.

Maas, Peter. 1996. *Love Thy Neighbour: A Story of War.* London: Papermac.

Magaš, Branka. 2003. "On Bosnianness." *Nations and Nationalism* 9 (1): 19–23.

Mahmutćehajić, Rusmir. 2000. *Bosnia the Good: Tolerance and Tradition.* Budapest: Central European University Press.

———. 2003. *Sarajevo Essays: Politics, Ideology, and Tradition.* Albany: State University of New York Press.

Malcolm, Noel. 1996. *Bosnia: A Short History.* London: Papermac.

Mann, Carol. 2001. "Une banlieue de Sarajevo en guerre: Les Amazones de la 'Kuca' ou la résistance des femmes de Dobrinja; Mémoire de DEA." PhD diss., Ecole des hautes études en sciences sociales, Paris.

Markowitz, Fran. 1994. "Soviet Dis-Union and the Fragmentation of Self: Implications for the Emigrating Jewish Family." *East European Jewish Affairs* 24 (1): 3–17.

———. 1995. "Discussion: Rape, Torture, Warfare . . . and Refuge." *Anthropology of East Europe Review* 13 (1): 44–50.

———. 1996. "Living in Limbo: Bosnian Muslims in Israel." *Human Organization* 55 (1): 1–6.

———. 2004. "Talking about Culture: Globalization, Human Rights and Anthropology." *Anthropological Theory* 4 (3): 329–52.

———. 2007. "Census and Sensibilities in Sarajevo." *Comparative Studies in Society and History* 49 (1): 40–73.

Mašović, Sulejman. 1998. "Genocide against Bosniaks." In *Religion and the War in Bosnia,* edited by Paul Mojzes, 145–49. Atlanta: Scholars Press.

Massey, Doreen. 2000. "Travelling Thoughts." In *Without Guarantees: In Honour of Stuart Hall,* edited by Paul Gilroy, Lawrence Grossberg, and Angela McRobbie, 225–32. London: Verso.

McCarthy, Justin. 1996. "Ottoman Bosnia, 1800 to 1878." In Pinson 1996, 54–83.

McMahon, Patrice. 2004. "Managing Ethnic Conflict in Bosnia: International Solutions to Domestic Problems." In *Reflections on the Balkan Wars: Ten Years after the Break Up of Yugoslavia,* edited by Jeffrey S. Morton, R. Craig Nation, Paul Forage, and Stefano Bianchini, 189–209. London: Palgrave Macmillan.

Merleau-Ponty, Maurice. 1962. *The Phenomenology of Perception.* Translated by Colin Smith. London: Routledge and Kegan Paul.

Mertus, Julie. 2000. "Nationalist Minorities under the Dayton Accord: Lessons from History." In Halpern and Kideckel 2000, 234–52.

More, Kenneth. 1975. "The City as Context: Context as Process." *Urban Anthropology* 4 (1): 17–23.

Moore, Patrick, with Ulrich Buechsenschuetz. 2004. "The Western Balkans: Waiting at NATO's Door." *RFE/RL Balkan Report* 8 (18) (May 27). http://www.rferl.org/content/article/1340979.html (accessed July 2009).

Mulaj, Klejda. 2005. "On Bosnia's Borders and Ethnic Cleansing: Internal and External Factors." *Nationalism and Ethnic Politics* 11:1–24.

Munasinghe, Viranjini. 2001. *Callaloo or Tossed Salad? East Indians and the Cultural Politics of Identity in Trinidad.* Ithaca, N.Y.: Cornell University Press.

———. 2002. "Nationalism in Hybrid Spaces: The Production of Impurity out of Purity." *American Ethnologist* 29 (3): 663–92.

Myerhoff, Barbara. 1979. *Number Our Days.* New York: Dutton.

Nederveen Pieterse, Jan. 2001. "Hybridity, So What?" *Theory, Culture and Society* 18 (2–3): 219–45.

Neidhardt, Tatjana. 2004. *Sarajevo kroz vrijeme.* Sarajevo: Arka.

Nora, Pierre. 1989. "Between Memory and History: *Lieux de Mémoire.*" *Representations* 26:7–24.

Okey, Robin. 2004. "Serbian, Croatian, Bosnian? Language and Nationality in the Lands of Former Yugoslavia." *East European Quarterly* 38 (4): 419–41.

Ong, Aihwa. 1996. "Cultural Citizenship as Subject-Making." *Current Anthropology* 37 (5): 737–62 (including comments).

Park, Robert E. 1926. "The Urban Community as a Spatial Pattern and Moral Order." In *The Urban Community,* edited by Ernest W. Burgess. Chicago: University of Chicago Press.

Pavlowitch, Stevan K. 2002. *Serbia: The History behind the Name.* London: Hurst.

Pejanović, Mirko. 2004. *Through Bosnian Eyes: The Political Memoir of a Bosnian Serb.* West Lafayette, Ind.: Purdue University Press.

Perica, Vjekoslav. 2002. *Balkan Idols: Religion and Nationalism in Yugoslav States.* Oxford: Oxford University Press.

Pinson, Mark, ed. 1996. *The Muslims of Bosnia-Herzegovina.* Cambridge, Mass.: Harvard University Press.

Pollack, Sheldon, Homi K. Bhabha, Carol A. Breckenridge, and Dipesh Chakrabarty. 2002. "Cosmopolitanisms." In *Cosmopolitanism,* edited by Carol A. Breckenridge,

Sheldon Pollock, Homi K. Bhabha, and Dipesh Chakrabarty, 1–14. Durham, N.C.: Duke University Press.

Ramet, Pedro. 1984. *Nationalism and Federalism in Yugoslavia, 1963–1983*. Bloomington: Indiana University Press.

Ramet, Sabrina P. 1999. *Balkan Babel: The Disintegration of Yugoslavia from the Death of Tito to the War for Kosovo.* 3rd ed. Boulder, Colo.: Westview.

———. 2005. *Thinking about Yugoslavia: Scholarly Debates about the Yugoslav Breakup and the Wars in Bosnia and Kosovo.* Cambridge: Cambridge University Press.

Renan, Ernest. [1882] 1996. "What Is a Nation / Qu'est-ce qu'une nation?" In *Becoming National: A Reader,* edited by Geoff Eley and Ronald Grigor Suny, 41–55. New York: Oxford University Press.

Republika Bosne i Hercegovine. 1993. *Nacionalni sastav stanovništva.* Statistički Bilten 234. Sarajevo: Državni Zavod za Statistiku Bosne i Hercegovine.

Richardson, Tanya. 2005. "Walking Streets, Talking History: The Making of Odessa." *Ethnology* 44 (1): 13–33.

———. 2008. *Kaleidoscopic Odessa.* Toronto: University of Toronto Press.

Riedlmayer, Andras. 1993. *A Brief History of Bosnia-Herzegovina.* Cambridge, Mass.: Harvard University. http://www.kakarigi.net/manu/briefhis.htm (accessed July 2009).

Robbins, Bruce. 1998. "Actually Existing Cosmopolitanism." In *Cosmopolities: Thinking and Feeling beyond the Nation,* edited by Pheng Cheah and Bruce Robbins, 1–19. Minneapolis: University of Minnesota Press.

Robin-Hunter, Laurence. 2001. "Brčko: Un microcosme de la Bosnie?" *Balkanologie* 5 (1–2): 93–106.

Robinson, Guy M., Sten Engelstoft, and Alma Pobric. 2001. "Remaking Sarajevo: Bosnian Nationalism after the Dayton Accord." *Political Geography* 20:957–80.

Rosaldo, Renato. 1989. *Culture and Truth.* Boston: Beacon.

Rotenberg, Robert. 1992. *Time and Order in Metropolitan Vienna.* Washington, D.C.: Smithsonian Institution Press.

Rothschild, Joseph. 1993. *Return to Diversity: A Political History of East Central Europe since World War II.* 2nd ed. New York: Oxford University Press.

Sahlins, Marshall. 1999. "Two or Three Things That I Know about Culture." *Journal of the Royal Anthropological Institute* 5 (3): 399–421.

Said, Edward. 1978. *Orientalism.* New York: Basic Books.

St. Erlich, Vera. 1966. *Family in Transition: A Study of 300 Yugoslav Villages.* Princeton, N.J.: Princeton University Press.

Scheper-Hughes, Nancy. 1995. "The Primacy of the Ethical: Propositions for a Militant Anthropology." *Current Anthropology* 36 (3): 409–20

Schwartz, Stephen. 2005. *Sarajevo Rose: A Balkan Jewish Notebook.* London: SAQI in association with the Bosnian Institute.

Scott, James C. 1998. *Seeing like a State.* New Haven, Conn.: Yale University Press.

Sekulic, Dusko, Garth Massey, and Randy Hodson. 1994. "Who Were the Yugoslavs? Failed Sources of a Common Identity in the Former Yugoslavia." *American Sociological Review* 59 (1): 83–97.

Sennett, Richard. 2000. "Reflections on the Public Realm." In *A Companion to the City,* edited by Gary Bridge and Sophie Watson, 380–87. Oxford: Blackwell.

Serotta, Edward. 1994. *Survival in Sarajevo: How a Jewish Community Came to the Aid of Its City.* Vienna: Edition Christian Brandstätter.

Short, John Ronnie. 2000. "Three Urban Discourses." In *A Companion to the City,* edited by Gary Bridge and Sophie Watson, 18–45. Oxford: Blackwell.

Shoup, Paul. 1968. *Communism and the Yugoslav National Question.* New York: Columbia University Press.

Silber, Laura, and Allan Little. 1997. *Yugoslavia: Death of a Nation.* New York: Penguin.

Simic, Drazen. 2001. "How Many Inhabitants Does Bosnia Have?" AIM-Sarajevo, April 28. http://tinyurl.com/nhg5gg (accessed July 2009).

Simmel, Georg. 1950a. "Metropolis and Mental Life." In *The Sociology of Georg Simmel,* edited by Kurt Wolff, 409–24. Glencoe, Ill.: Free Press.

———. 1950b. "The Stranger." In *The Sociology of Georg Simmel,* edited by Kurt Wolff, 402–8. Glencoe, Ill.: Free Press.

Simmons, Cynthia. 2001. "Urbicide." *Partisan Review* 68 (4): 624–30.

———. 2002. "A Multicultural, Multiethnic, and Multiconfessional Bosnia: Myth and Reality." *Nationalities Papers* 39:623–38.

Singer, Milton. 1991. *Semiotics of Cities, Selves and Cultures.* Berlin: Mouton de Gruyter.

Skok, Petar. 1971 *Etimologijski rjećnik hrvatskoga ili srpskoga jezika.* Zagreb: Jugoslavenska akademija znanosti i umijetnost.

Somun, Hajrudin. 2003. *Bosnia Today.* Malaysia: Limkokwing University.

Sorabji, Cornelia. 2006. "Managing Memories in Post-War Sarajevo: Individuals, Bad Memories, and New Wars," *Journal of the Royal Anthropological Institute,* n.s., 12:1–18.

Soysal, Yasemin N. 1994. *Limits of Citizenship: Migrants and Postnational Membership in Europe.* Chicago: University of Chicago Press.

Spangler, Michael. 1983. "Urban Research in Yugoslavia: Regional Variation in Urbanization." In Kenny and Kertzer 1983, 76–108.

Stalin, Joseph. [1913] 1975. *Marxism and the National-Colonial Question.* San Francisco: Proletarian.

Stefansson, Anders H. 2003. "Under My Own Sky? The Cultural Dynamics of Refugee Return and (Re)Integration in Post-War Sarajevo." PhD diss., University of Copenhagen.

———. 2004. "Sarajevo Suffering." In *Homecomings: Unsettling Paths of Return,* edited by Fran Markowitz and Anders H. Stefansson, 54–75. Lanham, Md.: Lexington Books.

———. 2007. "Urban Exile: Locals, Newcomers and the Cultural Transformation of Sarajevo." In Bougarel, Helms, and Duijzings 2007b, 59–77.
Stewart, Michael. 1997. *The Time of the Gypsies.* Boulder, Colo.: Westview.
Stokes, Gale, John Lampe, and Dennison Rusinow, with Julie Mostow. 1996. "Instant History: Understanding the Wars of Yugoslav Succession." *Slavic Review* 55 (1): 136–60.
Stolcke, Verena. 1995. "Talking Culture: New Boundaries, New Rhetorics of Exclusion in Europe." *Current Anthropology* 6 (1): 1–24.
Stroschein, Sherill. 2003. "What Belgium Can Teach Bosnia: The Uses of Autonomy in 'Divided House' States." *Journal on Ethnopolitics and Minority Issues in Europe* 3. http://www.ecmi.de/jemie (accessed July 2007).
Sucic, Daria Sito. 1996. "The Fragmentation of Serbo-Croatian into Three New Languages." *Transition* 2 (2). http://www.la.wayne.edu/polisci/kdk/easteurope/sources/sucic/html (accessed June 2009).
Sudetic, Chuck. 1998. *Blood and Vengeance.* New York: Penguin Books.
Svašek, Maruška, ed. 2006. *Postsocialism: Politics and Emotions in Central and Eastern Europe.* New York: Berghahn Books.
Tahmišečić, H. 1970. *Sarajevo.* Sarajevo: Zavod za Izdavanje Udžbenika.
Tanović-Miller, Naza. 2001. *Testimony of a Bosnian.* College Station: Texas A&M University Press.
Todorov, Nikolai. 1983. *The Balkan City, 1400–1900.* Seattle: University of Washington Press.
Todorova, Maria. 1997. *Imagining the Balkans.* New York: Oxford.
———. 2004. "Introduction: Learning Memory, Remembering Identity." In *Balkan Identities: Nation and Memory,* 1–24. New York: New York University Press.
Trumpener, Katie. 1995. "The Time of the Gypsies: A 'People without History' in the Narratives of the West." In *Identities,* edited by Kwame Anthony Appiah and Henry Louis Gates Jr., 338–79. Chicago: University of Chicago Press.
Ugrešić, Dubravka. 1998. *A Culture of Lies.* University Park: Pennsylvania State University Press.
United Nations High Commission for Refugees. 2001. "UNHCR's Position on Categories of Persons from Bosnia and Herzegovina in Continued Need of International Protection." http://tinyurl.com/mnt2rm (accessed July 2009).
Urla, Jacqueline. 1993. "Cultural Politics in an Age of Statistics: Numbers, Nations, and the Making of Basque Identity." *American Ethnologist* 20 (4): 818–43.
Valentine, Gill. 2001. *Social Geographies: Space and Society.* Harlow, England: Prentice Hall.
Velikonja, Mitja. 2003. *Religious Separation and Political Intolerance in Bosnia-Herzegovina.* College Station: Texas A&M University Press.
Voinovich, Vladimir. 1986. *Moscow 2042.* Translated by Richard Lourie. San Diego: Harcourt Brace Jovanovich.

Vucetic, Srdjan. 2004. "Identity Is a Joking Matter: Intergroup Humor in Bosnia." *Spaces of Identity* 4 (1): 7–34.

Vućinić, Vesna. 1999. *Prostorno ponašanje u Dubrovniku: Antropološka studija grada sa ortogonalnom strukturom.* Belgrade: Filozofski fakultet Univerziteta u Beogradu.

Wachtel, Andrew. 1998. *Making a Nation, Breaking a Nation: Literature and Cultural Politics in Yugoslavia.* Stanford, Calif.: Stanford University Press.

Weber, Max. 1966. *The City.* Translated and edited by Don Martindale and Gertrud Neuwirth. New York: Free Press.

Weine, Stevan. 2000. "Redefining *Merhamet* after a Historical Nightmare." In Halpern and Kideckel 2000, 401–12.

Werbner, Pnina. 1997. "Essentialising Essentialism, Essentialising Silence: Ambivalence and Multiplicity in the Construction of Racism and Ethnicity." In *Debating Cultural Hybridity,* edited by Pnina Werbner and Tariq Modood, 226–54. London: Routledge.

Wheatley, Paul. 1969. *The City as Symbol: An Inaugural Lecture Delivered at University College London, November 20, 1967.* London: H. K. Lewis.

Williams, Raymond. 1977. *Marxism and Literature.* Oxford: Oxford University Press.

Wilson, Thomas M., and Hastings Donnan. 1998. "Nation-State and Identity at International Borders." In *Border Identities: Nation and State at International Frontiers,* edited by Thomas M. Wilson and Hastings Donnan, 1–30. Cambridge: Cambridge University Press.

Wirth, Louis. 1938. "Urbanism as a Way of Life." *American Journal of Sociology* 44 (1): 1–24.

Wolf, Eric. 1982. *Europe and the People without History.* Berkeley: University of California Press.

Wolff, Larry. 1994. *Inventing Eastern Europe: The Map of Civilization in the Mind of the Enlightenment.* Stanford, Calif.: Stanford University Press.

Woodward, Susan. 1995. *Balkan Tragedy.* Washington, D.C.: Brookings Institute.

Wright, Susan. 1998. "The 'Politicization' of Culture." *Anthropology Today* 4 (1): 7–15.

Young, Iris Marion. 1990. "The Idea of Community and the Politics of Difference." In *Feminism/Postmodernism,* edited by Linda J. Nicholson, 300–323. New York: Routledge.

Young, Robert J. C. 1995. *Colonial Desire: Hybridity in Theory, Culture and Race.* London: Routledge.

Žarkov, Dubravka. 2007. *The Body of War: Media, Ethnicity and Gender in the Break-Up of Yugoslavia.* Durham, N.C.: Duke University Press.

Žiga, Jusuf. 2001. *Tradicija Bosne koju su izdali / The Tradition of Bosnia Which Has Been Betrayed.* Sarajevo: Vijeće Kongresa Bošnjačkih Intelektualaca.

Zimmerman, William. 1987. *Politics and Culture in Yugoslavia.* Ann Arbor, Mich.: Institute for Social Research, University of Michigan.
Zukin, Sharon. 1995. *The Cultures of Cities.* Cambridge, Mass.: Blackwell.
Zulfikarpašić, Adil. 1998. *The Bosniak.* London: Hurst.

Index

FRAN MARKOWITZ is a professor of cultural anthropology at Ben-Gurion University of the Negev in Israel and the author of *Coming of Age in Post-Soviet Russia* and *A Community in Spite of Itself: Soviet Jewish Émigrés in New York*.

INTERPRETATIONS OF CULTURE IN THE NEW MILLENNIUM

Peruvian Street Lives: Culture, Power, and Economy among Market Women of Cuzco *Linda J. Seligmann*
The Napo Runa of Amazonian Ecuador *Michael Uzendoski*
Made-from-Bone: Trickster Myths, Music, and History from the Amazon *Jonathan D. Hill*
Ritual Encounters: Otavalan Modern and Mythic Community *Michelle Wibbelsman*
Finding Cholita *Billie Jean Isbell*
East African Hip Hop: Youth Culture and Globalization *Mwenda Ntaragwi*
Sarajevo: A Bosnian Kaleidoscope *Fran Markowitz*

The University of Illinois Press
is a founding member of the
Association of American University Presses.

Composed in 10.5/13 Adobe Minion Pro
with Frutiger display
by Jim Proefrock
at the University of Illinois Press
Manufactured by Cushing-Malloy, Inc.

University of Illinois Press
1325 South Oak Street
Champaign, IL 61820-6903
www.press.uillinois.edu